THE DOOR TO THE FUTURE

BOOKS BY JESS STEARN

THE DOOR TO THE FUTURE

JESS STEARN

1963

DOUBLEDAY & COMPANY, INC. GARDEN CITY, N.Y.

Excerpts from *Memoirs of the Second World War* by Winston Churchill.
Reprinted by permission of Houghton Mifflin Company.

LIBRARY OF CONGRESS CATALOG CARD NUMBER 63–7721

COPYRIGHT © 1963 BY JESS STEARN

FIRST EDITION

For Freddie and Martha,

who are in it.

CONTENTS

CONTENTS

1 MEETING A NEW WORLD

It was impossible.

I could not believe it.

It didn't make sense.

How could anybody predict what was going to happen before it happened?

It was obviously absurd.

And so when a girl named Elle Kofler suggested I take her to a fortune-teller, I looked at her as though she were out of her mind. As a skeptical newspaperman, I felt that anybody who consulted a psychic of any kind, even for amusement, was vainly trying to escape into a dream world of flattering fakery.

"If they know the future," I told Elle, "why aren't they rich playing the market or the horses?"

"This one is really good," she said. "She hits me all the time."

I snorted, and made a mental note about Elle.

A year or so later, not having given a second thought to the incident, I was in Armando's, a smart New York supper club, when I noticed a dark, round-faced, black-haired woman of middle years, sitting alone in an upstairs lounge. "How would you like to have a reading?" she asked pleasantly.

"What kind of a reading?" I asked.

She said evenly, "About yourself—past, present, and the future."

I laughed rather impolitely, I am afraid, and said: "Save it for the ladies; they believe that stuff."

She looked at me with a quiet smile, and said as pleasantly as before:

"You have two children, don't you?"

Not terribly surprised, I nodded. Many men have two children.

"One is a boy, the other a girl," she said. I still was not surprised, though my hand lingered on the washroom door.

"The boy," she went on, "is the older, and favors you in appearance; the daughter is like her mother."

"That's pretty good," I conceded. "Who have you been talking to?"

"The boy," she continued as though she hadn't heard, "will grow up and be taller than you." Since I am well over six feet, this did seem a little noteworthy. "Your daughter," she said, "will be artistically inclined and will like horses; she will be quite a horsewoman." Though only six, she had just asked for a horse.

My hand slipped from the doorknob. "Your marriage broke up recently," she went on, "and you have been thinking of marrying another girl." Suddenly, I found myself easing into a chair beside the woman with dark, impassive eyes. "But you will not marry her." She paused. "You won't see her again."

I laughed. "That hardly seems likely."

She went on evenly. "You will not marry," she repeated, "not for seven or eight years, and you have not met her yet."

All this was in 1952. Ten years later, my twenty-one-year-old son was taller than I, my sixteen-year-old daughter has frequently sketched notes to me and has won many ribbons in horse shows. Through no doing of my own, I never again met with the girl with whom I had been considering marriage, and I was married seven years later to somebody I had not then known.

I have dwelt on this incident because it was my introduction to the world of the psychic, and though I found it only interesting at the time, it did make me aware of a world that I had been hitherto oblivious of.

Sometime after this, I was interviewing the celebrated motion picture actress Grace Kelly, then at the peak of her fame, when the conversation got around to fate and destiny, Miss Kelly being the probing intellectual type as well as a great beauty.

"You know," the actress said, "when I was still unknown in New York, having a difficult time getting even bit parts, a woman named Rava told me I was going to become a world-famous star."

She seemed rather amused that the prediction had materialized.

"That would have been a pretty good guess for anyone looking like you," I said dubiously.

"Perhaps," she said, "but she was rather definite about what I was going to do."

I shrugged as Miss Kelly went on. "But she was certainly wrong about one thing." She laughed. "She said I was going to become a princess."

I was not to think about this again, at least not for another year or so, when the Philadelphia-born beauty met Prince Ranier of Monaco and they shortly thereafter became Prince and Princess.

By now, I was beginning to grow conscious of experiences of friends and acquaintances. The head of a top model agency, practical-minded Eileen Ford, told me that a fortune-teller had predicted that she would, though only twenty-one herself, marry a younger man with the initials G.F. Her husband was only twenty when they married but his first name was Jerry. "I thought it stood for Jerome," she said, "but it was Gerard."

On television, a top TV personality, ridiculing the whole field of predicting, commented wryly to a psychic he was interviewing. "Before my wife and I were married, a fortune-teller told her that if she married me, she would commit suicide." He snorted. "Can you imagine anything more preposterous?"

It did not seem so preposterous, three or four years later, when that wife did commit suicide.

Long before he was abducted and carried off to Israel to face trial for the mass murder of six million Jews, Nazi Adolf Eichmann was informed by an Argentine fortune-teller that he would not live beyond the spring of 1962. In prison in Israel, awaiting trial, he grimly hurried his memoirs, explaining that he now believed in a prediction he had once ridiculed. He was executed June 1.

Before she had married once, Rita Daigle, a former Miss Rheingold, had been told by Anya, the palmist at a New York night club, that she would marry three times and have two children. "The initial 'J' will always be prominent in your life." Miss Daigle, then seventeen, laughed in disbelief and said, "When I marry, it will be for once and for all." But some dozen years later, she had married for the third time, and with a sigh of relief remarked, "Now I feel that's the end." She had two children and, remarkable coincidence, all three husbands were named James—the last James Kleid.

It was a completely new field to me, and one that I approached as I would any other event or story.

In an exploratory way, I made many tours of fortune-tellers, took experimental subjects along to see what was foretold for them, visited mediums and spiritualists around the country, amateur and professional sensitives—a pleasant name for psychics of all types and descriptions—and delved into not only contemporary experiences but also those of the past. I became acquainted with the work of the psychic researchers, but the tedious experiments, conducted with little or no imagination, left me singularly unimpressed. I held a deck of cards in my hand, as a research psychiatrist read the entire fifty-two correctly from their backs, and then smilingly explained that it was a trick. What more could a psychic do with cards?

It was in the boundless laboratory of life, not the confining laboratory of the university, not in experimental card tricks, but the spontaneous flow of events, that I hoped to find the answer to the riddle of the future.

As my investigation proceeded, my own skepticism never deserted me. Each incident stood by itself. If a psychic made an outstanding prediction, it did not follow that the next would be equally correct, and for that matter it might be a lucky shot or just coincidence. I dismissed trivial predictions of trips, romances, promotions, and monetary gains: these were the sort of things that happened to people in the normal course of living, and given time, they were invariably bound to happen.

The past was as illuminating as the present. Were the wondrous predictions of the seer Nostradamus sufficiently wondrous for the poet Goethe to have marveled, "Was it God that penned these signs?" And the Bible—Old and New Testaments—were they a collection of fairy tales, as modern sophisticates would like us to believe? And the prophets of old, Isaiah, Ezekiel, Paul, and John—and the greatest Prophet of them all—did their messages apply to us, just as they did to the people with whom they trod the earth?

Were the visions of the latter-day saints pure hysteria, or did these visionaries pry the veil from a panorama of events in brief, revealing flashes denied ordinary mortals? What spurred Joan of Arc on to fame and death at a tender age? What did the children of Fatima actually see in the isolated hills of Portugal, or were their visions a chimera of their unsophisticated young minds?

The belief in the psychic, I discovered, was not limited to the superstitious and the bored craving some glimmer of excitement, nor to the lonely and oppressed seeking a sign of another and better world, but shared by the keen, practical personalities of these and other times.

The Morgans and the Vanderbilts had consulted astrologers in their financial ventures; Hitler had his stargazers; H. G. Wells had his dreams that he prophetically put into writing; Pius V described the Battle of Lepanto as it was being fought hundreds of miles away. From his own dreams Galen, the great doctor of antiquity, learned to diagnose and treat cases not yet called to his attention. Abraham Lincoln conducted seances in the White House, with friends in attendance, and Napoleon, the most practical of men, flitting in imagination back to the scene of his triumphs, observed from his prison island: "Now if I can span the space from St. Helena, why not that of the centuries? Why should I not see the future like the past? Would the one be the more extraordinary, more marvelous than the other."

There were many kinds of psychics. The fortune-tellers, appealing to vanity and fear for a price, were only a segment of the practicing psychic field. There were the brooding mystics, with their fount in some obscure religion; the spiritualists, who believed they got their message from those who protectively returned in spirit; the astrologers, who measured the influence of the planets, but still had to be psychic to make their readings intimately interesting; and all the vast cult of savants, Swamis, and occultists who flourish in the dry, expectant air of Southern California where some breathlessly await long-predicted visits from outer space—visits, they are convinced, that our own flights into space may yet touch off.

And even before man's first space flights, there were predictions of a meeting with life of some form on other planets. It was certainly heady stuff.

One did not have to be a professional, it seemed, to claim psychic power. Many people of wealth and position, like Jeane Dixon of Washington, had predicted earth-shaking events—the assassination of Mahatma Gandhi, the partition of India; others saw the stock market crashes, 1929 and 1962, plane crashes, auto accidents, deaths, marriages, divorces, births—practically every conceivable event that could befall man, often foretold with such precise detail as to time, place, and sequence as to rule out normal logic and foresight.

But even in the face of predicted events that checked out, it was difficult for me to accept the evidence. I could somehow fathom telepathy and clairvoyance because they, like a television and radio antenna, tuned in or pictured events that had occurred or were occurring. But how could anyone tune in on something that wasn't even going on? I listened to many explanations of the universality of time; there was no time, there was no space! The past, present, and future were all the same, appearing differently only to the ordinary perceiver. But none of this registered with a mind like mine that had lived so many years with an eye on the clock. And yet, it became apparent that if psychics could read the past, they could read the future with equal facility. Time meant nothing to them.

To many scientific minds, precognition, even though inexplicable, was an actuality. Dr. Gardner Murphy of the Menninger Clinic in Topeka, Kansas, had stated flatly after years of research: "There is no need to apologize for regarding precognition as something real, when it is real, nor of regarding it as something impossible, when it is only impossible from the point of view of a frame of reference that probably none of us holds."

Precognition itself was a new word to me. I could not even find it in my dictionary. But Professor C. J. Ducasse of Brown University defined it as where the contents of a dream, a vision, or a hunch actually turn out to correspond to a later event, in precise and singular detail.

"If," Ducasse said, "I were to dream tonight that I received a letter from a friend from whom I have not heard for many years— that, by itself, is hardly evidence there was causal connection between my dream and the advent of the letter. If, however, the letter that I see myself receive in my dream is not an ordinary letter but, let us say, a letter in an oval envelope instead of a rectangular envelope, that itself would be an unusual feature. And if I noticed in addition that, in my dream, this envelope is white on one side and pink on the other, that the stamp is right in the middle of the envelope—all these would be extraordinary features, with strong indication this was not just a matter of chance."

Such an event, Ducasse stressed, must correspond to the precognitive experience in a manner that cannot be explained away as chance or coincidence, nor should it follow from the subsequent action of the person involved in the prediction.

There were numerous examples, of course, of a person himself making "predicted" events materialize by acting on the psychic's suggestion. It seemed conceivable that if anybody believed something enough, it might psychologically provide the impetus to bring the suggested event about. Nobody could have been more confident than racing driver A. J. Foyt when he began the five-hundred-mile race at the Indianapolis Speedway on Memorial Day, 1961. His favorite fortune-teller, reading the cards, had told him he was going to win. "I wasn't worried a bit even when I went into the pits with a bad fuel line," Foyt said later. "I knew something would get me across the finish line first."

But with three laps to go, it looked as if Foyt would have to settle for second place, when suddenly the lead car, driven by Eddie Sachs, went into the pit with a bad tire. And Foyt blazed past the side-lined Sachs to make his fortune-teller look like a prophet.

Yet Foyt's confidence itself could hardly have had anything to do with Sachs's misfortune—and any of a dozen other drivers might just as easily have capitalized on his bad luck.

In the field of research, as I discovered, the tendency was not to accept but to reject. In fact, at times this professional incredulity hung on in the face of all apparent reason. Like myself, few critical observers were inclined to seriously consider any instances of precognition—extrasensory perception of the future—except those they could vouch for themselves. I could hardly blame them.

But even the most skeptical of researchers, I discovered, have been confounded by their own skepticism. The Reverend Herbert Thurston, brilliant English Jesuit who launched a scintillating attack on the Malachy prophecies—the prophecies of the Popes— had with equal cleverness attacked prophecies predicting the onslaught of great wars. In *The War and the Prophets*, the English scholar wittily tore into a noted French psychic, Madame de Thebes, for her prognostications of World War I. Early in 1915, while Kaiser Wilhelm seemed to stand victoriously astride Europe, Father Thurston confessed to being left unmoved by her forecast. "Here is a specimen," he said, as though its absurdity required no further rebuttal, "culled from the *Almanac de Madame de Thebes* for 1913."

And Thurston quoted lightly:

"Germany menaces Europe in general and France in particular. When the war breaks out she will have willed it, but after it there will be no longer Hohenzollern or Prussian domination. I have said, and I repeat, that the days of the Emperor are numbered. And after him all will be changed in Germany—I say his days of reign, I do not say his days of life."

It seemed ridiculous at the time that the Hohenzollern rule should end after six hundred years; contradictory that its ruler should survive his downfall; and unthinkable that Germany should suffer so crushing a defeat. Disdaining even the consideration of any such eventuality, Thurston noted with cool tolerance: "In the Almanac for 1914, she continues in the same strain, but it would serve no good purpose to quote further."

But three years later, of course, the Kaiser did flee safely into Holland, abdicating his throne, and the Hohenzollerns became Hitler stooges.

Columnist Jim Bishop, a good reporter, could accept two supersensory incidents. Both involved his father, John, and he was witness to both. In January, 1943, his father reported a small round spotlight on the wall over his bed. His wife laughed and told him he was seeing things. But on investigating, she too saw the light without being able to discover the source. It appeared every night until January 23, when it suddenly disappeared. "Something's going to happen," John Bishop said forebodingly. "Something bad." That night late, as they slept, the phone rang. It was John Bishop's sister. "I don't like to wake you up, Johnny," she said, "but Momma just passed away."

The second incident occurred years later, August 2, 1957. Jim Bishop's mother had a heart attack and was taken to Monmouth Memorial Center near her New Jersey home. At ten-thirty that night, John Bishop said to his son, "Did you hear anything?" The columnist shrugged. "About what?" he asked.

"I could have sworn," the father said, "that I heard your mother calling me."

His son reassured him. "You're worried about her," he said, "and you're imagining things."

The father smiled bleakly. "I guess you're right," he said. He frowned uncertainly. "But I was reading in the kitchen and I heard her call: 'John! John!'"

Ten minutes later the phone rang. It was the family doctor. "Better come down to the hospital," he said. When they got there, Mrs. Bishop was already dead. The nurse was talking to the doctor. "I was working in the next room," she said. "It was about ten-thirty. Suddenly, I heard someone calling 'John, John,' but she was gone by the time I got there."

Jim Bishop could only wonder. "Some things are impossible for me to believe," he commented, "even in the face of evidence." But here were two incidents he had to believe; he had been part of them.

I have tried to maintain a similar approach. When people have asked me, "Do you really believe this stuff?"—and I have heard the question many times—I could only smile, remembering my own initial reaction, and say: "As with any other story, I am ready to believe what can be proven." I tried *not* to dismiss things just because I couldn't understand them.

I was frankly baffled by the report that Edgar Cayce, Virginia Beach mystic, had reached out in trance and identified a compound known as oil of smoke on the shelves of a drugstore in Louisville, where he had never been himself, and when even the proprietors didn't know they had the product. But at least, if the report were true, I could visualize the mind somehow doing what a closed television circuit could do, even though curing a boy's infected leg with this unknown preparation—all medically vouched for —could not be equated with any machine.

It was the future that tantalized me.

Edgar Cayce had predicted his own death.

He said he would disintegrate if he gave more than two readings a day. And then, yielding to wartime demand, conducting eight and nine a day, he died in a few months, weighing little more than sixty pounds.

On the other hand, the Dutch import, Peter Hurkos, was not able to predict as well for himself. But merely by touching objects —the art of psychometry—he could tell the owner all about himself, past, present, and future. Going to the scene of a crime, he could often solve that crime, sensitive, some theorized, to the auras, emanations, or odic life force clinging to that scene.

Many of the psychics I investigated had used tea leaves, playing cards, or crystal balls, or peered into palms, but these were only catalytic agents, I soon discovered, to facilitate concentration and detach the conscious mind. But nearly all tuned in on the subject's vibrations, the stuff of which, they said mysteriously, the soul or psyche was made.

Ordinary people, who didn't normally consider themselves psychic, also had flashes of precognition, generally under stress, in their dreams or through complete attunement with another person whose thoughts also were with them. Fully twenty-five percent of our dreams may be precognitive, but like Biblical dreams are often symbolic, requiring gifted interpretation.

But even so, how could anybody see what hadn't happened yet?

How could a Jeane Dixon, peering into her crystal ball for a distinguished Indian visitor she had never seen before, tell him he was soon going to be the prime minister of his country, Hyderabad, which had never had a prime minister before? And then as he was smiling in gratification, tell him that he would be thrown into prison, but would be surprisingly rescued later. And six weeks later, Mir Laik Ali, who had become prime minister on returning to his country, was jailed by his political enemies, but subsequently escaped in a dramatic disguise.

It seemed to me that if these things could be seen, it was only because there was a foreseeable future. And when the psychic was wrong, was it because the foreseeable future had changed, or was it merely that the psychic, only a human instrument at best, had erred in this particular prediction?

And what did this do to our belief in free will? If the future was predictable, did it mean that no action on our part could change it? And again, how had Mrs. Dixon tuned in?

It was a problem that more subtle minds had grappled with almost since the beginning of thought. I discovered that St. Thomas Aquinas, perhaps the greatest thinker of the Catholic Church, had theorized that there were two kinds of prophecy, that given by God in vision, which was inflexible, and that subject to changing conditions which the prophet had not anticipated intellectually.

But how was a person to gauge the flexibility of the prophecy that concerned him? Long ago, an eminent psychic researcher, Pope Benedict XIV, had tartly observed that the gift of prophecy cannot be produced on demand and occurs simultaneously in "fools, idiots, and melancholy persons."

And I had learned for myself that many with psychic ability were not necessarily kind, good, or spiritual people. So many seemed immersed, as were their neighbors, in the mundane business of making money and getting ahead. And yet, with all their claims for seeing the future, many apparently could do little for themselves. Just as I had asked Elle Kofler, so others asked me:

"If they can predict things, why don't they predict something good for themselves?"

There was an answer, of course.

The conscious mind is the psychic's worst enemy, and personal gain is high on the list of conscious desires.

The conscious desires had to be suppressed, I was told, before a psychic could properly function. As one veteran researcher explained, "It's all done with the subconscious." And apparently there were times when the psychic could perform better than at others.

Nevertheless, while not consciously seeking such help, many people have foreseen winning horses, numbers, and stocks. And some have successfully invoked such predictions, while not standing to profit themselves.

Every day there were glittering examples, it seemed, of the wondrous way this particular phenomena worked, and of a corresponding belief in these "hunches." Mrs. Althea Ottavio, a well-to-do businesswoman of Valdosta, Georgia, had dreamed that a 2–5 combination would win the daily double on the dog track of the Orange Kennel Club, near Jacksonville, Florida on May 29, 1961. From Valdosta, she drove with a friend, Mrs. Patricia Ann Hewitt, some one hundred and twenty miles to the track. The winning combination, which they had discussed with friends and relatives, was 2–5. Apparently, the dream had projected correctly, but not far enough. For on the trip, the two women were brutally attacked and killed, and the dream certainly did them no good. The combination ironically, paid $177 for $2.

The psychic did not appear as some isolated force, but was apparently interwoven in the everyday fabric of human life, with all its pain, joy, love, and tragedy. The night before her four-year-old son Philip mysteriously disappeared from their East Harlem, New York, apartment in June of 1962, Mrs. Rose Milano dreamed that her Uncle Carmen, dead seven years, had come to her, saying sinisterly, "I am going to take Phillie with me." She awoke with an uneasy sense of premonition, oppressed by the vividness of her dream. When the boy couldn't be found, but police were still hopefully searching, the distraught mother told her attending physician, Dr. Robert Baird, "I know he is dead. I dreamed that he would be taken from me." The next day, the boy's body was found by police. He had been the victim of a youthful sex fiend.

It can also be a beneficial force. While a posse of hundreds was searching desperately for three-year-old Stephen Papol in the tangled undergrowth of a Long Island state park in August 1962, Mrs. Rosemarie Finger, a neighboring housewife, told her husband, "I have a feeling—woman's intuition, if you like—that we'll find him near Parking Field Number Three." It seemed unlikely, since this was a mile from the area, and across a main highway from where the boy had disappeared while watching a ball game with his family. The husband laughed tolerantly; they broke away from the main searching party, drove to the parking lot, and walked along a thickly wooded fringe area, Mrs. Finger in the lead, calling "Stevie." Finally, they heard an answering cry. "That's a bird," the husband said.

"That's not a bird, that's a child," the wife responded. At her urging, he dug into the jungle-like underbrush, and there found a whimpering child, thirsty, hungry, and covered with scratches and insect bites. It was little Stevie.

Where do these visions come from? Is it necessary to know how electricity works to make it work, or even to see it at work? In California, actress Joanne Woodward told me of a dream that she had one night recently. In her sleep she had seen a child born to a close friend who had not been expecting that child for two or three months. When she awakened, she was so convinced of the reality of the dream that she telephoned her friend. The friend was not at home, and a member of the household informed her: "She was taken to the hospital during the night, and had the child in the morning."

The meaning of these visions or dreams is not always so clear.

The Irish-born medium, Eileen Garrett, probably the most tested of all modern psychics, once reported a vision in which she saw a dirigible in the skies over London and the passengers in evident distress. It had no significance for her, and she described it to a friend. He was equally baffled. Not long thereafter, the British dirigible R-101, bound for India, crashed with a heavy loss of life.

In a lesser way, but similarly, a fortune-teller told a pretty dancer from a Broadway musical that she saw her taking a short trip in a few days, and receiving an expensive ring. She could offer no explanation. The girl, Vivian Cooke, was thrilled, thinking it meant she was going home to Baltimore, and that her boy friend, whom she hoped to marry, would cement their relationship with an engagement ring. Instead, she took a trip to Bear Mountain that weekend, and seeing a sparkling object in the leaves at her feet, stooped and picked it up. It was an expensive ring, and she has it today, years later, though she has not yet been engaged—or married.

It was obvious that certain individuals, not necessarily receptive, in some unknown way evoked more responsive performances by psychics, as they sought to tune into a world unfettered by traditional barriers of time and space. I couldn't help but wonder if I was one of these catalyst agents. The most retiring sensitives seemed to become inordinately articulate, if not particularly prophetic, in my presence.

As time wore on, it was apparent that I was a good receiver. I was sitting in the Fifth Avenue Hotel in downtown Manhattan one evening, chatting with friends, when sensitive Marie Welt came up, took out her pencil searchlight, and started to scan my hand. Her brow furled in a reflective frown. "Have you been thinking of writing a book?" she asked.

I had written one book at this time, and it had not been very successful. I shook my head.

"Well, you're going to," she said.

One of my companions laughed dryly. "That's quite a prediction."

Without favoring him with a glance, she went on. "You will hear about this book in two days," she said. "A publisher will call you and ask you to write it."

I laughed. "You're certainly putting yourself on a limb, Marie," I said. "Better make it a week or two."

"It will be two days," she insisted firmly. She looked me in the eye. "Some things I see and they may happen or not, depending on conditions, but this I know." She reflected a moment. "It won't be easy; you'll hit a snag, and then it will look as though you won't do the book, but you will, finally."

Two days later I walked into my newspaper office in New York and saw a telephone memorandum in my typewriter. A Mr. Payne had called from the Avon publishing company and he would call back later. In about fifteen minutes the phone rang again. "This is Tom Payne," the voice said, "you don't know what I'm calling you about . . ."

"Oh, yes, I do," I cut in with some amusement, "you want me to write a book."

He appeared somewhat taken aback. "How did you know that?"

"Oh, I was just kidding," I said.

Mr. Payne, it developed, wanted to know if I would be interested in writing a book on juvenile delinquency. My name had been one of five recommended by the Youth Board of the city of New York, which works with juveniles, and for no apparent reason he had decided on me.

We met several times, without anything developing. His superiors had not shared his interest in the topic, and it looked as though the project would founder. Then one day, months later, he called excitedly, "Would you like to do the book for Doubleday?" he said. It developed that he had mentioned the project to an editor friend. I agreed, and the book was eventually written. It was called *The Wasted Years.*

Subsequently, I discussed the incident with an eminent psychic researcher, and he pointed out that a researcher, in some inexplicable way, often makes himself more sensitive to psychic phenomena by the very process of investigating. "Still," he said, regarding me steadily, "yours was not a good scientific case of precognition."

"And why not?" I asked, genuinely curious.

"Because," he said wisely, "certain forces had obviously been set in motion, and the clairvoyant, sensitive, fortune-teller, or what have you, somehow tuned in on them and anticipated their conclusion." He drew meditatively on his pipe. "It could be telepathy or clairvoyance, provided, of course, it happened as you say."

I couldn't help laughing. "You know, Doctor, if people could hear us discussing how to classify this event, it might remind them of the talking horse whose master expressed surprise because he spoke with a lisp."

He didn't seem to understand. "My point is," I said, "that whatever we call it, it still doesn't make sense."

I had still another experience to report. As a matter of research I had sent off a letter to a sensitive, Mary Ann Glenn, in Honolulu, perfunctorily asking a few obvious questions about her reported predictions. At the close of her reply, she remarked that I should not work so hard or I would be ill.

I wrote back that I had never felt better, and she then repeated mildly, "Be careful, I still see you ill."

I wondered what she was trying to do. Two weeks later I had a mild virus; the doctor prescribed antibiotics, and they caused an unexpected reaction. Weeks later I was still trying to get on my feet.

It may have been a lucky guess, the force of suggestion, or just one of those many coincidences that seem to dot our lives. Or maybe, as the researcher had suggested, I was prediction-prone.

But whatever it was, I had another experience to mull over. Now that I was absorbed in my research, I began wondering about Elle Kofler, the girl who had wanted to visit the fortune-teller. I wondered what she had been told, by whom, and how it had all worked out. Though she had been a publicist, working with the newspapers, I had not seen her for many years. I was unable to get in touch with her, when I tried, and no one seemed to know where she could be located. One morning after a few futile phone calls, I gave up on Elle Kofler, and ventured forth on an errand to Rockefeller Center, in the heart of Manhattan. I was walking along Sixth Avenue, in front of the RKO Building, when, lo and behold, who should I see in a teeming city of eight million but Elle Kofler. I greeted her as though I had seen her only the day before. "I was looking for you," I said.

She seemed mildly surprised. "Yes?" she said.

"Do you remember the fortune-teller you wanted to take me to?"

She nodded, with the glimmer of a smile.

"Well," I said, "as a matter of information, I'd like to know what it was that was predicted for you, and how accurate the woman was."

She hesitated, then frowned. "I'd rather not say," she said.

"Was she that wrong?" I asked.

She smiled thinly. "No, she was that right."

Would she reconsider?

She shook her head and gave me her hand. "If I do, I'll call you," she said.

But I felt somehow she wouldn't, and she didn't.

It was a dream world in more ways than one. The subject that absorbed me as a reporter had fascinated the leading scientific minds. Listening to accounts of four thousand dreams a year, the Swiss psychoanalyst, Carl Gustav Jung, contributed his theory of the collective unconscious to the world of the unknown. Not only were many of these dreams similar, Jung found, but they were reminiscent of the ancient myths and the passion for life of primitive peoples—things the collective conscious should have known little about. Did this mean that the individual in his dreams—too symbolical for ordinary interpretation—delved into a reservoir of the past common to the human race? Was there such a thing as genetic memory, which could dredge up the unrecorded past?

And was it possible, somehow, that these dreams, too, projected into the near or distant future, covering the complete life cycle, from the beginning of time to its end?

If there was such a thing as precognition, how could it be explained? Many had valiantly tried. Charles Richet, the distinguished French physiologist, was to report after thirty years of painstaking research: "It is a strange, paradoxical, and seemingly absurd fact, but one we are compelled to admit. The explanation will come—or will not come—later."

And its significance—what of that? Would that come later too, or are we on the threshold of knowing what it all means, without quite realizing how simple it is?

Just as I had noticed in myself, could other people become more psychically aware of the world around them? As one probed, it became obvious there was nothing very singular about psychic experiences. Instances of telepathy (mental communication); clairvoyance (perception ranging beyond normal vision); and precognition itself were commonplace.

Was man becoming more psychic in a world daily growing more perilous?

Prehistorically, both primitive man and the animals, I was told, were instinctually psychic, the better to survive dangers they could not otherwise have comprehended.

Now that the most terrible danger—total destruction—has become a hair-trigger possibility in the enlightened Nuclear Age, has nature revived this so-called extra sense in man to help him perceive the dangers into which his conscious mind has delivered him?

Or, with the advent of the Space Age, is he being prepared not only for a new form of miraculous travel, which we could not begin to visualize a generation ago, but for mental—or extra-mental—communication with a new and superior world in which the power of the human personality will blossom to gratifying fullness through the very recognition and exercise of its boundless potential?

2 THE NEW MASTER

Long before I saw Jeane Dixon, I had heard of her wonders. Living in Washington, where she operated a profitable real estate business, she was known as the Capital Seer. Over the years, she had read for many of the bigwigs in the passing Washington parade—Franklin Delano Roosevelt and Winston Churchill, Estes Kefauver and Everett Dirksen. She has correctly predicted every presidential election in the last twenty years, and confided to friends before the 1960 race that although Nixon would get the votes, he would not become President. In 1948, when Capital status seekers were scratching the Trumans off their guest lists, hers was the lone voice predicting a Truman victory—and her forecast was carried in the Washington newspapers before the event.

Hardly knowing the people involved, she has predicted murders, suicides, and divorces, and she has foreseen disastrous fires, accidents, and drownings. On demand, she has forecast the finish of horse races, and once she visualized the number of a raffle ticket that would win a car—and blithely rummaged through a stack of raffle books until she found the right one, for her husband.

Without special knowledge, interest, or background, she has predicted all manner of world events, ranging from the war in Korea, an anticipated stalemate, to a revolution in Brazil and the partition of India. Her fame is so far-reaching that foreign ambassadors have sought appointments with her for their rulers, more eager to see her than visit the White House.

Like no other psychic she has functioned in a goldfish bowl. On television once, she told a mocking former U. S. Ambassador to Russia—Mission-to-Moscow Davies—that Premier Malenkov, who had just succeeded Stalin, would himself be replaced in two years, and she described his successor. At the same time, she also predicted that Russia would win the race into outer space before there was any talk about outer space, and added a prediction—which never made the newspapers—that the Soviets would eventually dictate the peace.

Her predictions are generally impersonal, and she doesn't fret over them. When the wife of a Supreme Court Justice criticized her forecasting her husband's death, Jeane said calmly: "A greater power than mine has willed it. I only saw it." He died three months later.

She uses a crystal ball, but can see things just as well by glancing at people, or by communing silently alone. She never goes into trance, though she often prays for the guidance she needs.

Her visions come while she is perfectly relaxed, or under tension. There seems to be no format. She was sitting under a dryer in a Hollywood beauty parlor when a lovely actress in the next chair casually mentioned that she was preparing to fly across the continent. Although the blonde beauty was a stranger, Jeane reached out a restraining hand and pleaded, "Don't make that trip."

A few days later the plane crashed in the mountains, taking the life of Carole Lombard, Mrs. Clark Gable.

She had a similar vibration when her husband, James Dixon, was preparing to fly from Detroit to Chicago. She remonstrated so strongly that he went by train. He still got there before the plane, which crashed near a Chicago airport, killing all aboard.

Seeing so much tragedy in the making, she tries to keep her mind a blank, especially with friends, who are always wanting to be read. But often, unable to contain herself, she blurts out warnings, hoping she may avert disaster.

For weeks she urged friends not to get up in the same plane with Dag Hammarskjold, the United Nations Secretary-General, sadly refraining from I-told-you-so's when his plane crashed in Africa. Again she told a woman friend in government, "Keep away from that man or he will ruin you." The man wound up in jail, and the friend, involved in his disgrace, lost her job and political favor.

In her zealousness, she often does not realize how embarrassing her revelations can be. Introduced to a detective and his young lady at New York's Waldorf-Astoria, she exclaimed: "You two people should never marry."

As the detective and his fiancée smiled self-consciously, she rushed on: "You"—turning to the detective—"are still reliving what happened two years ago, and you aren't ready for marriage with anyone."

Both knew what she was talking about. Two years before, after twenty-five years of marriage, the detective's wife had died, and he felt then that nobody could take her place. But they married anyway.

Although she often reads the future at Washington benefits, the proceeds going to charity, Mrs. Dixon has never read professionally. "If I saw everyone who wants to see me," she said, "I would do nothing else." But she finds it difficult to put off all who press after her, even though the responsibility of directing other lives hangs heavily on her slim shoulders.

She wouldn't see Evelyn de Jong Davis, daughter of a noted neurologist, for months before agreeing to meet her at a charity bazaar, which she was attending anyway. Mrs. Davis was to recall vividly Mrs. Dixon's predictions. "She told me, a nobody, that I would be a success at finance. And now, five years later, I am a stock-market consultant in New York and financially independent. She told me that if I married, the marriage would break up, and now I am divorced."

Once a year now, Mrs. Davis travels to Washington to learn what will happen next. "She told me that an older man, posing as a friend, would take advantage of me financially—and now I am trying to get my money back."

I interviewed Mrs. Davis in December of 1961, and she turned out to be quite a prognosticator herself. She told me to get out of the market because it was going to tumble in four months, and in April of 1962 the worst market slump in years was on. But Mrs. Davis was not psychic, just knowledgeable, and maybe a little intuitive. "I leave the other for Mrs. Dixon," she said.

Unlike Edgar Cayce, Mrs. Dixon shies away from health readings, and intercedes reluctantly only where people are ill. Unable once to resist a mother's appeal, she read for an ailing child for whom the doctors had counseled immediate surgery. As the mother held the two-year-old boy Jeane told her, "If this child is operated on, he will die on the operating table."

The father, a prominent Washington attorney, preferred the medical opinion. The family took the child to a Philadelphia hospital for surgery. He didn't survive the operation.

Being in the Washington swim, Mrs. Dixon frequently gets into politics in spite of herself. On a visit to the White House in 1945, England's Winston Churchill asked her to predict the outcome of the first general election in years.

"Your party," Jeane told him, "will be turned back, and there will be a new Prime Minister."

Chomping on his cigar, the Englishman growled, "My people will never let me down after what I have done for them."

"Oh, don't worry," Jeane reassured him, "you will make a comeback."

History revealed Mrs. Dixon as the better political prophet.

Actually, politics made Mrs. Dixon a Capital celebrity. In 1948, when she insisted President Truman would be elected, a prominent Washington hostess proclaimed she would invite her to no more Republican parties until she publicly changed her mind. Jeane bristled and said: "My mind has nothing to do with it."

The politicians have been unable to decide whether they should court or avoid her. Early in 1956, shaking hands with Senator Estes Kefauver, she said, "You will not get the presidential nomination, but you will be Adlai Stevenson's running mate."

"On another occasion," recalled Martha Rountree, prominent Washington commentator, "she read her crystal ball for a flock of presidential hopefuls, and you never saw so many long faces in your life, including Dick Russell's of Georgia."

She may keep a prediction to herself, but she will never alter one. Before the Republican national convention of 1952, Bob Taft supporters asked her to pose with a crystal ball next to Taft's photograph, saying: "All I can see in '52 is Taft." Although Taft-minded herself, Mrs. Dixon rejected the bid, predicting, "Taft won't be nominated or elected."

She saw Eisenhower winning, and maintained a protective interest in him for eight years. In 1956, startled by what she saw in her crystal, she called an intimate of the President's and told him to get Ike to cut down his golf. "I was concentrating on the President," she said, "and saw a dark cloud gathering around him, which means sickness." A few days later, June 9, 1956, Ike was stricken with ileitis.

Before the last national election, she was consulted by a worried Republican leader, and told him, "Tell President Eisenhower to throw a guard around every precinct in the country. A Republican president will be elected but he will not be seated." And she still thinks, with some others, that Nixon carried Texas, New Jersey, and Illinois.

She has learned to live with her gift from childhood. When she was only fourteen, living in California, Hollywood stars would plague her to tell their fortunes. Once, she told Marie Dressler, then retired from the theater, that she would have her greatest success at fifty-seven. The old harridan clapped her thigh and laughed. "Guess I'm going to open a boarding house." But later, as Jeane foresaw, she rose to new fame on the screen.

Jeane became aware of her gift when she was too young to know it was unusual. She was eight years old when she asked her mother, "Can I see the letter with the black border around it?"

"I don't know what you're talking about," her mother said.

Two weeks later, an envelope edged in black arrived informing the mother that her father had passed away in Germany.

Jeane's parents were German immigrants of a practical turn of mind. The father, Frank Pinckert, had made a fortune in Wisconsin lumber, and had retired early, moving to Santa Rosa, California. There had been no psychics on either side of the family. Jeane's older brother, Erny Pinckert, had been an All-America football star at the University of Southern California and later played professionally with the Washington Redskins. She had four other brothers, and they were all normal. From childhood she was something special. When the mother didn't want to let brother Erny go out for football in high school for fear he might get hurt, pint-sized Jeane spoke up. "Don't worry, Mother, he's going to become famous playing football."

Marveling at the child's gift, the family took her to a celebrated gypsy fortune-teller who lived in a covered wagon outside Santa Rosa. The gypsy read the others, and then peering into Jeane's eyes, picked up the crystal ball and gave it to her. "Someday," she said, "you will tell others."

Though very much in the limelight, Jeane had managed to avoid the cult of personality. "The Bible," she observed, "says that all events are foreshadowed. I'm only the means of communication, and I must keep that communication line clear."

Strengthening this spiritual link, she goes to Mass daily; ministers the education of deserving youngsters, Negro and white alike; grinds up carrot juice for sick old ladies, and personally supervises a dozen pet charities. Even if she needed it, which she obviously doesn't, she would not take money for her readings. "The difference between extrasensory perception and spiritual prophecy," she said, "is materialism; and the more material you are the less clearly you see."

Just as she has no patience with psychics who misuse their gift, she has no use for psychic researchers who try to entice her into their laboratories. "I have no interest in card tricks or gadgets that measure brain waves," she said, "or scientist who would make a science of something they know nothing about."

While she piously feels that her power is spiritually derived, there are times, no matter how she strives, that she can't conjure up the future. "I can't turn it off and on like a spout," she said. Yet she has no such trouble with the past. For here her channels of feeling, as she calls them, tune her into the human personality and its history. Sometimes a touch of the hand will serve; sometimes, clothes, colors, or mannerisms—even a gesture—will activate this channel. In the spring of 1953, as something of a gag—to which she was not a party—she appeared on a Bob Hope television show in Washington. The comedian, with a broad wink at the audience, took her hand, and said: "I was playing golf with

President Eisenhower this afternoon. Now look into that crystal ball of yours"—he smiled impishly—"and tell me our scores."

Holding his hand, not hesitating, Mrs. Dixon said with a smile: "A 96 and a 92." The comedian was dumbstruck. Later, off-camera, he clapped a hand to his forehead and moaned, "That woman's ruined me at the White House; they'll never believe I didn't let out those scores." And that is how Ike's score—the 96—the best-kept secret of his administration, leaked out—just through a touch of the hand.

When I met Jeane Dixon for the first time I saw how readily this channel works. She rose, gave me a piercing look, and said as she took my hand:

"Many people have wanted to tell my story, but you are the one I have been waiting for."

I felt a slight chill up my spine—but didn't pursue the matter at the time.

There was little, superficially, to distinguish her from many other successful businesswomen. Her movements were quick and birdlike; she seemed unable to sit still—grabbing telephones, reaching for a pen, snapping out directions. "An overactive thyroid," I speculated. She was dark and slim, with shadows under eyes that held mine evenly without blinking. But she seemed youthful, her age indeterminate.

I had never seen hands like hers. They were seamed with heavy lines, crossing and crisscrossing. Noticing my interest, she remarked casually, "A German occultist said people with hands like mine are born only once in two hundred years."

We talked easily about my project. "I would like to feel free," I said, "to talk to anyone you have predicted for, and whoever witnessed these predictions."

"You can go anywhere, or see anybody you like," she said, "but politicians may not want to talk to you, and many others may prefer to keep the predictions confidential." She smiled in amusement. "People love to consult psychics, but they don't want anybody to know they do."

I had heard that she had read for President Roosevelt in the White House.

She grimaced unhappily. "That leaked out to one of the columns at the time. The cab driver who dropped me at the Pennsylvania Avenue gate must have told somebody."

"It was a little unusual, wasn't it?"

She shrugged. "What was unusual?"

"The President having a reading."

"Oh, Presidents are human too," she said. "They have the same misgivings, wonderings, and heartaches as the rest of us, perhaps more so."

"Did you know him at all?"

"Not before I was called in."

"How did you happen to be called?"

"He may have heard of me from one of his secretaries; I had read for a few people in the White House." She thought awhile, frowning. "And like many great men, I suppose he had wondered about many of the things that logic and science don't explain. Like other great leaders, Lincoln for one, he may have had occasional psychic experiences himself. He was certainly intuitive."

"When did you see him?"

She hesitated briefly. "Back in the fall of 1944, late November or early December, I'm not quite sure."

"Not long after his election then, and not long before his death?"

"I guess so." Suddenly, appearing ill at ease, she moved to change the subject. "There are so many other cases," she said.

"But only you can tell me about this case. There wasn't anyone else there?"

"No, we were alone."

"Did anyone else know about it?"

"I think so, but the White House seemed to be deserted that day. There were not even any guards at his door when I walked in, and I saw nobody in the hall. But someone must have given the outside guard my name. I just walked in, and following directions, headed for his room."

"Directions? Whose directions?"

Again she looked at me rather unhappily. "Oh, whoever it was that called me and made the appointment."

"Well, I didn't think the President would have called."

"No," she said slowly, "a woman called."

"Didn't you feel you might be the victim of a prank?"

"Not at all," she said.

"Was that psychic?"

"Not completely." She smiled.

The appointment was made three days ahead, for a Thursday morning at eleven. Jeane was told to be ready, say nothing, and wait for another call.

"Real cloak-and-dagger," I observed.

She nodded. "'A word to the wise,' I was told, 'is sufficient.'"

"It must have been important, what with the war going on and all?"

"Important enough," she said.

I smiled. "He wasn't getting advice on running the country?"

"Hardly," she said.

"Why can't you talk about it?" I asked. "After all these years, it certainly can't hurt anybody."

"I have never revealed anything I told anyone without their approval."

"That's not possible here," I said.

"Perhaps," she said, "you could get the information elsewhere."

I was puzzled. "From whom?"

"He may have mentioned it to one of the secretaries."

"I have a feeling this isn't the sort of thing he would discuss with his aides."

"Then why mention it at all?" she said. "It might only offend some people."

I thought about it a moment.

"It shows that one of the great political minds of our time was sufficiently impressed with the possibilities of psychic phenomena to invite a psychic into the White House, and the nature of the conference would indicate how important he thought it."

She nodded thoughtfully. "I'll think it over."

I proceeded to check the Dixon predictions, beginning with the baby who had died on the operating table. The family would no longer discuss the incident, but I learned that after the child's death the mother had phoned Jeane from the hospital, sobbing, "The doctors say that I can never have another child."

Jeane consoled her. "What has happened is God's will, but you will have two more children."

"But my blood is wrong."

"Never mind what they tell you," Jeane said, and she gave the dates on which the children would be born. "Let me know if I am right," she said.

All this had happened in the mid-fifties, and a well-known Capital newspaperman, it developed, had talked to the family not long thereafter in the course of doing a story on Mrs. Dixon. "The family confirmed every bit of the story as you have it," *Parade* magazine's Jack Anderson told me, "and though we didn't use any of the details, we did confirm the prediction."

He wondered curiously, "Why won't they discuss it now?"

"Family trouble," I said. "They'd prefer to forget it."

"Well, they verified it all—the operating-table bit, and the two kids being born on the predicted dates."

Anderson seemed the hard-boiled newspaperman. "You're not a believer, are you?" I asked.

He smiled wryly. "We started to do the *Parade* story on Mrs. Dixon tongue-in-cheek, but so many predictions began to check out—divorces, problems with domestics, political prognostications —that we changed the slant."

"And now you're a believer?"

"Hardly," he said. And, chuckling, he added: "I understand she told friends that Nixon was going to beat Kennedy."

"She still says he won, but they didn't count all his votes."

"That sounds like a quibble," he said. "As I got it, she flatly predicted that Nixon would be President."

"Didn't you cover the presidential prediction for 1960 in your story?" I asked.

"You might check it," he said. "Our story appeared in 1956."

I picked up a tattered issue of the magazine, the last paragraph catching my eye. It spoke for itself. "As for the 1960 election, Mrs. Dixon thinks it will be dominated by labor and won by a

Democrat. But he will be assassinated or die in office, though not necessarily in his first term."

Through physical necessity, Jeane takes her psyche to work with her. In the Dixon realty office, which Jeane manages with her husband, she is regarded as both nut and prophet. The day twenty-two-year-old secretary Patricia Crist came to work, her new boss told her: "You're a very pretty girl, but you won't marry until you're twenty-seven, and your first child will be a boy."

And what happened?

"I thought she was a little kookie at the time since I was going out with somebody I liked," Pat told me, "but in May of 1958 I was twenty-seven and that July I got married."

As we chatted, a big good-looking young man came in with a child in his arms. "That's my husband now," she said, "and my only child, a boy."

The husband, Bert Ridenough, was that practical article, a salesman. He had not been terribly impressed by the prediction.

"Girls are getting married at twenty-seven all the time, and it's always a boy or a girl."

He reflected a moment. "But she is odd."

"What do you mean?"

"Last Christmas I bought a camera for Pat, and while picking her up I ran into Jeane, and mentioned casually I'd been shopping. A radiant smile lit up Jeane's face," Bert recalled.

"And what a beautiful present you picked out for Pat," she said, "It's lovely." She looked off into space as though she were trying to visualize it. Somehow, this irritated Bert.

"How do you know?" he said tartly. "It's still in the store."

She lowered her voice. "We mustn't let Pat know. It must be a surprise."

"What is it?" he said insistently.

Jeane appeared surprised that he should ask. "Why, it's one of those self-developing cameras that prints pictures in seconds. Pat will love it."

I stood there watching Ridenough shake his head reminiscently. "I don't know how," he said, "but she guessed it."

"What was it?" I asked.

"A Polaroid camera."

"It wasn't precognition," I said. "She probably read your mind."

He laughed. "Is that all?"

At Dixon realty, the help can never be sure the boss isn't peering over their shoulders, even when she isn't around. In the summer of 1955, Mrs. Dixon's togetherness with her staff was so notable that it made the Washington front pages. She had been at Emile's, a beauty parlor on nearby Connecticut Avenue, relaxing under a hair dryer again when suddenly a vision of danger hit her. She bounced up, elbowed her way past an attendant, grabbed a phone, and frantically dialed her office. As a clerk, George Miller, answered the phone, Mrs. Dixon blurted out: "Mr. Mitchell is having a heart attack. Get a doctor and ambulance right away."

Miller looked back to a cubbyhole where Justice Mitchell, a salesman, sat complacently reading a newspaper. "Please, Mrs. Dixon, I was just talking to Mr. Mitchell, and he never felt better in his life."

"Call the ambulance," she snapped, oblivious of the people staring at her.

As Miller swung around for another look, Mitchell slumped suddenly to the floor. The phone slipped from Miller's hand, and he almost passed out himself. Pat Crist retrieved the phone and called an ambulance. As Mitchell was carried past Miller on a stretcher, a doctor inquired, "When did you first discover him?"

Miller said sheepishly, "When the phone rang, just before it happened."

Miller, working elsewhere now, will always recall the doctor's expression. "He looked at me," Miller said, "as though they were carrying out the wrong person."

At seventy, Justice Mitchell was retired and living in Wayne, Pennsylvania, a Philadelphia suburb. "I would have been dead a long time," he told me, "if Jeane Dixon hadn't made that call. My eyes had rolled back and my pulse had stopped when they got me to an emergency hospital. Those few minutes saved me."

Though not completely recovered, Mitchell was still grateful to his old boss. There was one convalescent problem, however. "So many people called or wrote the hospital, asking how they could contact Jeane Dixon, that I couldn't get the rest I needed," he recalled with a reminiscent sigh.

A few weeks after I spoke to him, Mitchell was dead. "You had better call him right away if you want to check with him," Mrs. Dixon had enjoined me. "He won't be around very long."

As word of Mrs. Dixon's prowess got around, the gambling fraternity was naturally interested. But the overtures didn't really pour in until word got around how her raffle ticket had won a new Cadillac for her husband at a wartime benefit at Fort Myer, Virginia. The offers were made in person and by telephone. "They would call up, offering her all kinds of cuts if she'd only give them a number or a horse," Pat Crist reported. "Or their wives would come in and pretend interest in Mrs. Dixon's charities just so they could get to meet her, perhaps overhear something, and report back to their husbands."

On one occasion, without realizing she was the center of all this interest, Mrs. Dixon mentioned a curious dream she had the night before. "I saw three numbers," she said, "and when I woke up, I couldn't get them out of my mind."

A nattily dressed stranger, with fifty-dollar shoes, who had dropped in to pick up his charity-minded wife, carelessly asked: "What were these numbers?"

"Three-four-five," she said, "and it doesn't mean a thing to me."

"In that order?" he asked.

She nodded.

But the numbers meant something to the caller. He played them across the board and two days later sent Jeane an expensive new crystal ball. It had cost him a thousand dollars. The psychic was completely baffled.

"What's all this about?" she asked.

He was more than frank. "That's your share," he said. "I made ten thousand dollars on that number, and you get ten per cent. Let's keep working together, and you can have all the crystal balls you want."

She promptly returned the ball, cut the gambler's wife from her charity, and kept her dreams to herself thereafter. "That crystal ball," she lamented to a friend, "had horrible vibrations; I couldn't see a thing in it."

When the right people request it she occasionally concentrates on sporting events, but never makes a bet herself. Before the 1953 Kentucky Derby, Jockey Club friends in New York inquired about the chances of Alfred Vanderbilt's unbeaten Native Dancer, a top-heavy favorite. Peering into her crystal ball, she told a friend, Mrs. Estelle (Mike) Friedrichs, former White House secretary: "I see a dark horse winning, but I see a gray horse too."

"That gray horse would be Native Dancer," Mrs. Friedrichs said.

Mrs. Dixon's face knit in a perplexed frown. "I see the dark horse across the finish line first, but I see the gray winning some money too. Is that possible?"

"Why, yes," Mrs. Friedrichs explained. "The second and third horses share the money too. Place and . . ."

"That's it, place," Jeane cried triumphantly. "I see the gray one second."

There was an unexpected sequel to this prognostication a few days later. With the unbeaten Dancer the glamour horse of the year, the impending race was being discussed at nearly every Washington cocktail party Derby week. "Just kidding, over a drink," recalled former advertising executive Oliver Presbrey, "I happened to mention that Native Dancer was such a sure thing I'd been thinking of betting a thousand dollars on him." Presbrey smiled. "Two dollars would have been a good-sized bet for me."

He had noticed Jeane looking at him quizzically, but thought nothing of it. But the day before the race, back in New York, he received an urgent wire from Washington. It was from Jeane. "Bet Dancer to place," she enjoined, "or you'll lose your shirt."

As it developed the Dancer did place, the lone defeat of a glorious career. He was nosed out by a dark horse—Dark Star.

Presbrey was to have another experience with Jeane. With his wife, commentator Martha Rountree, he had bought a country place in Warrenton, Virginia, and was happily ensconced there weekends and holidays. One day as the couple discussed the problems of a new home with Jeane, she suddenly threw her hands up in horror. "Get that house insured, Martha," she said, "you're going to have a fire."

She saw nobody hurt—only the fire. "I don't care where you buy your insurance," she said, "only buy it soon."

Within a week, there was a fire with heavy damage at the Presbreys' Warrenton place. "Naturally," Miss Rountree sighed, "we were underinsured."

As the originator of one television show, "Meet The Press," Miss Rountree was so impressed with Jeane that she arranged to put her on another show, "Washington Party House," a program reflecting the Capital social scene. "I was hoping," she said, "that Jeane and her crystal ball would liven things up."

She was not to be disappointed.

The program emanated from Washington's NBC outlet on May 14, 1953, while Jeane's friends were still talking about her Dancer prediction. A coterie of these admirers had decided that she should answer TV questions on Nepal, since she had recently read for a brother of the King of that principality, and would know something about her subject. She had also been tutored on that remote land by Mrs. Virginia Wallace, an executive of Washington's big Woodward & Lothrop Department Store, who had long been fascinated by the Dixon psychic powers.

Having heard a good deal about the spontaneity of the Dixon forecasts, and having seen some of it for myself, I was surprised that it was thought necessary to groom her with special information. "That certainly wouldn't have made for a fair demonstration of Mrs. Dixon's psychic talents," I told Mrs. Wallace.

She was not at all ruffled. "Anybody who knows anything about psychic powers," she explained, "knows they can't be turned on like the television. So I thought that in the event Jeane got nothing psychically, it would be nice if she could fall back on some topic she could discuss intelligently."

It seemed plausible—and well-conceived.

Certain that her protégée would put on a good performance, Mrs. Wallace had invited a goodly audience to review the television offering on her luxurious houseboat at the foot of the Capital's Maine Street. She was sure that they would learn all about Nepal, and leave convinced that psychics were reasonable, intelligent people after all.

But fate decreed otherwise. Instead of discussing Nepal, which she had just brushed up on, Jeane, on the television screen, began rambling on about Russia, of which she knew nothing. "Imagine my consternation, in front of all my guests," Mrs. Wallace said, "when Jeane started making a fool of herself on television. There, I thought, went all that we had tried to build up with our work on Nepal."

Mrs. Wallace was also angry, for she thought that Jeane had taken off on her own, but actually the crystal-ball gazer was as surprised as the watching Mrs. Wallace. As the cameras focused, bringing Jeane's image to millions around the country, former Ambassador to Russia Joseph Davies had unexpectedly taken over the questioning. With an easy smile, the New Deal's leading authority on Stalin's Russia began discussing the recent rise to power of Stalin's successor, the round-faced, puffy-eyed Malenkov. "How long," he asked with a patronizing grin, "will Malenkov be Prime Minister?"

Martha Rountree, hovering on the sidelines, gulped helplessly, even as Virginia Wallace stewed unhappily miles away.

Only Jeane remained calm. She peered intently into her crystal ball, and said with an easy conviction that matched the Ambassador's: "He will be the Premier for less than two years, and then he will be removed."

The Ambassador's smile broadened. "No Russian chief of state is ever replaced," he said with emphasis. "He either dies, like Stalin, or is shot." His eyebrows went up. "You know, I happen to know something about this subject, I wrote a book about it."

Jeane stood her ground. "I'm sure you're better informed than I, Mr. Ambassador, but I still see Malenkov being replaced." She looked Davies in the eye. "And his replacement will be a portly military man with wavy hair, green eyes, and a goatee."

Davies snorted. "I've been in Russia for years," he said, "and I never saw a Russian who looked like that."

"I'm in no position to contradict you," Jeane retorted, "but that is what I see." She took another look into her crystal ball, and her face suddenly grew grim; her eyes burned with a new intensity, and the words now came streaming out. She was oblivious not only of Davies, but of the curious knot of people who had grouped around her.

Like a prophetess of old, her voice soared: "I see a silver ball spinning into space, coming out of the East, which leads me to believe that Russia will be the first to put a satellite into orbit. And I see the ball changing into a dove, then sinking its claws into the scalp of a completely bald man, but not drawing blood. And then, it looks to the East, meaning that someday Russia will determine the peace."

There was an awkward silence as she finally stopped. She had been much too serious for anybody to laugh; her figure, as she tautly held out an arm, far too impressive. And she herself, as she glanced around, was sobered by the realization of what she had predicted. She had gotten more than she had counted on, but she knew she was right. "The newspapers mentioned the space prediction," she said later, "but nobody referred to the bit about Russia dictating the peace."

Meanwhile, turning off her television set, Virginia Wallace apologized to her guests for Jeane's performance. But twenty-three months later Malenkov was replaced by Marshal Bulganin, a portly green-eyed military man with a goatee, and in 1957 the Russians cracked the space barrier with their sputnik.

Mrs. Wallace's misgivings have since turned to pride. "That dove must have landed on Khrushchev—he doesn't have a hair on his head—and the Russians seem to be getting their way wherever they turn."

This was all very nice, but I still wondered about the White House interview with Roosevelt.

At a party at the Sulgrave Club in 1944 given by Capital hostess Perle Mesta for her friend Harry Truman, Jeane had foreseen that Truman, recently-elected Vice-President, would some-day be President.

"Was this before or after you read for Roosevelt?" I asked, pursuing my inquiry.

"After."

"Then you already knew about Roosevelt?"

She nodded. It had been several days since we had discussed her sitting at the White House, and she seemed calm and relaxed, no longer uneasy when Roosevelt's name was mentioned. "I have decided to tell you about the session with the President," she said. "My friends, including a former White House secretary, advised against it, but I made my own decision."

"What influenced you?" I asked.

She regarded me with her penetrating blue eyes. "Whatever power I have," she said, "was given me to be used for others, and can be taken from me if it is misused."

Her face took on a glow. She smiled, and impulsively reached over and took my hand. "When I first saw you I sensed that you would bring better understanding of this power—God's power—to an unbelieving world. And so I must do what I can to help you."

I listened silently, not wanting to do or say anything to break the mood.

Although it had been many years since she had sat down with the President, their meeting was as fresh and vivid as the day it took place.

"It was good of you to come," Franklin Roosevelt had said, as he pointed to a chair next to his. She sat quietly, waiting for him to speak, noticing how careworn he seemed. "For several days, since receiving that first phone call," she recalled, "I had kept my mind clear, so that all my communication lines would be open."

The President's desk was bare except for a miniature flag and the figure of an American eagle. He had cleared his desk, and his visitor had his complete attention. As they chatted, he seemed intrigued by the lines in her hands. "They are very old hands," he said.

"Yes, they've always been old hands," she agreed.

His mood suddenly changed and he turned to the war raging around the world. "Wars," he observed, "can never bring lasting peace."

She knew that he had not called her in to discuss the war, but she nodded understandingly and said:

"Mr. President, if you can make the Russians understand we are their friends, it will save much trouble later on."

"I've had a feeling about Russia for some time now," he said. "Something I feel quite strongly." He glanced up with a smile. "Would you call that being psychic? This feeling tells me that the Russians will never want to bomb us, and it tells me that our great trouble one day will be with another ally—of both ours and Russia."

"Do you mean China?" she asked.

He nodded, and suddenly the voice that had appeared so resonant, seemed to tire and fade. He sat a moment staring, and then sighed almost imperceptibly, speaking softly as though thinking to himself: "It is important to finish the things we start in this life." He looked into space, pausing a moment before he continued. "But as a rule," he said finally, "man doesn't live long enough to complete the work so important to him."

As she sat wordlessly, intently alert, the President toyed with one of the ornaments on his desk, lifted himself a little in his chair, and cocked a quizzical eye at his guest. "Tell me," he said, in a matter-of-fact tone, "how much time do I have to get my work done?"

It was almost as though she had been waiting for the question. Concentrating deeply, Jeane Dixon reached over and took the President's hand. "I felt an unselfish vibration as big as the world," she recalled of the man whose politics she had never approved. "His spirit was strong, though his body faltered."

As she held his hand, she felt his eyes on her, waiting for her answer. And as that answer came, she weighed the words carefully. "If I were in your place," she said slowly, "I would try to get everything done as quickly as possible."

He smiled. "Can you be a little more definite?"

Her voice came back crisp and impersonal. "Not later," she said, "than the middle of the coming year."

He seemed lost in thought awhile. "I understand," he said at last. "I had been hoping for more time."

Jeane returned her hand to her lap. "Are there any other questions, sir?" she asked.

He smiled again, patting her hand. "You have told me all I need to know."

She got up and bowed.

"Thank you for coming," he said, "and God bless you."

The interview was over. It had lasted just twenty minutes.

At the study door, she took her last look at the President. He was deep in thought, unaware even that she was still in the room. "I felt a great wave of pity," she said, "for the lonely man behind the big desk, for he knew as well as I, the truth of what he had just been told."

Outside the President's door, she saw the first White House aide, a lone guard. She smiled sadly, her thoughts with the man who had but four months to finish the important work he had started, and walked slowly into the crisp morning air.

3 MRS. DIXON PREDICTS

"As you know," Mrs. Dixon said, "I persuaded my husband to cancel his flight, and it saved his life."

There was no question in the Washington seer's mind that her gift, used judiciously, could make life easier for her fellow man.

"Why else," she asked, "was it given me?"

But I had checked out some remarkable predictions of tragedy by Mrs. Dixon, made well in advance, and the tragedies had still occurred.

"Maybe," I said, "you only saw the plane crashing, and assumed your husband was on it." I coughed politely. "That would still mean that you had seen correctly."

"But without my premonition," she protested, "he would have taken that plane."

"Actually," I said, "if you hadn't stopped him, something else might have—he might have missed the airport bus, or become ill."

She was plainly puzzled. "What I am driving at," I explained, "is that you have given people all kinds of warnings, and they still haven't been able to help themselves."

I thought back on several remarkable predictions—a mother who had been warned of her daughter's murder, and who could still do nothing to forestall it; a New Jersey artist, warned of a tragic fire, who still did nothing to avert that fire.

She had foreseen the deaths of Supreme Court Justice Frank Murphy and Dag Hammarskjold, both in the midst of life, and they had died as she anticipated.

"What would have happened," I asked, "if that mother with the sick child had listened to you, and not the doctors who wanted to operate?"

She considered a moment. "Just as I saw that child dying on the operating table, I saw it living had there been no operation."

She looked doubtful when I suggested that she might have insight into future events only because those events were inevitable. "How could you see Malenkov replacing Stalin, and Bulganin replacing Malenkov, unless these events were slated to take place?"

She frowned, conceding, "I was sure in both cases."

I recalled aloud the case of little Lisa, a teen-ager with an impeccable family background, whom Mrs. Dixon had shocked by predicting that she would be behind bars in six months.

"If her parents had been different," Mrs. Dixon said, "it would have never happened."

There could have been a thousand and one "buts," but it happened all the same. I had talked to the girl myself, trying to determine whether such a prediction could have been logically and plausibly made. She herself had laughed uproariously when Mrs. Dixon had made her prediction, cautioning her to stay at home nights lest she get into trouble.

Several weeks later, driving a borrowed car, the girl, then sixteen years old, was picked up for a driving violation. And when a friend, previously liberal with the car, claimed that it had been taken without permission, she was booked on a delinquency charge.

Her family, inexplicably, would do nothing to help her. Probation officers told her about a girls' school she could go to, and she agreed. "It was a school for girls, all right," she recalled, "wayward girls, and the windows had steel bars."

There had been numerous other predictions for Lisa—and all have come true so far. "When I was most despondent," Lisa recalled, "Mrs. Dixon told me I would be out of the institution by my eighteenth birthday, and the judge freed me that very week."

She was still estranged from her family when Mrs. Dixon predicted that she would be a bridesmaid at her brother's wedding in the spring of 1962, and wear blue. "Oh, don't be silly," she had commented, "he wouldn't even invite me."

But when the wedding bells pealed, she was there in blue.

She had been wearing contact lenses for five years without the slightest discomfort, when Mrs. Dixon warned her to get rid of them or she'd have difficulty within the month. "Two weeks later," she recalled, "I developed an eye infection and almost lost the sight of one eye."

It was curious that Lisa should not have heeded the warning when the seer had been so right before. Lisa smiled, as she observed: "You never get over your surprise that anybody should be able to predict something that hasn't happened, and"—she hesitated—"you do get the idea they're trying to brainwash you a little."

Actually, Mrs. Dixon had talked Lisa out of an early marriage. "I see you marrying at twenty-two," she had said. "Any marriage before that will not work out, and he will be a man old enough to understand you."

Lisa, nineteen, when I spoke to her, seemed reconciled to her fate. "I am waiting," she said, "until I am twenty-two."

Unlike Lisa, Dag Hammarskjold never had the benefit of a Dixon warning. "If I had told him," Jeane said philosophically, "he wouldn't have listened." But she seemed intent on telling the rest of Washington, long before the plane crash, and right up until it occurred, in September 1961, not to fly with the UN

Secretary-General. "When I was considering a flight abroad," recalled Eleanor (Lady) Baumgardner, confidential aide of late Supreme Court Justice Frank Murphy, "Jeane Dixon told me, 'Whatever you do, don't get on the same plane with Dag Hammarskjold.'"

Just as clearly, years before, she had foreseen the death of Justice Murphy himself, but had veiled her prediction because she did not think that her warnings could avert a natural death. Murphy was already vacationing in his native Michigan, waiting to be secretly married within a week to a Forest Hills, Long Island, socialite, when Jeane, with the inscrutability of a Nostradamus, took Miss Baumgardner's hand at a Washington dinner party and said sympathetically:

"Lady, I see you with a new job soon, in a new house, and I see the death of an older man very close to you."

"Jeane," Lady replied, "I wouldn't think of giving up my apartment. I've been with Justice Murphy for seventeen years, in Michigan, the Philippines, and Washington, and wouldn't dream of leaving him, and everybody in my family is well, thank you."

Fleetingly, the thought had crossed Lady's mind that Mrs. Dixon might have meant Murphy, but the fifty-five-year-old jurist had never seemed in better spirits. "I had the Justice's wedding ring in my purse," Lady recalled, "and was flying out to Detroit that week with his fiancée for the wedding."

And then the wire came. The Capital's most eligible bachelor had suffered an unexpected heart attack. "We flew out as planned," Miss Baumgardner said, "but for an entirely different occasion."

After the Justice's untimely death, Eleanor Baumgardner changed her job, joining the Supreme Court secretarial pool; then, quite unexpectedly, she became foster mother to a sick friend's children, and took a house in Georgetown to give the children a home. The older man, of course, was Justice Murphy.

In contrast to her Murphy prediction, Mrs. Dixon was singularly direct in telling a mother of her daughter's murder. "I felt," said Jeane, justifying herself, "that Nancy's death was avoidable."

Everywhere in Washington, people had remarked on the beauty

and verve of Nancy Hathaway Rogers, a mischievous, red-haired minx, whose life had ended tragically at twenty-four. Her death had been a cruel blow to her family and it was with some trepidation that I approached her mother to check on the Dixon-forecast, even though ten years had already elapsed.

"Do you mind talking about Nancy?" I asked thrice-married Mrs. Kitty Von Ammon Denny Jordan, formerly of Washington, now of Los Angeles, and a beauty in her own right, as we sat together in a New York restaurant.

Mrs. Jordan shook her head slowly. "The years have made things easier, and I can think back on it now without getting upset."

"Do you think Nancy's death could have been averted?" I asked.

She sipped her tea slowly. "I think there was very little anyone could do about it."

As I watched her, I could see easily enough where her daughter must have gotten her good looks. She was an elegantly handsome woman, lightly showing her years. She had obviously developed a compensating philosophy of life, and I sensed immediately that I could ask her any question without causing her distress. I was curious about her reaction to Mrs. Dixon's first warning remarks.

"But hadn't Mrs. Dixon warned you?" I asked.

"Yes, on two occasions. The first time she said, 'If you don't get Nancy out of town, something will happen to her.'"

"Did she explain?"

"She saw a murder or suicide; she couldn't quite make her mind up at the time. But the result would be the same for Nancy."

"Did she say how soon?"

"In two years or so."

"Did you take her seriously?"

"I knew that there would be no sense telling Nancy; she would only have laughed. But we did persuade her to visit my husband's ranch near Bremerton, Washington."

"Did she go alone?"

"She was joined by her husband, Robert Dean Rogers, an ex-serviceman."

But bored by ranch life, missing the Capital tempo, Nancy returned to the Washington social swim. She took an apartment by herself in a Maryland suburb, breaking off with Rogers, with whom she had not been getting along.

Months later, Mrs. Dixon repeated her warning and stressed its urgency. "Whatever you do, Kitty," she again told the mother, "get Nancy out of town; the net is closing in on her. There is no time to lose."

The mother knew Nancy would not listen. "All I could do," Mrs. Jordan said, "was hope and pray."

The Jordans were in New York. Kitty's husband, Major George Racey Jordan, author of the controversial book *Major Jordan's Diary*, was speaking at the Waldorf-Astoria Hotel, when the first word came.

Bizarrely, it was both murder and suicide. As Nancy returned home to her apartment that night, a jealousy-crazed Rogers, failing at reconciliation, had shot her three times, and then turned the gun on himself. Washington newspapers carried the details. "Estranged Mate Kills Wife, Self," one headline went. A subhead said: "Silver Springs Couple Found Dead: Reconciliation Attempt Fails." The beauty had fled to the bathroom in a futile attempt to reach a fire escape. Her body was found draped over the edge of the tub. Adding a further macabre twist, the body was identified by Robert Denny, a Washington newspaperman, who had dashed out on the story when the first reports flashed into the city room. He was Nancy's half-brother.

In her grief, Kitty attributed Nancy's fate to a higher power. "We must learn to accept what we cannot alter," she said. But her husband was more realistic.

"Rogers wasn't right upstairs," Major Jordan said. "He had been wounded in the war and was forever picking shrapnel from his back. After the marriage broke up, he snapped."

"Were you aware of Mrs. Dixon's prediction?" I asked Jordan.

"My wife told me."

"Did you take it seriously?"

"We can't live by this sort of thing," he said, "or we'd be paralyzed. Our own actions shape the course of our lives."

"Then how do you account for Jeane Dixon seeing the event virtually as it happened, discounting any possible action by you or Mrs. Jordan?"

"I don't try to account for it. When these things occur and can be verified, I don't question their authenticity, but our own efforts still largely determine what happens to each of us. Nancy chose her own life."

He seemed very sure of himself.

But without knowing it, Major Jordan had figured in another Dixon prediction. And the death of a man he did not know had contributed significantly to the shaping of his own life—and marriage.

"Shortly after World War II," Kitty Jordan explained, "I told Jeane of my intention to marry a Navy Commander. 'You'll never marry that man,' she told me. 'As quickly as he came into your life, he'll leave it.'"

"And how quickly was that?"

"We had met at a party, and had fallen instantly in love."

Upset by Jeane Dixon's prediction, yet still impressed by a seer she had never known to be wrong, Kitty had said, "Then I guess I won't marry anyone."

"Oh, yes you will," Jeane said. "A tall well-built man, with reddish hair and two front teeth set wide apart."

"Not in a million years would I marry a man who looked like that," Kitty rejoined.

Womanlike, Kitty told the naval officer of Jeane's prediction. "He was furious," she recalled, "saying Jeane was only trying to break us up, and really didn't see anything at all."

"And what did break you up?"

She sighed. "His plane crashed on a Navy mission near the Potomac. He left my life as quickly as he had come into it." Her face was as calm and as impassively beautiful as when she had discussed her daughter.

"But you are happily married now?" I asked.

"George and I were married fourteen years ago, just as Mrs. Dixon predicted."

As she spoke, I recalled with a start my first impression of

Major Jordan. He was tall, powerfully built, with red hair, and he had two front teeth spaced widely apart. "I had not even met him," Kitty said, "at the time of the prediction."

"Do you think Jeane influenced you?" I asked.

"Lord no," she laughed. "I realized at once, of course, that George fit the description. But I never expected to marry him; he wasn't my type."

Was Jeane Dixon, the prophet, always right, as many of her friends insisted?

Mrs. Jordan mused a moment. "In twenty years, I have never known her to be off. She was confused at first about Nancy, seeing murder or suicide, but that was a matter of interpretation, since both did occur."

Months later, I was to see Mrs. Jordan again in Beverly Hills, California. Her husband had been ill, requiring an operation, but she was as brave and staunch as ever. I did not tell her, as I suddenly recalled, that Mrs. Dixon had predicted her husband's illness. I am sure it would not have surprised her, but it might have upset her, coming as it did while she was still concerned with his sickness. "I am sure," she said, "that George will soon be well," and you almost thought it was Mrs. Dixon talking. She was that confident.

Still, checking through Mrs. Dixon's predictions in Washington, I had found what I considered errors. "You predicted some time ago that Nehru would soon be replaced," I mentioned one day, visiting her office.

Mrs. Dixon took no offense. "The time element is often very difficult," she said. "I made the Nehru prediction three or four years ago, without setting a time limit. Asked about it later, I gave five to seven years. I'm still within the deadline."

It seemed to me that I had caught her in an inconsistency. "Why should time be difficult when you have pinpointed so many things so well?"

"Time varies," she said. "To the man on the ground time represents twenty-four hours; to that man in orbit, it's an hour and a half."

"But you have predicted specific dates."

"The dates actually flashed before me, as part of a vision. But with Nehru I only saw him losing out, and got the general impression that it was an approaching event."

"After taking Goa from the Portuguese, Nehru seems stronger than ever," I observed.

She smiled. "So did Malenkov, and Bulganin—before they were replaced." She looked up. "And I see Khrushchev disappearing quickly when he goes." She slapped her hands together for emphasis.

"Any human being can be wrong," I suggested tactfully.

"I'm only an instrument; the source itself is never wrong."

"But instruments are human and can be faulty."

"True, but then I see nothing." She sat back and smiled, as though there were nothing more she could add. Meanwhile, I reflected. Was the hand of God on Jeane Dixon as she and many of her friends obviously believed? Or was she a glandular freak, a throwback to primitive, instinctual man? But whatever it was, God or glands, her power was never more strikingly displayed than in the strange case of Emma Ench.

It was another of those apparently incredible Dixon stories, only more so.

Jeane and Emma Ench had met in the Dixon office in Washington in November of 1954 to discuss a Christmas display that Emma, an artist, was preparing in her Paterson, New Jersey, home. It was a benefit for the Damon Runyon Cancer Fund, one of Jeane's pet charities.

To an admiring group, Emma passed out photographs of her miniature models. Picking one up, Jeane suddenly dropped it as though it had burned her fingers. There were many witnesses.

"A look of great concern immediately came over Mrs. Dixon's face," recalled Lorene Mason, a Washington secretary, "and she said to Emma as she picked up the picture: 'Emma, please be careful, or you're going to have a terrible fire in your home.' When Emma smiled indulgently, Jeane said, 'Emma, whatever you do, make sure everything in the display is fireproofed.' "

For the rest of the meeting Mrs. Dixon seemed strangely preoccupied. "Never as long as I live," Miss Mason said, "will I forget the expression on her face. She appeared to be reliving a nightmare."

Twice again Jeane warned Miss Ench of fire. "In fact, when she kept mentioning it," said Miss Mason, "Emma finally laughed good-naturedly and said, 'Oh! Jeane, you're just trying to use that fire as an excuse for not visiting us in Paterson.'"

Jeane did not join in the laughter. "Promise me," she insisted, "that you will fireproof everything, and make sure that you are adequately insured."

"Everything will be fireproofed," said Miss Ench. "There is nothing to worry about."

After the meeting, Mrs. Dixon stood motionless as though in a trance. "Poor Emma," she murmured. "Poor, poor Emma."

The Christmas display was a great success. Opening shortly before Christmas, it lasted two weeks beyond the new year, and hundreds of people paid to see the exquisitely fashioned models of nursery-rhyme figures, carved from cotton and celluloid, in the basement of the Paterson home.

After the show was over, Emma threw a party for the children who had helped her stage the spectacle.

The Paterson *Morning Call* of January 17, 1955, told the rest. There had been a marshmallow roast over the fireplace; a marshmallow flew off a stick held by a seven-year-old girl, and plopped into a display that was powder dry. In a flash, flames roared through the basement. There was no panic. The fifteen children were led safely to the only exit not cut off by the blaze. Their elders were not as fortunate. Emma's father, Peter Ench, her brother, Richard, and her close friend, William Farren, suffered severe burns. Emma herself, herding the youngsters to safety, was the most cruelly burned. Her nylon dress, catching fire, made her a living torch. She died within a few hours in the hospital. Before the year ended, her father and Farren both succumbed. Four other adults were less seriously burned.

Luck had been against Emma Ench. Witnesses recalled that on the morning of the fire, remembering Jeane Dixon's prediction, she had expressed concern over the crackling dryness of the evergreens, and said that she would take the display down immediately after the party.

There had been other reminders of the Dixon warning. A week before the display opened, Mrs. Estelle Friedrichs, the former White House secretary, who had been at the Washington meeting, visited the Paterson home with a friend, Mrs. Elwood Meyers of Wayne, New Jersey. Mrs. Meyers, a puppeteer, who had not met Miss Ench before, recalled that the artist had invited the two of them to the basement to see the display—titled "Land of Let's Believe."

They sat there, comfortably sipping cocktails, when Mrs. Friedrichs, craning her head around the room, suddenly remarked, "Just look at all those evergreens, celluloid figures, and cotton snowballs—what a fire they would make." Then, with a start, she turned to Emma. "Remember what Jeane Dixon said about a fire; is all this going to be fireproofed?"

Emma laughed. "Of course, it is."

But it never was.

Mrs. Meyers' husband was badly burned. Her daughter escaped, and so did she, one of the two adults so fortunate. The other was Emma's sister-in-law, Grace Ench. "Grace's baby had been crying for no apparent reason," Mrs. Meyers explained, "and Grace decided to take her upstairs. I went along. When we reached the head of the stairs, the baby stopped crying, and as we looked back, the entire basement was in flames."

There was another ironic twist of fate. Emma Ench's brother, a Catholic priest, surveying the display prior to the party, had urged her to introduce a Nativity scene. "You have depicted all the other well-known tales of the holiday scene," he pointed out. Then, Mrs. Meyers said, he pointed to the fireplace, and observed, "That would be the perfect place for it."

But Emma had another use for the fireplace.

Not everybody is impressed by the Dixon predictions. Even in Washington, where she has amazed so many, Mrs. Dixon has her detractors. "Oh, anybody might guess that Hammarskjold would be killed in a plane crash," a skeptical reporter observed. "He was always flying around to the damndest places."

"But she seemed to pinpoint it pretty well," I said.

"Predict enough things about enough people, and some are bound to hit," the reporter persisted.

Hammarskjold's life had perhaps been more dangerous than most, but he might just as easily have been shot or hit by a car as crash in a plane. Or so it seemed to me.

"Coincidence," the reporter said, "the sheerest coincidence."

"But I understand she practically picked the day."

"Who told you?"

"I got it indirectly."

He paused triumphantly. "There you are; somebody who told somebody, who told somebody else. The usual way these stories grow."

That day, as the newspapers were filled with the Hammarskjold crash, I visited the *Parade* magazine offices in downtown Washington. Opal Ginn, a *Parade* staffer, asked casually. "Have you heard that Mrs. Dixon predicted the Hammarskjold crash?"

"Two or three people said something about it," I replied.

"You might check Mr. Nicholson," she said, "he's the vice-president of the bank downstairs, the American Security and Trust Company. I understand she told friends of his when it was going to crash."

Mr. Nicholson had all the reserve of the banker bracing himself for a loan. "Can I help you?" he asked carefully.

I asked if he knew Mrs. Dixon and he nodded noncommittally.

"I understand she told friends of yours that the Hammarskjold plane was about to crash."

He shook his head, and I started up to leave.

"No," he said, "she told me."

I sat down again. "How did she say it?"

"She told me not to go up in a plane with Hammarskjold for the next couple of weeks."

"How long ago was that?"

"A couple of weeks ago."

"Did she give you any reason?"

"She said it wouldn't be healthy, and"—he drawled softly—"I guess she was right."

"How did she happen to tell you?"

He shrugged. "You'll have to ask her that."

"Do you think it was a lucky hit?" I asked.

"She's a remarkable woman," was all he said, not answering directly.

"Did she make any other predictions that you know of?" I asked.

He scratched his chin reflectively. "Some years back, when I was with the National Metropolitan Bank, Mrs. Dixon came in one day and my assistant, young George Earnshaw, who was going on vacation, mentioned that someone else would be handling her account while he was gone."

As Nicholson told it, Mrs. Dixon seemed pleased. "Fine, Mr. Earnshaw," she said. "Where are you going?"

"To Virginia, on a hunting trip."

Jeane's face froze in alarm and she put out a restraining hand. "Please, Mr. Earnshaw, don't take that hunting trip. Promise me." She tugged at his sleeve. "If you make that trip, you won't come back."

Earnshaw looked at her as though she were mad. The two men exchanged glances, and Earnshaw said reassuringly, "All right, Mrs. Dixon, I'll call off the trip."

She breathed a sigh of relief, and walked happily from the bank.

And what had happened to the young banker?

Nicholson stared at the ceiling. "That was a Friday," he said. "On Monday, Earnshaw was trudging contentedly through the fields with a rifle; he shot something and began to run forward, and then he fell down. When they reached him, he was dead, a heart attack, they said."

I looked at Nicholson and Nicholson looked at me.

"Tell me," I said, "do you believe he would have been all right if he had listened to her?"

The banker shrugged and looked me squarely in the eye. "I don't know what to believe," he said. "All I know is, I don't want her predicting for me."

4 THE SAGE OF VIRGINIA BEACH

We were talking about Bridey Murphy and how Morey Bernstein visited the Cayce association before writing his controversial
book on reincarnation. "Cayce told us to look for him," Hugh
Lynn Cayce said.

The son of the "miracle man of Virginia Beach" dug up a
Cayce reading for August of 1926, in which Cayce had suggested
that trustees of the Association for Research and Enlightenment
turn to "a New York connection" for financial help. And he gave
six names. Bernstein was one.

I was no more impressed by this than by Bernstein's book,
which had tried to establish a case for reincarnation via a tape
recorder. There were an awful lot of "Bernsteins" in New
York.

"Did you gain anything from Bernstein's visit?" I asked.

"Bob Adriance, our president, and Everett Irion, our business
manager, both men of independent means, came to us after
reading about Cayce's work in *The Search for Bridey Murphy*.
They put our association on its feet financially."

Hugh Lynn smiled. "But I can show you an even more surprising name; Cayce told us to look for him, too."

He riffled through a pile of readings that the late seer had
given in his miraculous healing of the sick, and then with a
straight face, handed me three separate files. "This man," he
said, "is mentioned in all three."

I scanned the files perfunctorily; they all went back to 1931.
And then, as my eye ran down the first file, it was caught
by one name—my own. There was a reference on March 3,
another on June 1, advising the group to contact a "Stern"—

phonetically, the same as my own. I smiled now as I began to surmise why I had received so warm a welcome at ARE headquarters, but again, I was not terribly impressed. There were an awful lot of "Sterns" in New York.

Under Hugh Lynn's watchful eye, I checked the third file and another name suddenly stood out—that of David E. Kahn, and this was the man, Cayce said, who should contact the man with a name like mine. I knew David E. Kahn. I had met him years before, quite by chance, and now, with a start, I recalled that he, a Cayce trustee and New York businessman, was the first to ever talk to me about Edgar Cayce.

Not only that, but I had briefly recorded his experiences with Cayce for a New York newspaper in June 1956, some twenty-five years after the original reading. But even so, what help could I—a reporter—be to the Cayce group?

Hugh Lynn smiled. "Morey Bernstein didn't see how he could be helpful, either."

I looked through the readings again; there was my name, Kahn's, and two or three others. For some reason, one stuck in my mind. And that night at dinner, oddly, Hugh Lynn Cayce mentioned this name. "An old classmate from Washington and Lee is down from New York," he said, "and he called saying he wanted to talk about something."

"His name's in one of the readings with your friend 'Stern,'" I said lightly. "Maybe he wants to make a contribution."

He certainly was in a position to do so. He had done well financially since leaving college but, as Cayce had once predicted, had not done so well in another department. In college, Hugh Lynn told me, he had been one of eight students for whom Edgar Cayce had given life readings, discussing past incarnations and the present, too. In this incarnation, Cayce had warned the young man to watch himself with women, for they would bring trouble all his life. While by no means an unusual forecast for any red-blooded American college boy, this prediction almost immediately made Cayce look good. In a few weeks the student was expelled over a girl, and, transferring to another college, was again thrown out for the same reason. After college the problem continued. At last count he had been married three times.

Later, I learned he had expressed interest in the Cayce movement, wondering now in his middle years what it was all about. What was there to reincarnation? How had Cayce been able to predict things? How could he help the sick when he didn't even see them and knew nothing about medicine anyway? Was there any evidence of survival?

I was unsympathetic. "I just don't see how anybody can buy reincarnation," I told Hugh Lynn. "It's unprovable, untenable, obviously the product of wishful thinking."

"You have seen people predict correctly, and not understood how they did it," he said.

"But at least," I said, "there were ways of checking these things out."

Hugh Lynn smiled. "Reincarnation, when you think about it, is no less remarkable than what my father, with no medical background, did in curing people he had never seen of ailments he had never diagnosed."

"But these things can be checked, too, so that even if we don't know how it was done, at least we know it was done." I studied Hugh Lynn closely. He was a pleasant-faced, middle-aged man with none of his father's psychic powers. He had made a lifelong job, as recommended by Cayce in his readings, of explaining his father's work. But even so, nothing of the mystic had rubbed off. He could have been the proprietor of a small-town general store. He spoke with a slight Southern drawl, and he spoke moderately. He was not trying to convince me of anything, least of all that his father could predict the future. "Cayce didn't like to make predictions," he said. "He believed in free will, and didn't like to influence people who might be susceptible to suggestion."

For one who didn't care to predict, Cayce had certainly made plenty of predictions. He had predicted the stock market collapse, Norfolk's pre-eminence as a port, a best-selling book; he foresaw England losing India, the end of Prohibition, Hitler's defeat, the rise of the yellow races, Russia as the dominant power of Europe

—and earthquakes, typhoons, volcanic eruptions, the formation of new land.

In the past, successfully, according to some, he had traced the history of antiquity and its cultures, describing in detail the Lost Continent of Atlantis, which, except for a classic reference by Plato—and other ancient Greeks—has been generally dismissed as romantic rumor.

How did he see it all?

Through merging his own subconscious, his followers felt, with that of a Universal Consciousness that had existed since the beginning of time, recording everything that had ever happened. And he remembered so well, his followers insisted, because he had lived in all these ages, his soul ever recurring in a new body.

It was a philosophy not easy to accept. Yet in the sleeping state Cayce would correctly mention names, places, and events he knew nothing about in the waking state. The subject of his reading could be hundreds of miles away; he would merely close his eyes, fall off to sleep, and say, "I have the body," and often, as though he were there, describe what that person was doing at the time.

If given a fictitious name or address he wouldn't attempt a reading. "He always needed the time and place," secretary Gladys Davis Turner said, "before the reading would start."

Once, a list of names was handed him, the name of a woman in Ohio at the top and further down a man in New York. All were to have readings. "We had better read for the man from New York first," Cayce said, "because he has to go pretty soon." A checkup the next day revealed that the New Yorker, even as Cayce was discussing him, was getting ready to leave his apartment because of an emergency.

There were many examples of this omnivision. Years before, Cayce had a request for a physical reading from Noah Miller, a ship's captain, who had suffered a severe back strain while unloading his freighter in Jacksonville, Florida. The appointment was made, but the busy Miller got his times confused. "I was thirty miles from the ship," he told me, "when Cayce was to have given me the reading for my back."

Back in Virginia Beach, closing his eyes, Cayce frowned as he tried to reach Miller. "I cannot find the body," he said. And then, still groping verbally, "it is not on the boat." But after some hesitation, he proceeded with the reading anyway, explaining that enough of Miller's presence pervaded the ship's cabin for him to tune in. It was just a little bit more fantastic than the average Cayce story.

"How could all that be?" I asked Miller.

The captain looked at me with a merry twinkle in his blue eyes. He was a rugged man of the sea, with a leathery skin as tough as rawhide and a disposition that matched. He was emphatically not the mystic type.

"How could all that be?" he intoned. "You'll have to ask Cayce."

"All right then," I said, "how did you happen to consult him?"

"That's easy," he said, with a touch of Irish brogue. "The back was so bad, the doctors said they'd have to operate, or I might never walk again." He stretched his arms and yawned. "I didn't have time for operations, and I had a big, hungry brood to feed, so I figured I had nothing to lose with Cayce." He smiled. "I'd heard he never lost a patient."

With Cayce's advice his back soon mended and he became a convert to Cayce-ism, like thousands of others who were miraculously helped, even while eminent medical men wagged their heads and said it wasn't possible.

"Do you really think," I asked Captain Miller, "that Cayce knew you weren't in your cabin?"

The old salt rejoined with a grin. "Now don't go trying to make Cayce a reasonable man. He was a man by himself, and the proof of the pudding, lad"—he winked roguishly—"is in the healing."

"How about this so-called presence of yours—his reading you when you weren't there?"

Miller guffawed. "'Even when I'm not there,' the man says. And how was he reading me, when I was hundreds of miles from the man, and him lying there with his eyes closed, and never seeing me in the first place anyway?"

"But still if he needed your body to read you, how could a presence suffice?"

Miller laughed out loud. "What's a wee thing like a presence that even my dog can sniff?"

"Not from five or six hundred miles," I said. Then thinking of one possible explanation, I asked: "Did you ever hear of the odic force, Captain?"

Miller threw up his hands. "Odic force, you're giving me. All I know is that Cayce cured me, and he knew I wasn't in the cabin, because he put it in his report the very same day."

Virtually all Cayce predictions were made during life readings, delving into past lives and this one, too. The most momentous predictions often stemmed from trivial questions. Ironically, it was a New York City clothing man's concern about his business that led Cayce to perhaps his most dramatic prediction—the destruction of New York City, forecast roughly for 1998. The reading had occurred in 1941, and the textile executive, after hearing about his previous incarnations, had pointedly requested information about the current one. "Is the present location of my business safe until the expiration of my lease in January 1943?" he asked. "I have felt for many months that I should move away from New York City."

Cayce observed that New York was not the ideal place to live because of its tensions, and then: "There will continue to be the kind of vibration that will be disturbing to the body, and eventually those destructive forces, though these will be in the next generation." Later he elaborated: "Portions of what is now the east coast of New York, or New York City itself, will disappear."

And how about moving to the West Coast? Cayce shook his head in trance. "Los Angeles, San Francisco—most all of these will be among those places which will be destroyed even before New York."

Unfortunately, the clothier, absorbed with business, did not ask how this destruction was to occur, and the Cayce faithful in these cities do not know whether they have an H-bomb, earthquake, or tidal wave to look forward to.

Perhaps because he bit off so much, Cayce was never popular with the psychic scientists. His more than fourteen thousand readings, from 1901 to his death at Virginia Beach in 1945, were an investigator's dream. Even as the readings were given they were transcribed, and copies kept for the subject and the file. There was a name and address for every reading, and the time lag needed to prove or disprove his remedies and forecasts. But the "scientists" preferred to stand off and sneer at what they didn't trouble to investigate.

He was driven by an urge to help people, and did not accept money for his readings until he gave up his early occupation as a photographer to devote himself exclusively to his readings—and then only to support his growing family.

Cayce did not pretend to be infallible, and when anybody said he was wrong he insisted on returning whatever they had paid. Once, he warned a professional man to guard against a blood disorder with a rigid regimen. The man, given a clean bill of health by his doctors, then attacked Cayce as a fraud. Three years later he died of leukemia—the deadliest blood disorder of all.

Cayce needed a reason to go off into trance. He had to have a problem—his own, somebody else's, or the world's. There had to be an expressed desire, preferably written, before his subconscious took over. "That need," said Hugh Lynn, "seemed to establish a mental bridge."

Going to "sleep" was simple, even enjoyable. He would lie down on a couch, loosen his clothing, breathe deeply, and then with hands calmly folded over his stomach wait for a white light to flash before his closed lids. "When his eyes fluttered, signaling the light, the request was put to him," Hugh Lynn said.

The conscious could and did obtrude. When angry, upset, subjected to pressures and prejudices, he was not at his best. And only when his predictions came spontaneously, did he himself have confidence in them.

In the same way, when he sought something for himself or his family, he usually could not get it. Yet, though he could do little for himself in the market, for instance, he helped others make fortunes. And while his searches for oil were futile, millions were made in oil for others on land where he could not find oil himself.

"If the seeker seeks for that which is for the self and not for the help, the cheer, and the aid for others," he explained once, "this becomes a stumbling block, and thus confusion arises even in the experience of the entity [Cayce] trying to aid."

In his lifetime Cayce had always been ready to help anybody who needed help. And none profited more from his counsel, or accepted it more readily, than his old friend, Dave Kahn. "Toward the end of my life," Kahn told me, "Cayce told me I would develop an interest in Canadian forest preserves—and now I'm looking that way for timber for the fallout shelters my firm is contracting to build."

"Tell me," I asked Kahn, "did you ever talk to any Stern, Stearn, or Sterne about Cayce's work, and try to enlist his support?"

"You're the only Stearn I discussed Cayce with," Kahn said. "What's it all about?"

Briefly I reviewed the three references that Hugh Lynn had showed me. Kahn laughed out loud. "Cayce made a heluva lot more remarkable predictions than that," he said.

Few people were more familiar with Cayce than Kahn. Now in his sixties, he had known Cayce since he was thirteen years old when Cayce had delivered an apparently miraculous physical reading over a next-door neighbor in Lexington, Kentucky. "The doctor said this woman was incurably ill," Kahn recalled. "But Cayce went to sleep, diagnosed the ailment, and prescribed a remedy. The doctors wouldn't believe it—they never believed it—but the woman got well."

Over the years, everything that Cayce predicted for Kahn had come true. But Kahn's faith in Cayce was so absolute that this very faith may be given credit for fulfilling certain predictions. Cayce had predicted that a youthful Kahn would head a giant furniture empire, and Kahn worked with such confidence, industry, and conviction that his elders put him at the head of a big furniture combine at thirty-two. The depression wiped him out, but he came back. "Cayce told me I'd have my ups and downs."

Still, Cayce made many predictions that no foreknowledge on Kahn's part could have possibly induced.

During World War I, Lieutenant Kahn was assigned to the staff of Major General E. St. John Greble, whose division was expected to move overseas momentarily. "That week," Kahn recalled, "I called Edgar Cayce and asked whether I would have a chance to see my family before I sailed."

Cayce's secretary called Kahn with the result of the reading, and the next morning, as the General discussed departure plans, his ebullient aide remarked, "Sir, we won't be leaving for weeks, and when we do go, you won't be with us."

"What are you talking about?" the General snapped.

That week the division's sailing orders were countermanded, and weeks later, as the division finally got orders to move, the General summoned his aide. "Kahn," he said, waving a sheet of paper, "how did you know I wouldn't be going with the division?"

As Kahn told him about Cayce, the General laughed good-naturedly, as though it were all too ridiculous to talk about, and said: "For a while, I thought you might be reading my mail before it was written."

Greble mentioned that he had been reassigned to training duty.

"I know," Kahn said, "and you're going to offer me a spot."

The General looked at him curiously. "More Cayce?" he said.

Kahn nodded and said, "Thanks, General, but I'd like to go across."

Kahn had no fear of the fighting overseas, for Edgar Cayce had told him he would return unharmed. "I was a blooming hero, volunteering for everything," Kahn recalled, "but Cayce had told me nothing would happen to me, and Cayce was never wrong."

Returning as a captain, Kahn persuaded Cayce to use his powers in the search for oil and thus make enough money to fulfill a lifelong dream of founding a college based on his metaphysical beliefs.

The postwar oil boom, fed by the country's first mass production of automobiles, was on, and it seemed a simple thing for Cayce to cash in on his subconscious connection with the so-called Universal Mind to determine where rich oil fields lay. The first reading, with Kahn asking Cayce where they could find oil, took them to Comyn in the Texas panhandle. "We had raised several thousand dollars for oil leases because of investor confidence in Cayce," Kahn recalled, "and pursuing the readings, we wound up in a tract surrounded by other tracts on which major companies had dug wells. The other drillers were bringing in oil on all sides of us, but we knew nothing about the preparations and cost of digging to depth. We ran out of money and got rid of our leases, which was rather frustrating at the time, since even if I hadn't had confidence in Cayce, from the nearness of the other strikes it was obvious that we were sitting on a sea of oil."

Kahn decided it might be less expensive—and wearing—if they were to look for oil in shallow ground. So Cayce obediently went into trance, and came up with the name Luling, which neither Cayce nor Kahn had heard of before. They consulted a Texas atlas and discovered that Luling, in the year of grace 1921, was a small, virtually forsaken hamlet of some four or five thousand in Caldwell County, between San Antonio and Houston. With a new grubstake, they proceeded to south Texas to try Cayce's luck.

Scouting the bleak countryside, Kahn tied up three thousand acres with oil leases, while the neighbors openly sneered. Nobody had yet hit oil in this area. "But I knew Cayce was right," Kahn said. "After the rains the water would wash down on the surrounding lowlands forming pools that the cattle shied away from because of the oil slick mingled with the water."

Novice Kahn dug until they ran out of money, and with all the digging not one well had been brought in. The two men traced their separate steps homeward. In New York, Kahn ran into a man named Edgar Davis, a former U. S. Rubber Company official, who had become interested in the occult while developing rubber plantations in the Far East. Davis was impressed by what Kahn told him about Cayce's predictions. He formed a syndicate and dug in Luling himself. They sank a fortune in six dry wells before they, too, went broke, but Davis was the determined type. He raised more money, borrowing from Frank Seiberling, the Akron, Ohio rubber man, and continued digging. In 1922, he brought in his first gusher. "Four years later," Kahn recalled, "he sold out to the Standard Oil interests [the Magnolia Petroleum Company] for twelve million dollars."

In his way, Davis paid his debt to the Cayce image. For more than two years, from 1926 to 1928, he supported a play on reincarnation, *The Ladder,* on Broadway, losing more than a million dollars in the venture, as he couldn't even give away tickets.

By now Edgar Cayce had decided that it was not the Lord's will that he should ever have money. And he never again speculated for himself. He rededicated himself to trying to help people, telling himself in trance: "Let that mind be in you, as was in Him who thought it not robbery to make Himself equal with God, yet took on Himself the burden of all, that through His privation in body and mind, there might come blessings to others. Not self, but others."

Although he was to never play the stock market himself, Cayce did pass out advice on the market, and one broker, at least, made millions in the years before the crash. With some of these profits he helped found an infant college in Virginia Beach rooted in the Cayce beliefs, but the college vanished in the depression along with the Wall Street profits.

But why should the depression have affected Cayce?

If Cayce was such a complete know-it-all, why hadn't he known the crash was coming? It seemed a fair question.

"Oh, Cayce knew." Hugh Lynn laughed. "But he couldn't convince anybody—they all thought the market was never going to stop going up."

"Maybe Cayce didn't make it emphatic enough," I said. "His inverted prose is rather difficult to follow at times."

However, Cayce had given not one but many warnings, all unheeded. The first warning came on March 5, 1929, some seven months before the October debacle: "Better that a few points were missed here and there, even in a spectacular rise or fall, than to be worrying where the end would be. Forget not the warning here."

Later that day, interpreting a broker's dream, he was more

specific. "This is an impression of a condition that is to come about, a downward movement of long duration, not allowing latitude for those stocks that are considered very safe. Dispose of all held, even the box [shares]; signifies great changes to come."

And then a month later, on April 6, Cayce described not only the actual market break, but the nationwide panic and the sweeping financial changes: "There must surely come a break where there will be a panic in the money centers not only of Wall Street's activity but a closing of the boards in many other centers and a readjustment of the actual specie."

But many were to profit by confidence in Cayce. Harold J. Reilly, a New York physiotherapist, first heard of Cayce in the early 1930s, when patients wandered into his Broadway health establishment saying Cayce had sent them. Reilly gave them the massages and baths Cayce had ordered, and they got well. In November, 1933, Reilly had a problem of his own, and turned to Cayce. "I thought that if he could send people he hadn't seen to a physiotherapist he had never heard of, then he could help me." And so during a life reading at his country place in Oak Ridge, New Jersey, the shrewd Irishman slipped in a question asking whether negotiations to move his institute into Rockefeller Center would be successful. "I couldn't get the space I required," Reilly explained, "and I was ready to give up."

And so he asked Cayce: "Is it advisable to continue my efforts to secure an establishment in Radio City?"

"Advisable to continue," the sleeping Cayce said, "and should culminate in the latter portion of the coming year, when those influences from the efforts of others from without are attracted to the activities of the entity [Reilly], and bring better relationships."

So confident was Reilly of Cayce's prediction that when the long-sought lease was finally offered him thirteen months later in December of 1934, as Cayce had predicted, he enlarged his demands.

"I asked for an extra thousand feet, which I now felt I needed," Reilly said. "Cayce had told me I was getting it, and Cayce was always right." Reilly's associates were horrified, but he remained calm and stayed that way, even as the Rockefellers approved the addition, and he moved into the Center as forecast.

For years Cayce continued to send him patients, and all who did as Cayce told them were helped. And the reverse, too, was true. "He told one man, a millionaire Florida land developer," Reilly said, "that he would disintegrate if he didn't take relaxing therapy as he was told, but the patient demanded something more strenuous, and went elsewhere. Two weeks later he was dead."

In the realm of therapy, Cayce is still very much alive, as a new generation of practitioners are applying the remedies he dredged up out of his dreams. In Galien, Michigan, Dr. George O'Malley, an osteopath, learned of Cayce in Christmas of 1959, when a friend gave him Tom Sugrue's book, *There is a River*, featuring the Cayce cures. Intrigued by Cayce's philosophy—and his treatments—O'Malley obtained files of Cayce readings on many diseases. He noticed that castor oil packs were recommended in hundreds of instances; Atomidine, an iodine derivative, in many others. Where an eye specialist had failed, O'Malley relieved a corneal ulcer with two drops of Atomidine in the eyes daily. But his most outstanding success came with castor oil packs. Even as the surgeons prepared to operate on one fifty-four-year-old woman for an abdominal obstruction, O'Malley kept applying his castor oil packs. When a snowstorm caused a three-hour delay in the operating schedule, the packs were continued, and an hour before the rescheduled surgery, the obstruction cleared up. O'Malley reported similar success with ulcerative colitis, chronic appendicitis, foot swelling. He doesn't know why it works, but work it does. "I am searching for more information," he told me, "about how and why castor oil packs work so well." He has a clue. "It has been brought to my attention that castor oil, when applied to the skin, stimulates the production of hyaluronic acid, an enzyme that breaks down connective-tissue barriers and speeds up passage of tissue fluids."

But how did Cayce know all this, when he didn't even know what the word hyaluronic meant?

Unjustly attacked as a mercenary, Cayce thought nothing of giving free readings when there was hardly enough money in the larder for himself and his family. "He was sending patients to me, and not charging them a dime," said Dr. F. F. Dobbins, a Staten Island osteopath, whose first Cayce patient came to his office before his telephone number was even in the book. A Staten Island mother, concerned about a sick child, had asked Cayce to name an osteopath in her neighborhood, and Cayce had said: "See Dobbins."

As with Reilly, neither Cayce nor Dobbins had ever heard of each other. Scores of patients were subsequently sent to Dobbins. Asked to explain the outstandingly successful "Dobbins method," the osteopath observed dryly: "I did what Cayce told me to and they got well."

No prophet has served his own home area with more honor. In August of 1922, Cayce incredibly predicted that the neighborhood port of Norfolk, Virginia—"Norfolk and its environ"—taking in Newport News, Hampton, and Portsmouth, would be the busiest port on the coast in thirty years. One year recently Norfolk's shipping load reached forty-nine million tons, against thirty-nine million for New York City proper, and twenty-nine million for Philadelphia.

Even closer to home, Cayce had predicted that Virginia Beach would grow north when everybody else felt it would grow south. "He was the only one," said W. Russell Hatchell, long-time city manager of the Cape Henry resort, "who had that idea. And if anyone had followed Cayce, he could have bought blind and been a millionaire today."

Cayce himself influenced the ARE to buy to the north, but most of the property was lost in the depression. "No matter how right Cayce was," his son said, "he couldn't help himself financially."

Cayce is undoubtedly the only psychic in history who ever predicted that a book would be a best seller, and then, better than any editor, told how the book should be written. He even named the publisher. On August 29, 1943, veteran chief of the White House Secret Service, Edmund Starling, having received permission to write his memoirs, asked Cayce what he should do to make the book successful.

Cayce agreed that author Tom Sugrue, already picked to collaborate, would be ideal. Then Starling asked:

"Who would be the publisher to do the job?"

"Simon and Schuster," Cayce replied.

There was a pause, and Starling asked: "What is the best approach to Simon and Schuster?"

"Just that it may be written. They will be waiting for it."

He was asked to suggest a title, and said that "in the White House" should be included; the book, eventually, was called *Starling of the White House.*

The book, Cayce emphasized, should stress human interest and be free of politics. "From the beginning with Theodore Roosevelt to the end in another Roosevelt, there are great human-interest stories."

"Would it be better to open with the Wilson Administration or the Coolidge?"

"The Coolidge, and then begin at the beginning, with the climax of course in the Wilson Administration, with warnings to the nation."

"How much should be said of the present-day visitors at the White House known to me?"

"Enough to indicate the needs of the warnings, not to laud any particular President but principles. Not belittle any, as it will not be the purpose, nor should it be sarcastic. It will then be not merely a best seller, but for many years the ideal of many an American."

After the reading, Starling went back to Washington to mull over what Cayce had said, and Dave Kahn, a friend, who had gone to Virginia Beach with him, boarded a train for New York. What happened thereafter requires all the documentation that it has. When Kahn arrived at Penn Station in New York City, it being wartime, a long line of people were waiting in the rain for cabs. But Kahn grabbed the first cab that hove into view, and then as he was riding off, down the line he saw a man standing forlornly holding a bag. He motioned to the stranger, asking if he wanted a lift uptown. "I don't know why I picked on him," Kahn said, "when there were so many others there."

Inside the cab the two men introduced each other. "My name is Kahn," Dave said, "Dave Kahn."

"Mine is Schuster," said the other quietly. "Thanks for the lift."

Kahn looked at him quizzically. "You wouldn't be from the firm of Simon and Schuster—M. Lincoln Schuster?"

"I'm Max Schuster," the stranger said.

Kahn beamed. "You may not know it, Mr. Schuster," he said, "but you're going to publish a book about Starling of the White House, Tom Sugrue is going to write it, and what's more, it's going to be a best seller."

Politely, the publisher murmured that Simon and Schuster was always happy to have a best seller.

And then the two men said good night.

Later, questioned by a reporter, Schuster confirmed the meeting with Kahn, and the conversation. "About this time," the reporter said, "you must have been shrinking over to a far corner of the cab."

Schuster laughed. "Frankly, he didn't seem like a crackpot. I was rather convinced by what he told me."

"But weren't you surprised?"

Schuster smiled. "In the publishing field we're used to surprises."

The reporter persisted. "What did Cayce say about the prospects for the book?"

"Kahn quoted him as saying it was going to be a best seller, and at the last count we had sold copies in the six digits. The book has become a legend in the publishing field." He shrugged. "I wouldn't mind another just like it."

I recalled now how Tom Sugrue, a respected colleague, had himself been scornful of Cayce's reputed powers until he had met Cayce years before the Starling reading, and become an eager convert. Even so, to his great detriment, Sugrue had not always followed Cayce's counsel. Long before he did his Cayce book, Sugrue had had a Cayce reading for a debilitating affliction. Cayce, prescribing a course of treatment, advised that relief would be slow. But impatient with the snail-like progress, which Cayce had anticipated, the Naugatuck Irishman took himself into a hospital, ignoring Cayce, and underwent a series of fever-cabinet treatments. He emerged virtually paralyzed head to toe, requiring help to be dressed, fed, and put to bed. But Cayce, in trance, had given him something to hope for, Sugrue was to later recall. He had said that before his death the writer would have complete mobility of his right leg, partial mobility in his left.

Years later, mindful of the dead Cayce's prediction, Sugrue cheerfully underwent an operation that the doctors thought would make it mechanically possible for him to walk again. The operation was a success, and joyfully moving his limbs, he reminded a visiting friend of the Cayce prophecy. But postoperative complications set in, and a few days later Sugrue was dead. "It was unfortunate," the friend observed, "that Cayce wasn't alive to clarify his prediction."

As Cayce became better-known, pressure for get-rich-quick deals and scientific experiments mounted. But he resisted both. When asked about horse races or other gambling ventures, even though in trance, he became visibly upset, and might not read again for weeks at a time. As he grew older, he had no patience, too, for parapsychologists' experimentations, considering them trivial. In 1935, Dr. Joseph B. Rhine of Duke University wanted Cayce to prove himself by Rhine standards. An associate, Dr. Lucien B. Warner, was to arrange a test, the question to Cayce being:

"Please describe contents of package in filing case in Room 215, Schermerhorn Extension, Columbia University, New York."

Cayce didn't approve the questions, or the test, noting in trance: "Unless such experiences create such in the lives of individuals that interest or apply themselves in the study of such lives, then it is indeed of little thought, nor has it any place in man's experience, and is not worthy of consideration of any sort."

But Hugh Lynn, remembering how his father had once ticked off the fifty-two cards in a bridge deck face down, urged him to co-operate for the recognition it would bring. Cayce finally agreed, but the ARE board declined, deciding that the mystic's participation in an experiment he considered meaningless would be a mockery of his own reading, and not in the least comparable to the wonders he was performing daily for ailing mankind.

However, Cayce did treat Warner to a demonstration with some point. Criticizing a novel by Warner, which was still in manuscript form, Cayce picked out one page by number—page 179—and said that the rest of the book should conform with the philosophies presented on this page. Marveling, Warner said later that his 179th page, describing a scene in a chapel, was the only "part of the book which might be referred to as philosophical."

Cayce had other experiences with Rhine. In 1936, the Duke researcher asked Cayce to read his three-year-old daughter, Betsy, ill in Durham, North Carolina. When the Cayce diagnosis and treatment arrived, Rhine said it was inaccurate—because it didn't conform with the medical diagnosis—and spurned the free offer of an electrical wet cell recommended by Cayce. By speech and written word, Rhine has since blasted Cayce and the Cayce movement. In 1955, speaking before a Dallas group, he made a slighting reference to Cayce's reading of his daughter; witnesses reported him saying the treatment called for "a machine or battery which he learned much later was sold by a front for Cayce or the Association."

Again in 1960, writing to a Mrs. Doris Patterson of Ardmore, Pennsylvania, who was doing some research, he renewed his charge, despite the free offer of the machine for which he had once expressed thanks, that the mystic had tried to make money on a machine. "In addition to the diagnosis, which cost me twenty dollars," he wrote, "[the machine] would have added forty dollars to the bill, since he was the only producer of such therapeutic devices." His advice to the researcher Patterson was: "I only wish all those who are giving time and money to this old collection [the Cayce files] would put their energies to better use."

As it happened, Cayce neither made machines nor got kickbacks from those who did. He lived and died poor, and without the constant encouragement of his wife, Gertrude, who shared his work and privations, it is doubtful that he could have continued that work. Twice he was arrested like a common criminal, herded into court with his family, and accused of practicing medicine. In both instances, in New York and Detroit, the presiding magistrates, after listening to Cayce, not only dismissed him, but indicated interest in his powers.

The newspapers considered him a quack, and he felt the lash of their scorn. In New York, a tabloid carried a screaming head-line, "Mystic Arrested With Blonde In Hotel," and ran a photo-graph showing him with his pretty secretary; his wife, standing on the other side of him, was cropped out of the picture.

Cayce's physical readings, which made up most of his life's work, have been principally responsible for his many conversions —the converts arguing that if Cayce could cure people without seeing them, then he could do anything. I myself have seen how this conversion works. One night recently I was having dinner with friends at the Leslie Newmans' in Lynnhaven, Virginia, not far from Virginia Beach. As I sat at the groaning board, listening to the patter of small children, and watched Mrs. Newman ladle out generous portions of food, I thought that I had never observed a more characteristically American scene. It was so down-to-earth that I can remember thinking that I hoped nobody would ask me about an earlier visit to the Cayce foundation, as I had no wish to keep explaining that my interest was purely professional. And then, suddenly, I overheard the wholesome-looking, maternal Mrs. Newman casually mention Hugh Lynn's name, as she helped one of her infant grandchildren bring his spoon to his mouth.

"Do you know the Cayces?" I inquired.

Without interrupting her serving she said: "I knew Edgar Cayce very well."

"Were you a member of the Association?" I asked.

She shook her head. "Not in those days."

Meanwhile, her equally brawny husband, a construction man with arms like hams—who had toiled all day long at his bulldozer —kept his head buried in great mounds of food, oblivious, appar-ently, to the conversation in the greater need of replenishing his strength. Mrs. Newman glanced over at him fondly, and put another heaping portion on his platter. "We got to know Edgar Cayce during the war," she said. "We had heard reports of his cures, and we thought he might help some friends of ours. They lived in Ohio, where Leslie comes from, and their little girl was suffering with such a bad case of boils, the doctors said they'd have to operate within a week to save her."

The distraught parents, the Mapeses in Port Clinton, Ohio, were ready to try anything. "So," Mrs. Newman continued, "I went to Edgar Cayce, and asked if he would read for little Sharon Ann, who was less than two years old at the time." Her mind seemed to drift back over the years. "He was very busy then, some magazine had just printed a story about him, and dozens of people were wanting to be read every day, and any more than two was a strain. He looked tired and pale, as though he could use a reading himself, but he couldn't turn down a child; he said he would fit her in, if I would have a written request from the mother at his house at three o'clock on Friday." This was Tuesday, so Mrs. Newman called Mrs. Mapes in Ohio, and instructed her to send the name and address special-delivery.

At the appointed hour, Mrs. Newman took the Mapeses' slip to the Cayce house in Virginia Beach. "While Mr. Cayce went off to sleep," she recalled, "Mrs. Cayce read off Sharon's name to him, along with the town. But Mr. Cayce, lying there, eyes closed, asked for the street address. Mrs. Cayce turned to me, but I didn't know the address, and I was afraid the reading wouldn't go on, when Mr. Cayce suddenly cried out, "I have it, I have the body, it's on Harbor Road.'"

As Mrs. Newman, telling her story, mentioned Harbor Road, Leslie Newman stopped eating long enough to exclaim: "That's what convinced me, Cayce telling her the name of the street, when my wife didn't know it, and it didn't even have a sign on it."

Newman resumed his gastronomical activity, as I asked Mrs. Newman:

"How about Cayce's treatment—how did that work out?"

She laughed. "Mrs. Mapes did exactly what Mr. Cayce said, and the baby was well in a week." As a matter of fact, the child had started to improve in twenty-four hours, as he had predicted it would.

"And what was the treatment?"

"It was quite simple. He recommended plantain, the fuzzy, weedlike green plant that grows in any back yard; the leaves from this were to be cut in strips and mixed with an equal quantity of milk, brought to a boil slowly. This was to be used as a lotion. Internally, he recommended a mixture of sulphur, Rochelle salts, and cream of tartar. Then he took her off fried foods and recommended liquids."

All this had been prescribed in trance.

Mrs. Newman had asked Cayce if the child's condition warranted an operation. He replied negatively.

"And what did the doctors say to all this?" I asked Mrs. Newman.

She smiled. "They told Mrs. Mapes she was proceeding at her own risk."

"And when it worked?"

"Oh, they said then that the treatments had nothing to do with it; Sharon Ann would have gotten better anyway."

Leslie Newman had now finished his dinner. "And what did you think about it all?" I asked.

He shook his big head and said in a booming voice, "When he gave the name of that street, like I said, he convinced me. That did it. I would have believed anything he said after that."

Though Cayce is dead these many years, there is considerably more interest in his movement today than while he lived. People all over the country keep asking questions about his life and work; thousands have made a shrine of the ARE headquarters at Virginia Beach, others have flocked eagerly to classes in psychic development based on his teachings. He is slowly becoming a legend.

Many of his followers, to be sure, are incurable cultists and fanatics, more intrigued by the Lost Continent of Atlantis, whose culture Cayce traced in trance, than his lessons for living on this earth. But these are a minority. To most, Cayce is a tangible, reassuring link to the Great Unknown, to the mysteries of this life, and what may lie beyond.

And reincarnation, which assertedly gave Cayce greater powers to foresee things, was one of the reassurances to which so many Cayce-ites clung. At first thought, it seemed incredible to me that practical-minded people, who had made their mark in the world, could seriously consider it. "You don't really believe in reincarnation?" I asked incredulously of a hard-bitten businessman I had known nearly twenty years. He was not at all abashed. "There's no proof, obviously," he said, "or there would be nothing to debate, but since matter can be neither created nor destroyed, why should not the human soul survive and live again?"

"But matter has a physical quality to it."

He smiled. "But as Cayce pointed out, the mind, or soul, could easily control matter. It built skyscrapers, leveled mountains, created and destroyed whole civilizations. Certainly the mind is the greater force."

"You have the conclusion you want," I said, "now you are groping around for reasons that will justify it."

He looked at me somberly. "Practically everything that ever happened in my life Cayce told me to look out for—business developments, my relationships with other people, even the extent of my life—and it has all worked out. So why shouldn't what he told me about the past be as accurate as what he told me about the future? It's all out of the same bottle."

I laughed, thinking he had chosen an unhappy simile.

He explained what he meant, ignoring the interruption. "The stream of consciousness—Cayce thought that everything that had ever happened was recorded somewhere, just like every experience or illness of man is registered within him."

I had the feeling that my friend, along in years, was trying more to convince himself than me. "This stream of consciousness," I said, "what did it tell Cayce about your past?"

"Oh, I had three or four lives before. In one I was a Roman centurion; in another an Egyptian overseer, and most recently I was a Norseman and came over with Eric the Red when he found America."

"Anyway," I said, "you always had a good job."

He laughed. "Yes, I was always telling people what to do."

"That must be pleasing to the ego," I said.

Again he laughed. "I asked Cayce once whether any peasants ever came back."

"Even granting this theory," I said, "nobody knows whether they've lived before."

He shook his head. "Cayce did about himself, in trance, of course. He remembered it all, and that's why he was able to see so much we don't know about."

"Even so, without the remembrance of previous existence by ordinary people, what difference does reincarnation make?"

He had the grace to smile sheepishly. "The idea is that what you have done or haven't done in one life is going to affect this life or the next."

"And if you do badly on one existence, you pay in the next?"

"It advances some reason for the unjust deaths of children and the massacres of adults. If these people have lived before and are going to live again, God does not then become an indifferent spectator to a chamber of horrors, but the fount of an endless order of human existence, in which death itself is only an interlude."

I looked at my businessman friend with some surprise. "You have that pretty well thought out."

"Oh, that's pretty much Edgar Cayce."

"And you'd like to believe?"

He shrugged. "I have an open mind."

"But what did reincarnation have to do with Cayce's powers of precognition?"

"Cayce had been through it all so many times, gaining wisdom each time, that he knew what the pattern of the future was."

"And yet he believed in free will?"

"Always within the pattern that he saw as set. For instance, he read for a business friend of mind during the war, and suggested he contact a certain General for the government contract that he wanted. And he predicted that the General, though usually unapproachable, would see him right away, even though he didn't know him, and give him the contract."

"But why?" I asked.

"Cayce said that in a previous incarnation these two had been friends, and when they met they would feel an instant trust, as though they had always known each other—not an uncommon feeling among people meeting for the first time."

"And did he get the contract?"

My friend smiled. "Why don't you ask him?"

I called the businessman with Washington connections. "Sure," he said, "I saw General Somervell in the Quartermaster Corps, we hit it right off from the start, and he gave me the contract." His laugh came rippling over the phone. "Of course, I didn't tell him that Cayce said I knew him well two hundred years ago—he might have thrown me out."

5 LITTLE *NO* NEW YORK

In a dream, Edgar Cayce saw himself reborn in the year 2100 A.D. in Nebraska. Wanting to know what shape the country was in, he flew about in a cigar-shaped metal flying ship, traveling at supersonic speeds, and finally settled down on the ruins of a great city, which swarms of workmen were laboring to rebuild.

"What is this place?" the wandering Cayce asked.

The workman looked up surprised. "Why, New York City," he said.

The dream was so vivid that Cayce decided to ask himself what it meant. He went into trance and pointing out that the Bible often meant literally what it said, quoted significantly from Scripture: "Though the heavens and the earth pass away, my word shall not pass away."

All this occurred in 1936, five years before Cayce's predicted destruction of New York to the textile man worried about his business.

And this was not the first holocaust seen by the man who told wondrous stories of one lost continent in the Atlantic, and another in the Pacific. He had made many predictions of earthquakes, new land formations, and changes within the earth's crust and under the ocean beds, and some of these have already come true. Others appear to be comfirmed by the recent finds of the International Geophysical Year.

With his predictions of earth changes he has even made converts in the ranks of the geologists, though it is not professionally safe for any to acknowledge this conversion. One prominent geologist, head of geology in a major university, was attracted to the Cayce readings when he learned that Cayce had attributed history's Great Flood to the sinking of the last remaining portion of the continent of Atlantis, and not exclusively to the melting icecaps of the frozen north. He was already inclined to this view from more tangible evidence of radiocarbon datings of ancient ocean sediments when he discovered Cayce.

He examined other Cayce readings, and found his interest in Cayce's Universal Mind growing. In August of 1926, Cayce had predicted that because of the influence of the planets Jupiter and Uranus, there would be strong atmospheric disturbances between October 15 and 20 that year with "Violent windstorms, earthquakes in California and Japan, and tidal waves following to the southern portion of the isles near Japan."

Thirty years after the prediction the geologist shot down to Washington and checked through the weather records of both the Library of Congress and the United States Weather Bureau. October, 1926, was an exceptionally stormy month. "A storm that smashed Cuba on October 20 was one of the most severe on record," the geologist reported. "In the vicinity of the Kuril Islands, near Japan, hurricanes hit on October 14 and 15. There were typhoons in the Philippines. On October 22, California was shaken by three tremblers. Quakes hit Japan on October 19 and 20." But the only reported tidal wave was far south of Japan in the Solomons.

By now the geologist's excitement was mounting. He turned to another Cayce forecast, a gradual shifting of the center of the earth with respect to its axis, beginning in 1936. "Still checking the official records," the geologist said, "I learned that from the years

1934 to 1938, the earth had undergone its maximum polar shift, as measured at International Latitude stations. In time, these shifts might bring about deep-seated changes in the earth, and touch off cataclysmic disturbances that could be building up right now."

Within a few decades, Cayce had predicted, the waters of the Great Lakes now emptying into the St. Lawrence River and the North Atlantic might empty instead into the Gulf of Mexico. "It is well known that in a few thousand years there will be enough tilt," the geologist said, "for the upper Great Lakes to wash into the Mississippi drainage by way of the Chicago River. Cayce's readings, however, indicated that the rate of rise of the earth's crust along the northern shores of the Great Lakes will speed up suddenly."

The world will not have long to wait to see how right—or wrong—Cayce was. In the period between 1958 and 1998, give or take a year, he has predicted, besides New York's destruction, that:

The earth would be broken up in the western portion of America.

The greater portion of Japan will go into the sea.

The upper portion of Europe will be changed as in the twinkling of any eye.

New land will appear on the east coast of America, where Atlantis purportedly once stood as a symbol of culture, and in the Pacific, where the continent of Lemuria once flourished.

After his 1941 prediction of the New York calamity, Cayce had still another vision of disaster. Two years later, consulted by another worried businessman, he advised this worthy to move everything he owned from Manhattan island proper. "The mainland," he said, "will be safer."

Although these predictions weren't to be tested for another thirty-five years or so, the geologist was already struck by minor materializations of the Cayce prophecies. Solemnly, he quoted from an article in a leading British scientific journal dated April 1960, showing the beginnings of new land rises in the Atlantic:

"'Evidence of a tremendous submarine upheaval off the coast was obtained from preliminary naval soundings. In one case the depth of water was found to be 45 feet where previously it was charted at 1200 feet. In a position about 9 miles from shore, soundings showed a depth of 1200 feet instead of the charted 4500 feet.' "

In another few years land is expected in the Atlantic. "And Poiseda," Cayce said, "will be among the first portions of Atlantis to rise again. Expect it in sixty-eight or sixty-nine. Not so far away."

Even though zealous research has backed up Cayce thus far, the geologist has not dared to lend his name to his research, or make any claims openly for the material he has dredged from the dead mystic. "Can you imagine," he said, "quoting a mystic in the classroom? I would be barred from teaching anywhere in the country."

We had met rather furtively, like a couple of thieves in the night, not far from the college campus where he lectured daily in traditional geology. As we sat and talked, I wondered how far the geologist's preoccupation with Cayce went. Was he, for instance, interested in reincarnation? "Only as it can be checked out," he told me seriously. "But if Cayce was right about past earth changes, Atlantis and all that, and if he is right about future changes, then—conceivably—he could be right about reincarnation."

"If you are so sure that Cayce is right," I said, "why not come out and say so publicly?"

He smiled bleakly. "I wouldn't mind for myself, but I have a wife and children to support." He frowned a moment. "However, as I continue my investigation of Cayce's geology, checking it against available records, I may write a paper and put my name on it." Actually, he had already done so, showing how certain sedimentary deposits confirmed part of Cayce's axis-tilt concept, but colleagues had talked him out of publishing.

He had made a thoroughgoing study of Cayce in his various aspects. "When you check phases of Cayce's readings that can be proven, with statements more difficult to document, you realize that his undocumented earth changes are no stranger than what has been proven."

Cayce's first realization of his gift, was an example. When Cayce was a boy of nine, witnesses reported, he went to sleep with a schoolbook under his pillow. When he wakened in the morning, he astonished family and friends by remembering everything in the book—including pages he could not have read.

Religiously motivated, he had a sublime confidence in God. Once, a mother had departed gratefully after thanking him for helping her ailing daughter, and then, forgetting something, had turned back. At the doorstep she overheard Cayce, standing where she had left him, praying fervidly: "Thank you, God, for permitting your servant to have helped this child."

His conscious visions were many. One day, working in his garden, he had looked up into the sky, and had seen chariots of fire spreading their flames through the heavens. Shaken, he had fled to his study and locked himself in; through the door his family could hear his voice raised in prayer. Only much later was he able to explain: "I got the sudden impression of a world catastrophe, and I knew then a great war was coming with death for millions." He had foreseen World War I.

He had also foreseen World War II in much the same way. While greeting twenty scout leaders gathered for a meeting in his home, he had abruptly turned and left the room. "I saw another war," he explained later, "and three of those fine young men not returning." And these three, a witness reported, were the only ones of the scout group to die when war came.

The geologist had examined—and believed—all this. That much was clear. But I couldn't help wondering why the thought of death should upset anyone believing in reincarnation.

The geologist smiled philosophically. "After all, it is the living who sorrow, not the dead."

"Have you any reason at all, apart from Cayce, for believing in reincarnation?" I asked.

"There are some indications," he said. "We are always meeting people we feel we have known before. Some people discover talents and powers at an early age they had no way of acquiring in this world, like Mozart writing music at the age of five, and another child prodigy of eighteen months playing popular tunes on the piano." He looked at me. "And nearly everybody has had that feeling at one time that he's been to a certain place before, and done it all before."

"That's been explained away as precognition," I said, "and there's still another theory that all child prodigies are freaks of genetic memory—just as some people inherit coloring, dispositions, brains, etc., from their ancestors, so, too, can they inherit memory."

He laughed. "That's more fantastic than reincarnation."

I studied him closely. He was a friendly, affable man, good-looking, with several college degrees. But for all his pleasant appearance, solid background, and earnest demeanor, I wondered whether he might not be a sort of crackpot. "How," I asked, "can you consider yourself a scientist, basing your conclusions on sound evidence, when you believe in something like reincarnation for which there is not the slightest scrap of real evidence?"

The lines around his mouth suddenly tightened and his pale blue eyes fixed on mine. "I can be a Baptist or a Lutheran and be a geologist in good standing, so why not a reincarnationist?" He held up a hand as I started to say something. "As to believing in reincarnation, I have no present evidence that would satisfy a scientist, but I am exploring the possibility, using Cayce's readings as a barometer. If he knows more than the geologists about geology, as he knew more than the doctors about medicine, then maybe he knows more about life and death than some of the clergy."

I returned to Cayce's dream, the date of 2100 A.D. somehow striking me as at odds with the predicted destruction of great cities toward the turn of this century. "Dreams are often only symbolic," the geologist said, "and even so, if Manhattan island itself were destroyed, how long might it be before it becomes habitable again?" He shrugged. "It all depends on how the destruction took place, and who was left to pick up the pieces."

"How about Los Angeles, San Francisco, New York, and places like that, disappearing before the end of the century?" I asked. "Was Cayce predicting an H-bomb or what?"

"I don't know, specifically, what Cayce had in mind, but the whole thing is possible geologically, without a bomb." He looked at me with a new seriousness. "Did you see the report in *Life* magazine, November 7, 1960, on the 'not-so-solid' earth, revealing some of the great scientific discoveries of the International Geophysical Year?"

I shook my head.

"Well, let me read a bit of it to you." His brow furling in a frown, he read: " 'Well-known places, apparently rooted with comfortable firmness, now seem to face uncertain futures. California, for example, may be gradually splitting away from the rest of the Continental U.S. as part of a great shifting of the Pacific floor. The Hawaiian Islands, surrounded by a deep moat, seem to be slowly sinking into the ocean. . . . New land seems to be rising in the Red Sea, in the Caribbean and in the Gulf of California.' "

Back in 1934, lying on his battered couch in Virginia Beach, Cayce had said: "The earth will be broken up in many places. The early portion will see a change in the physical aspect of the west coast of America. There will appear open waters in the northern portions of Greenland. There will be seen new lands of the Caribbean Sea, and dry land will appear. . . . South America will be shaken from the uppermost portion to the end; and in the Antarctic off Terra del Fuego will be land, and a strait with rushing waters."

"What's supposed to happen in California?" I asked.

He shrugged. "What's happened before? Part of San Francisco came down in 1906, and nearly all of it could come down again. Some geologists in California live in reinforced steel homes. All the way out into the Gulf of Alaska there is a major crack in the earth's crust, and the strain has been building up for nearly sixty years, since the last great quake. There are a lot of auxiliary flaws too, extending from San Francisco down through Bakersfield."

But the greater earth change, according to Cayce, would be on the North Atlantic seaboard. "Watch New York, Connecticut, and the like."

Sitting there listening, it all seemed very academic to me. "When is all this taking place?" I asked calmly.

For his part, he was equally detached. Cayce was asked this question and said: "When there is the first breaking up in the

South Pacific, and the sinking or rising in the Mediterranean and the Etna area, then we may know it has begun."

"And?"

"And it has already begun. The Seismological Society of America reported, in July of 1960, a series of earthquakes near Mount Etna in Italy, and said that Mount Etna itself erupted with a violence unmatched in modern times. In southern Greece, small boats sat on the sea bottom after the water level fell three feet; the bottom of the old Venetian harbor at Crete has appeared in many places."

Cayce had warned that Pelée would rumble and toss before the great breakups came in California and Nevada, and Pelée was the great foreboding goddess of the Hawaiian volcano. The geologist smiled grimly. "Recent activity in the Hawaiian volcanoes indicates that perhaps Pelée is getting ready."

Already in the South Pacific, the geologist noted, the subterranean forces were building up a head of steam, heralding the formation of new land forecast by Cayce, on the site of land that had long ago disappeared in the ocean. Again, he quoted confidently from the *Life* report: "'IGY found the amount of heat radiating from the crest of the rise near Easter Island is seven times greater than heat flow elsewhere on the earth's surface, leading to the surmise that the rise [East Pacific Rise] is welling up with molten rock from the planet's depths and may some day be dry land.'"

The earth changes will be world-wide. "The catastrophes foreseen by Cayce in California, New York, Japan, and other places will themselves be capped by a global catastrophe." But there will be ample warning. "There will be upheavals in the Arctic and the Antarctic," Cayce had said, "and there will then be the shifting of the poles, so that where there has been a rigid or a semitropical climate, there will be a more tropical one, and moss and fern will grow."

Without batting an eye, the geologist told me IGY research bore out Cayce's statements of climatic changes from polar slippage. "Confirming Cayce," he said, "the IGY revealed a relatively weak layer of the earth's crust at a four-hundred-and-thirty-mile depth.

And at this level, the 'more solid skin of the earth may slide over its inner part, as though the skin of a grapefruit were to slide over its pulp.'"

It sounded a little weird to me.

"And how would that induce climatic changes?" I asked.

He read on in his low-pitched voice: "'Some geophysicists believe that the whole upper part of the earth has done this from time to time in the past. They find evidence that the lands and seas which are now at the north and south poles once were in quite different locations. During IGY, coal, which is the remains of temperate-climate plants, was found in the Antarctic. One cause of this might have been global slippage of the upper rock layers.'"

Behind thick-lensed glasses, the geologist regarded me triumphantly. "Now listen to what Cayce had to say about these changes." And he quoted from the old sage of Virginia Beach: "'The extreme northern portions were then the southern portion, or the polar regions were then turned to where they occupied more of the tropical and semi-tropical regions. The Nile entered into the Atlantic Ocean. What is now the Sahara was an inhabited land and very fertile. What is now the central portion of this country or the Mississippi Basin was then all in the ocean. Only the plateau existed, or the regions that are now portions of Nevada, Utah, and Arizona formed the greater part of what we know as the United States. That portion along the Atlantic seaboard formed the outer portions, then the lowlands of Atlantis.'"

It was all pretty fantastic stuff, but as the geologist pointed out, the desert areas had to be fertile once, or oil, the carbonized product of millions of years of decomposition, would not have been found underground. And, of course, every schoolboy had learned of the glacier sweeping down on North America, even if he hadn't been told about the tilting axis, which the geologist said did all this.

It was all going to happen again, Cayce said, just as so many other phenomena in the universe seemed to repeat themselves as part of an orderly pattern: "What is the coastline now of many a land will be the bed of the oceans. Even many of the battlefields of the present [1941] will be oceans, seas, bays, and the land over which the new order will carry on their trade with one another."

It was all very plausible, according to the geologist.

But it was easy to predict the future, which we had no chance of prejudging. How had Cayce done with a past that could be checked out?

"Has Cayce ever discussed anything in the past," I asked, "that he couldn't have reasonably known at the time, but that was confirmed after his reading?"

The geologist took this one in stride. "Oh sure," he said. "Stonehenge, for one. As you know, this mound of curious stones near Salisbury, England, baffled scholars for centuries, without anyone quite knowing how they got there. Well, in 1944, a year before he died, Cayce gave them the clue: 'In the Holy Land where there were those breakings-up in the period when the land was being sacked by the Chaldeans and Persians . . . among those groups who escaped in ships and settled in portions of the English land near what is now Salisbury; and there builded those altars that were to represent the dedication of individuals to the service of a living God.'"

It sounded to me like the old fable of the Lost Tribe of Israel. "But where's the confirmation?" I asked.

The geologist smiled, shuffling through his papers again. "Here's something from the Encyclopedia Britannica of 1956 that indicates the migration of a Semitic group from the eastern Mediterranean." This migration had taken place around 1800 B.C., roughly the same period as the flight described by Cayce. The structures [mounds] "'are unknown elsewhere in prehistoric northern Europe,'" the geologist quoted from the Encyclopedia, "'and imply influence from the contemporary Mycenaean and Minoan architecture of the Mediterranean.'" He paused dramatically, then: "'The probability of such influence was startlingly confirmed in 1953 . . .'"

He put down his glasses. "And that," he said, "was eight years after Cayce's death."

Titillating the more romantic of his followers, Cayce constantly

referred to the Lost Continent of Atlantis, speaking of two separate upheavals and sinkings, the last of which resulted in the sinking of fragmentary remnants of the continent into the Atlantic.
As Cayce told it, some survivors made their way to Egypt, changing that country's civilization from a simple agrarian to a complex
social structure. Others escaped to the American mainland, forming
the Mayan and Incan societies in Central and South America, and
still others found a haven in the Spanish Pyrenees. It was truly
a romantic picture. But the geologist was as solemn as though he
were describing the Paleolithic Age.

"But what," I asked, "makes Atlantis so important?"

"Merely that everybody in the field is afraid to depart from
traditional concepts without some undeniably tangible evidence;
so if we can establish an Atlantis as a bridgehead, we can then
work backwards, showing that the shifting axis principle, an inherent part of Cayce's reading, must then be correct."

He smiled. "And if this is correct, how can we say that Cayce
was wrong about anything, until we have shown him wrong?"

Even so, I couldn't fathom the absorption of the Cayce claque
with the Lost Continent, and their disconcerting way of mentioning Atlantis in the same breath as Europe and South America.

"Isn't it a little strange," I said, "the way some of these people
immerse themselves in Atlantis legends, like children with the
Wizard of Oz stories?"

The geologist smiled tolerantly. "Not all of it is cultist. If an
advanced civilization existed as Cayce pictured it on Atlantis, we
may have gone through all this turmoil before, passing through
many progressive stages of technology before we reached the
grand finale."

"But outside of wishful thinking and a few fresh-water plant
remains on the crest of the mid-Atlantic ridge," I said, "what
possible basis is there for a continent mentioned so briefly in antiquity, and then only in passing?" He had mentioned the finding
of these plant remains—diatoms—in passing.

"Geologically speaking," he observed, "there is evidence for
Atlantis in the mid-Atlantic ridge, which has a crack along its
crest that is fifty miles wide and a thousand feet deep. And the

civilization it spawned—like ours, a highly technical and powerful one—may have dealt itself the blow causing the area near the Sargasso Sea to disappear."

According to Cayce, this eruption occurred some 17,500 years ago, 7500 years before the final destruction. And, as he saw it in his trance, it was as though a mighty array of H-bombs had with all the fury of frustrated nature struck the land: "The turning of the etheric rays' influence from the sun produced what we would call a volcanic upheaval, and the separating of the land in several islands, five in number."

The Sargasso Sea, as I recalled, was an almost legendary stretch of the North Atlantic covered with floating seaweed and superstitiously regarded as a graveyard for ships. It lent a nice touch to this latest science fiction. I regarded the geologist mildly. "How can you accept the fantastic," I asked, "just because Cayce went into trance and his dreams took over?"

He didn't seem at all disconcerted by my attitude. "Well, there's nothing about the earth the IGY turned up that Cayce hadn't discussed," he returned, "and he was ridiculed for much of that before these teams of scientists came up with similar revelations."

"But you can't say he's right about Atlantis because he was possibly right about the tilt of the axis and global slippage."

He turned this one over for a moment. "I agree that a civilization existing seventeen thousand years ago capable of utilizing the etheric rays of the sun as a source of power is foreign to all present-day concepts. But ancient maps showing both England and Antarctica in an unglaciated state have been found, and A. H. Mallery, the great map authority, says it's quite possible that these areas were mapped from the air because of their detail and precision."

As he talked his face began to lighten. "The importance of Cayce's discourses on prehistory," he observed, "lie not so much in their possible revelations about earth changes, but in their view that the lives of nations and other large groups repeat, rather like the lives of individuals in the reincarnation theory. America is Atlantis all over again, according to this view. And as for the 'reality' of Atlantis, I would only ask, as a geologist, 'Why is it that we know so much about man back to about five thousand years ago, and beyond forty thousand years? Why do we lose sight of him in the intervening period? Could not something like the lost Atlantis be the answer?'"

6 EVERYMAN PSYCHIC

Virtually every major discovery made by the leading Andes explorer, George Michanowsky, has been achieved through a psychic impulse.

"I would see it all clearly in a daydream—the direction, the scene itself—and then my steps would take me there."

Thus the venturesome New Yorker saw the largest pyramid in the Andes, one which holds the unsuspected secret of an ancient culture that may show a kinship to the Egyptian; in the same way he tracked down in the heart of Bolivia the legendary river, the Khaweera Kelkata, a subtributary of the Amazon invisible from air because of the dense virgin foliage. In the Central Andes, not far from the home of the Aymara Indians, the intrepid head of the Amazonia Foundation mapped the hitherto uncharted Centinela peak.

When he had his first vision of a high-situated pyramid he shrugged it off, because everybody *knew* there were no pyramids at that elevation in South America, but the same compulsion that had made an explorer of him in the first place, drawing him to the Andes, drew him on to the great mound near the mountainous Bolivia border, a discovery that may someday yield its wonders to the archeologist.

But his most unique vision was about the jaguar. That one puzzled him for nearly a year and a half, and he would have brushed it aside except that it kept repeating itself vividly.

And then one day, exploring the approaches to the Illimani peak he found his jaguar. It wasn't the leopard-like animal he would have expected. It was a sizable, cracked remnant of an incense burner, with an ornamental encrustation—the ceramic head of a jaguar.

And on the back of it, in a land that was not supposed to have known the imprint of the white man until the conquering Spaniards, he saw the mark of two Maltese crosses and an Egyptian cross.

With this record over the years, Michanowsky has learned to trust these visionary impulses. But when he was a student abroad and first felt the urge to travel to the Andes, he was rather troubled by the insistence of the impulse. And when he got there he was even more baffled. "Looking around, I felt, somehow, as if I had seen it all before."

As a modern explorer, Michanowsky doesn't rely only on the psychic, of course. With the co-operation of the Bolivian Air Force, he has been photographing unmapped foothills of the Andes with infrared beams, cutting through previously impenetrable overgrowth for a startling revelation of what lay below. The pictures revealed well-constructed roads built long before the Spaniards got there. It was *one* discovery that science could take chief credit for.

And Michanowsky's case is not unusual.

Anybody can be psychic—without even trying.

What we think of as intuition, or imagination, even a mere hunch, is often a psychic indication of a future event. It enables a scientist, like Einstein, to visualize a complex principle he had no way of proving; leads a Da Vinci to draw models of airplanes, helicopters, and submarines materializing five hundred years later; and a Rudyard Kipling to describe a secret well in a castle discovered many years later.

Winston Churchill, unable to sleep, looks out a window, and gets a dark vision of war and millions of young men dying; Lincoln dreams of his own death, and sees his body lying in state in the White House.

In the same way, a mother turns to her daughter, knitting tiny garments for an expected child, and tells her she may as well stop knitting; that child will be born dead.

A housewife in the middle of preparing dinner sees her son wounded in the foxholes of Europe, and twenty-four hours later he is hit by a sniper's bullet.

An actress, poring over her ouija board, tells an unbelieving business executive he will look for a new job in two weeks, but cannot bring herself to mention to him the death she sees in another year.

An airline hostess who has never seen a horse race picks Derby winners for her startled passengers.

In the midst of war, many fighting men quietly know when and how they are going to die—the poet Rupert Brooke in World War I, and an unsung Georgia teen-ager in World War II.

Even though we may not realize it ourselves, nearly all of us, some researchers say, have varying, if small, amounts of these psychic flashes, which we dismiss as coincidence. And yet the animals, considered less sensitive than ourselves, constantly reveal their sixth sense: the dog howling before his master dies hundreds of miles away; the cat, blindfolded and sacked, finding its way home over unfamiliar ground; the ants building stronger mounds before a rigorous winter; fish avoiding storms by swallowing pebbles and sinking beneath their accustomed depth before the hurricane strikes.

Instinctual behavior is in itself often psychic: eels crossing the Atlantic to a breeding spot in Holland they have never seen; salmon fighting and slashing over rocks to swim up an Oregon river and die; young swallows winging south over a route they have never been shown; and certain caterpillars becoming butterflies and then, as butterflies, returning to the original homes.

Unlike the animals, man is not uniformly psychic. Yet many people, says Dr. F. Regis Reisenman, psychic researcher extraordinary, are psychic without knowing it. This latent sense cannot be invoked at will, but often occurs as the need arises. Whenever the conscious is detached, the psychic force may assert itself, Reisenman pointed out. "During the sleep state, at the point of death, under hypnosis, in the stress of fear, or even completely relaxed."

A staff psychiatrist at St. Elizabeth's in Washington, D.C., he has tested thousands of people, discovering: "While psychic ability can't be developed in people who haven't got it, many have three to eight per cent of it contrasting with the Hurkoses and other psychics who are right eighty per cent of the time and more."

Man is naturally psychic, Reisenman said, a carry-over from caveman days when he had to be psychic or die. But what he doesn't use, he may eventually lose. "If primitive man hadn't been able to sense the danger lurking around every corner," the doctor stressed, "he would never have survived the hostile jungle." And even today, though he no longer needs his sixth sense for survival, man's psychic experiences continue. "So often," Reisenman said, "he keeps them to himself for fear of ridicule, or dismisses them as coincidence, though he knows it is something else."

Still, researching the field, the Washington psychiatrist has found it fraught with fraud and phonies. "For every real experience, ten may be manufactured."

Investigating phony psychics, Reisenman had picked up many of their tricks, and could read off every card in a pack merely by scanning their backs. Still, he was only seven or eight per cent psychic himself, he said, as he offered to demonstrate for my wife and myself in his home outside Washington. "Take these slips of paper," he told me. "Write the names of people you've known well on each slip, four living and four dead." At the far side of his study, well outside the doctor's range of vision, I scribbled the names of eight persons intimately known to me. I then arranged the slips in two piles, living and dead, as directed, and folded them into tiny squares with the names concealed. Then I mixed them up, until I didn't know which was which myself.

The doctor didn't bother to examine the slips and, holding each square over his head, he called "Living" and "Dead." Only once did he hesitate, and then he released the slip as though it had burned his fingers. "This fellow went fast," he exclaimed.

I unfolded the remaining slips. He had correctly called four living and three dead. Then I opened the slip so hastily dropped. With a start I saw my scrawled "Bob"—for Robert (Bob) Sullivan, a close friend and colleague who had died four years before. "Did he go suddenly?" Dr. Reisenman asked.

Sullivan had dropped dead while shaving.

I looked at Reisenman curiously. He appeared rather satisfied with himself. "How did you do it?" I asked.

"Mostly it was a trick," he said. "I know fifty tricks like it."

"But the one slip you dropped—how could that be a trick?"

He smiled. "That was the only thing that wasn't a trick; that may have been psychic."

Smilingly, he refused to give away his tricks, but he did try to account for his apparent hit, psychically. "It may have come through your odic force," he said casually. "Everyone connected with an event, or the people involved in an event, have this odic or life force; it remains on everything they touch or go near for an indefinite period, and the psychic can bring it in, like a bloodhound finds a scent."

"Do you have to sniff around like a bloodhound then?"

He laughed. "It's difficult to define the infinite in terms of the finite. But let me say that it comes in flashes, snatches of pictures, like a newsreel—and sniffing might help if you concentrated at the same time."

The doctor was in good form. He rubbed his hands, jestingly hitching up his shirtsleeves. "Would you like to try another trick?" He passed out some additional slips. "Write out two questions," he instructed, "and then fold the slip into a square so that I can't see your question—and I'll answer it without looking at it."

I asked about the prospects of children and my book. My wife, with the New York City mayoralty election near, asked him to tell her who would be mayor, and her brother's name.

He touched the paper squares, but did not open them. "Your book," he said to me, "should be a best seller, and you will have one child, a boy." These, of course, could have been educated guesses, with some logical chance of working out.

He turned to my wife. "Wagner," he said, "will be the next mayor of New York." And then pausing: "Your brother's name is Harold."

My wife and I exchanged glances. She looked slightly shaken.

"You made one mistake," I said. "My wife's brother's name is Bill, but she had an uncle, not very much older than she, whom she referred to as her brother. His name was Harold."

He laughed. "My one mistake was the only indication of extra-sensory perception. The rest was a trick."

How did he do it? He shrugged. "It's anybody's guess. Mine is the odic force."

In Florida, California, Washington, wherever I went, people told me of psychic experiences once they knew they would not be laughed at. And they were not unusual. In his Smith College class of a dozen students, Professor Ralph Harlow stated that fully half reported psychic experiences within their family circles. In Key West, Florida, a retired Navy officer, thirty-nine-year-old Kermit Waters, renting me a car, told me of comrades in arms knowing when they were about to die; a housewife, Marcia Smith, told me of her mother predicting she would marry a rejected suitor—the husband I was having cocktails with.

In sunny Southern California, where the climate seems to lend itself to absorption with things psychic, Janice Sarnoff, wife of NBC executive Thomas Sarnoff, has had so many premonitions and precognitive experiences that she thinks nothing of them. One day, while shopping in downtown Beverly Hills, she suddenly felt an overwhelming impulse to return to her home high in the neighboring hills. As the young mother drove anxiously toward her house, where a nurse kept watch over her children, her alarm grew as she noted black clouds of smoke billowing toward the sky. Not far from her home, police had put up a network of road blocks ringing the fire zone. "I was the last car," she told me, "to get through."

Only recently, she had a vision that a close friend, Cecily Jean Gavin, wife of actor John Gavin, was having a child. She called up Mrs. Gavin to congratulate her on being pregnant. "Don't be silly," the actor's pretty wife said, "my other child is only seven months old."

"I know you're pregnant," Mrs. Sarnoff insisted.

Mrs. Gavin laughed good-naturedly. "It's just not possible right now."

Two or three weeks later, the medical diagnosis confirmed the Sarnoff prognosis.

It was not unusual to find friends entertaining friends at parties with titillating forecasts of the future.

In a smart salon on New York's Central Park, I overheard a beautiful brunette with a faint German accent tell a friend quite correctly: "Your husband was married before to a dark beautiful woman, and has two children, a son and a daughter—the daughter living with the mother."

The amateur clairvoyant was Gisela Becker, wife of a prosperous manufacturer and mother of three.

As her husband looked on, she explained that she normally read the cards and was seldom, if ever, wrong. "Unlike the professionals," she said, "I don't make up things to please anybody." She motioned at her husband. "We met in Germany," she said, "and one day I suddenly saw a blonde woman in the cards and realized that it was his wife. I told him I would not see him anymore." But she looked at the cards again, and though he had not yet thought of divorce she saw him proposing. "And then," Gisela said, "after the divorce we got married."

I expressed doubt that these would be scientifically endorsed cases of precognition. Our hostess, who had joined us, smiled indulgently. Gisela and my wife seemed to share her amusement. "When you were away recently," the hostess explained, "Gisela and I visited your wife, and Gisela, reading the cards, said you were down South, resting and working, as you were. And then she predicted that your closest friend, an older man, would die in two or three weeks." She paused. "That was a month ago."

I looked at Gisela. She smiled prettily, like a Dresden doll. "It should have happened already," she said.

I nodded with a pang. "One week ago," I said, "without any warning."

At twelve midnight I had received a phone call from another sensitive, Bathsheba Askowith, and without preliminaries she had said, "Call Virginia."

"Why?" I had asked. "She will be asleep."

"Call her," she said in an urgent voice, "she needs to hear from you."

"It is very late," I said, and then a sudden thought struck me. "Is anything wrong, have you been talking to her?"

"I have not talked to her for six weeks, but I know she wants to talk to you."

I had already learned not to argue with psychics. The Belmonts, Walter and Virginia, dear friends of mine for more than twenty years, operated a pet shop in Rockefeller Center; Bathsheba knew Virginia Belmont slightly and had never met Walter Belmont.

It was not until the next morning, at her shop, that I got hold of Virginia Belmont on the phone. I had no need to ask her anything; her voice broke on the phone. "Walter died yesterday," she said.

After we had talked awhile I said, "Your friend Bathsheba called me."

"I know," Virginia said. "She called me earlier today, to say that she had let you know, and could she do anything to help."

"You had not spoken to her recently?" I asked.

I could see her shaking her head over the phone. "Not for weeks," she said.

In war it was different. Death was always just around the corner, never a surprise. But Kermit Waters *knew* that nothing would ever happen to him. "I had boys come to me on Guadalcanal and give me rings and watches to take home, but I knew nobody would have to say good-bye for me," the former Navy flier told me.

Waters had flown more than one hundred missions against the Japs in World War II. He had gone in the Navy an enlisted man and come out an officer. He operated several profitable businesses in Key West—car-rental service, gas station, investment trusts. He was a man of a practical bent.

He cocked a shrewd eye at me. "Do you know," he said, "no matter how thick the fighting, I always knew nothing would happen to me. I just felt it."

I laughed. "A chance bullet in the right place might have changed your feelings."

"Not a chance," he said. "The boys who were going to get it knew it; I never had that feeling."

"I'm sure a lot of boys felt they were going to get it before every battle."

"Not the boys I knew," he said, shaking his head. "We were in Guadalcanal with a Navy heavy-bombing group, assigned to the Thirteenth Air Force, when one of the crew, Al Montgomery, came into the B-24 where I was standing guard one night. We discussed the raid on Bougainville for the morning, and Monty said to me, 'Something bad's going to happen.'"

Waters had smiled. "What do you mean, Monty?"

"I don't think I'm going to get back."

Waters had tried good-naturedly to rally him out of it. Monty didn't respond. "When you get back," he said, "will you visit my mother, and tell her good-bye from me?"

Montgomery lived in Augusta, Georgia, some seventy-five miles from Waters' home in Statesboro. He promised. And then the eighteen-year-old Waters did his best to help and reassure his friend, who was only a little older than himself.

"Would you want to get off the crew and go back to ground duty?" he asked.

Monty shook his head. "That wouldn't help any."

They had been bombing the daylights out of the Japanese at Bougainville, getting a cargo ship unloading just the day before. "We have to pay for everything we get, Monty," the teen-age Waters philosophized.

Monty thought it over, and seemed to brighten in the recognition that his life was buying something. "I hadn't thought about it that way before," he said. And suddenly he smiled.

It was a furious battle over Bougainville. The Japs seemed to be waiting for them. The raiding party from Guadalcanal lost six fighters and a bomber. "There were twenty-eight holes in our bomber, but we made it back," said Waters. Despite his own preoccupation, he had kept an eye on Monty's bomber. "It was hit, then fell behind the formation and crashed. It floated for a few minutes, but there was no radio response before it sank. Monty had known what he was talking about."

Waters kept his word. Back in the States, he visited Monty's mother. "She wouldn't believe he was dead," Waters said. "She was corresponding with a New Jersey mother who also thought her son alive. All I could do was say good-bye for Monty and leave."

The skeptical were equally vulnerable, I found. I was with a friend, Tom Kelly, managing director of New York City's Vanderbilt Hotel, when Kitty Steele, a television actress asked if we would like to "play" the ouija board. I declined, but Kelly laughingly agreed. As I watched, Miss Steele's fingers flew across the surface of the well-worn board. Suddenly she frowned. "Tom, I don't know what this means, exactly, but they see you in a new job."

I asked: "Who are 'they?'"

The attractive Miss Steele said patiently: "The people I get from the other side."

She quickly retraced her fingers over the board, as if she were checking back, but her fingers traveled to the same letters and numerals as before, spelling out the same message. "Two weeks," she said, frowning again. "I get two weeks."

She turned to Kelly. "Have you been thinking of leaving your job, Tom?"

The Irishman from New Orleans laughed until the tears ran down his cheeks. "Don't try that power of suggestion on me," he jibed. "I've been there for years, and I have no intention of leaving what I built up."

Kelly and I left the Steele apartment together.

"A fine girl, Kitty," he said with a wag of his handsome head, "but she takes that stuff entirely too seriously."

Two weeks later, Kelly was out of the Vanderbilt. I never saw him again myself, but learned that the change had come without warning. In the next year his trail took him to hotels in Buffalo, St. Louis, Philadelphia, and Havana, as Miss Steele confided, "I am terribly worried about Tom. He's in for a rough time."

"Does he know about it?" I asked.

She sighed. "I didn't have the heart to tell him."

She would no longer play the board for Tom in absentia. And as I left her one day, she was staring out a window, eyes moist, murmuring, "Poor Tom."

Not long after that, Tom died suddenly. A friend called Kitty to break the news. "I know," she said, "but there was nothing anybody could do."

Amateur psychics often find it difficult to veil what they have seen, the very vividness of a vision apparently compelling them to blurt it out. Mrs. Lillian Jackson Moyer, living in Altoona, Pennsylvania had a reputation not only in the family, but among neighbors for second sight. She was of Scotch-Irish descent, a strain producing many mystics, and claimed descent from President Andrew Jackson, a man who always seemed to know how things would turn out.

It was not uncommon for her to look out a window, as a friend was walking by and say darkly, "What a pity. He won't be with us next week."

And the sad part of it, her family said, was that she was invariably right. She was as frank with her family. In February of 1948, as her daughter, Mrs. Pauline Falconer, was knitting booties for an expected child, Mrs. Moyer said abruptly, "You can stop your knitting; your child will not live."

While the statement itself should have been enough to induce a miscarriage, the mother retained the child. And right up to the birth the doctors assured her that she would bear a normal, healthy child. But the unexpected happened. On May 8, the day she gave birth in a Chicago hospital, her own doctor was unavoidably delayed by an emergency. Internes handled the delivery. "My baby," Mrs. Falconer said, "was asphyxiated by its own cord, its oxygen supply cut off. It could not have happened once in a million cases."

The death vision often reveals itself obliquely at friendly, informal sittings, though the result is the same. Mrs. Catherine Cook, widow of a prominent attorney in Baltimore, was working the ouija board with her sister, Mrs. Sarah Anderson, when she looked up with surprise. "Did you know that David will be coming home soon, in three or four weeks?"

David was Mrs. Anderson's son, and he was in the Army.

"Impossible," Mrs. Anderson said. "He's in Europe and can't get back for another year."

"Well," Mrs. Cook drawled, "they insist he'll be home soon."

"Ask why he should be coming home," Mrs. Anderson demanded, as her sister's fingers flew over the board, and the two of them spelled out the words.

"They say he's coming home for a funeral."

The sister laughed at the utter absurdity of it. "Why, nobody's even ill," Mrs. Anderson said. But three weeks later, Colonel Anderson did make a quick trip home to attend a funeral—his father's.

Not otherwise psychic, Mrs. Cook receives messages only when she's playing the board. "I only do it for fun," she said.

Predicted events need not have the finality of death to be impressive. They can be—and very often are—quite trivial in nature. On May 2, 1959, my wife and I were on an Eastern airliner bound for Florida, when the hostess, an attractive girl with an engaging smile, suggested we make a small wager on the Kentucky Derby being run that day at Louisville. I remember the date well because we had been married that morning, and I remember the horse.

"Do you have a tip?" I inquired.

"Oh, no," she said, "I know nothing about horses."

Even my wife was puzzled. "Then how can you be so sure?" she asked.

"I pick the Derby every year," she said.

"Do you have a bet down?"

"I wouldn't even know how to make one."

"Do you study the entries?" I asked.

She laughed. "I never look at them."

"Then how do you even know who's running?"

"When somebody reads off the names, one suddenly hits me and I know he's the winner." She shrugged. "It's happened three or four times in a row now."

"And who's the winner?" I asked rather ungraciously, naming the favorite and obvious choice, "First Landing?"

"Oh, no," she said, "Tomy Lee."

As the pretty tout romped off down the aisle my wife said, "What do you think?"

I replied grimly: "I think we should travel National."

In Miami, over the car radio, we heard the race, the most thrilling Derby in years. The winner? Tomy Lee, of course.

Lay people with psychic ability often have special interest in the field. The comedian Jackie Gleason has a large library on the occult and has privately researched dozens of mediums—only one of whom impressed him. But he has found things happening in his own life that he can't account for logically. "Sometimes in the morning," he confided to columnist Hedda Hopper, "I'll wake up and know I'm going to meet a certain person I haven't seen in ages." Besides this quite common tendency, he has a more remarkable facility. During preparations for a show, for instance, he would often overhear stagehands discussing the assembly or repair of equipment that were different or unusual. Without thinking, he would blurt out: "I know how to fix it." But then he would realize that he didn't actually have the slightest idea what was wrong, since the problem was usually something that called for technical knowledge that he didn't have. "But I'd look at it," he related, "and tell them what to do. Nine times out of ten it worked. And I don't know where the knowledge comes from, because it's something I've never learned."

Keeping to the whimsical, Ron Cochran, the television commentator, told me of the time he was watching the Jack Paar show, and a magician asked comic Joey Bishop to think of a card. As Bishop pondered, Cochran, in his own living room, turned to his wife and said, "It's the three of diamonds." Mrs. Cochran laughed, but her husband insisted, "I know," he said, "I can see it." Moments later, the magician triumphantly held up the three of diamonds. He had guessed it—and so had Cochran. But the commentator could not convince his wife. "To this day," he said, "she thinks it was a trick, and that I was in on it."

It was Cochran's only vision, and he only regretted it didn't serve some useful purpose.

After nearly every major disaster—a train wreck, the crash of a big airliner, or the sinking of a ship, the reports of life-saving premonition pour in. There were so many of these reports after the *Titanic* foundered on an iceberg, with a loss of fifteen hundred lives, that one wag quipped that more people had been saved by the *Titanic* than lost by it. However, there were many well-authenticated predictions of the tragedy. Like Cochran, one of the *Titanic's* scheduled passengers had only one vision, but this involved something more important than a three of diamonds—his life. On March 23, 1912, three weeks before the "unsinkable" ship's maiden voyage from Southampton, J. Connon Middleton, an English businessman, had booked passage for a business appointment in New York a week later, he dreamed he saw the *Titanic* floating on its side, and her passengers and crew floundering around her like so many helpless ants. The dream left him with an oppressive feeling, but he was too ashamed to mention it, or cancel his passage. However, a week before the sailing, associates in the United States cabled that he defer his trip. Gratefully, he canceled out. And then, a few days before the sailing on April 10, having a clear conscience, he related his dream to friends and relatives. It had been unsettling because of its vividness, and because normally he "didn't dream." In his dream, friends reported, Middleton appeared to be floating in air just above the wreck. It could not have been more real. But had it not been for fate, he would still have sailed. "How foolish it would seem if I had postponed my business on account of a dream," he told his wife.

As the *Titanic* eased into the English Channel to the start of its memorable voyage, the English sportsman, Jack Marshall, and his household, sat on the roof of their home overlooking The Solent to catch a glimpse of the breath-taking beauty. Suddenly, Mrs. Marshall grabbed her husband's arm and cried: "That ship is going to sink before it reaches America."

Her husband patted her hand reassuringly while the servants looked discreetly away. But Mrs. Marshall's agitation only increased. "The *Titanic* has watertight compartments," somebody said, "it can't sink."

Mrs. Marshall became furious. "Don't stand there staring at me," she shouted. "Do something, you fools. I can see hundreds of people struggling in the icy water. Are you all so blind that you are going to let them drown?"

Joan Grant, Mrs. Marshall's daughter, recalled in the autobiography *Far Memory* that for the next few days everyone was careful not to mention the *Titanic* to her mother. "It must have been almost a relief for her when everyone knew that the *Titanic* had struck an iceberg; not nearly so lonely as waiting until it happened."

Mrs. Marshall had other premonitions. Three years after the *Titanic* sank, the Marshalls were planning a voyage home from America through the submarine-infested North Atlantic. "The stateroom tickets . . . were on the sitting-room mantelpiece, although we were not sailing for another three weeks," Joan Grant recalled, "when mother suddenly stared at them and said, 'The *Lusitania* is going to sink on that voyage, Jack. Change the reservations.'"

Marshall had the reservation moved up. "We will sail the day after tomorrow . . . on the same ship," he said.

"Oh, that's all right," the mother replied calmly, "the *Lusitania* is not going to sink until the voyage we were going on. I suppose she will be torpedoed, as it is too warm for icebergs."

Long before the *Titanic* was in blueprints, novelist Morgan Robinson had dramatically previewed the 1912 disaster. His fictional ship was the same size as the 880-foot liner, proud of its watertight compartments, light on lifeboats, and it collided with an iceberg in the North Atlantic in April. The loss of life was comparable, and as some men were heroes, others cowards—just like on the *Titanic*. Robinson's ship was called the *Titan*.

Robinson's *Titan*, like Jules Verne's submarine, was not unique. Nearly every gifted writer, thinker, statesman, or inventor, Dr. Reisenman had insisted, owed much of his success to his ability to anticipate events that could not be logically foreseen. Before he became Prime Minister, Winston Churchill had an unmistakable vision of World War II some twenty months before it broke out. Although for years his had been virtually the lone voice in Commons to warn of Hitler's might, Churchill's vision did not stem from political logic, but was triggered by an emotional reaction to Anthony Eden's resignation as Foreign Minister—and bolstered him for the coming crisis. As only he could, Churchill described the vision in his *Memoirs of the Second World War*:

"Late in the night of February 20 [1938] a telephone message reached me as I sat in my old room at Chartwell (as I often sit now) that Eden had resigned. I must confess that my heart sank, and for a while the dark waters of despair overwhelmed me. In a long life I have had many ups and downs. During all the war soon to come and in its darkest times I never had any trouble in sleeping. In the crisis of 1940 when so much responsibility lay upon me, and also at many very anxious moments in the following five years, I could always flop into bed and go to sleep after the day's work was done—subject of course to any emergency call. I slept sound and awoke refreshed, and had no feelings except appetite to grapple with whatever the morning's boxes might bring. But now on this night of February 20, 1938, I lay in my bed consumed by emotions of sorrow and fear. There seemed one strong, young figure standing up against long, dismal, drawling tide of drift and surrender, of wrong measurements and feeble impulses. My conduct of affairs have been different from his in various ways; but he seemed to me at this moment to embody the life-hope of the British nation, the grand old British race that had done so much for men, and had yet some more to give. Now he was gone. I watched the daylight slowly creep in through the windows, and saw before me in mental gaze the vision of Death."

After he came to power, Churchill was to have another vision —and another wretched night. In July of 1945, with the Germans beaten, England held its first general election of the war. Assured by Conservative leaders that the day had gone well for his side, the Prime Minister retired early, not even thinking of the prediction made by a Mrs. Dixon in Washington. And then: ". . . just before dawn, I woke suddenly with a sharp stab of almost physical pain. A hitherto subconscious conviction that we were beaten broke forth and dominated my mind. All the pressure of great events, on and against which I had mentally so long maintained my 'Flying speed' would cease and I should fall. The power to shape the future would be denied me. The knowledge and experience I had gathered, the authority and good will I had gained in so many countries would vanish. I was discontented at the prospect and turned over at once to sleep again. I did not wake till nine o'clock, and when I went into the Map Room the first results had begun to come in. They were, as I now expected, unfavorable. By noon, it was clear that the Socialists would have a majority. At luncheon my wife said to me, 'It may well be a blessing in disguise.' I replied, 'At the moment it seems quite effectively disguised.'"

Others not so great had their visions of great affairs. A good many know of Lincoln's much-told dream of his own assassination. But how many know that a mother, watching her baby in its crib, had a terrible presentiment, as her glance fell on a clenched little fist, that the child would one day do evil to his country? That Mother was Mary Anne Booth, and the son, her ninth child, John Wilkes Booth.

The mark of Cain was already in his hand.

Recalling her mother's vision, Asia Booth, whose own life was to be wrecked by the deed, had written in 1852, thirteen years before her brother fired the fatal bullet into Lincoln's head:

> "Tiny, innocent, white baby hand,
> What force, what power is at your command,
> For evil or good?
> My God, let me see what this hand shall do.
> In the silent years we are tending to."

And then the answer from a mother's intuitive heart:

> "The flame up-lept
> Like a wave of blood
> An avenging arm crept into shape,
> And the country shone out in the flame,
> Which fading resolved into her boy's own name."

As a schoolboy, Wilkes had his palm read by an itinerant fortune-teller. Gleefully, he told the troubled Asia about it. Shrinking from the handsome boy, the gypsy had said, "I've never seen a worse hand, and I wish I hadn't seen it. All I can tell you is that you'll die young and make a bad end."

Lincoln, too, had his presentiment long before he took his place in the White House. Leaving Springfield for Washington, he sadly told friends he would not be back. And with the war over four years later, the martyr President was able to discuss his celebrated dream a few days before his assassination with the detachment of a man who had finished his job. The dream was so vivid that, waking, he had turned to the Bible for reassurance. And he found none. Wherever he turned there was an allusion to dreams consistent with his own somber thoughts. The reality of it oppressed him.

"There seemed to be a death-like stillness about me. Then I heard subdued sobs, as if a number of people were weeping. I thought I left my bed and wandered downstairs. There the silence was broken by the same pitiful sobbing, but the mourners were invisible. I went from room to room, no living person was in sight, but the same mournful sounds of distress met me as I passed along. It was light in all the rooms, every object was familiar to me; but where were all the people who were grieving as if their hearts would break? . . . Determined to find the cause of a state of things so mysterious and so shocking, I kept on until I arrived at the East Room. There I met with a sickening surprise. Before me was a catafalque, on which rested a corpse wrapped in funeral vestment. Around it were stationed soldiers who were acting as guards; and there was a throng of people, some gazing mournfully upon the corpse, whose face was covered, others weeping pitifully. 'Who is dead in the White House?' I demanded of one of the soldiers. 'The President' was his answer. 'He was killed by an assassin.'"

Many writers have been remarkably prophetic when their readers thought them only imaginative. In his fantasies, H. G. Wells foresaw space travel, germ warfare, interplanetary warfare. He dreamed of an irresistible monster on caterpillar treads, and planted in Churchill's head the idea for the first tanks in World War I. Jules Verne, of course, foresaw the long-voyaging submarine, which may have been a forerunner of our nuclear submersibles. Heinrich Heine, writing a hundred years before, warned Europe of the Nazi tide: "The cross is brittle and the day must soon come when it will pitifully break. . . . A drama will be enacted in Germany, by the side of which the French Revolution will seem like an innocent idyll . . . let it not be imagined that the great actors have yet appeared . . . And only when that hour comes will real battle begin."

Before the Civil War, Andrew Jackson Davis, the unschooled mystic of Orange County, New York, wrote of air-conditioning, Pullman travel, autos, airplanes, diesel engines, and described not only the combustion engine but the fuel that would power it—gasoline. "Carriages will be moved by a strange and beautiful and simple mixture of aqueous and atmosphere gases—so easily condensed, so simply ignited, and so empowered by a machine somewhat resembling our engines as to be entirely concealed and manageable between the forward wheels."

With striking precision, writers continue to anticipate startling events. A year before the Russians planted two spacemen in orbit in August 1962, author-columnist Bob Considine started a short story describing how two Red cosmonauts flew close together in space, conversed, and otherwise filled their time in their unprecedented junket around the earth. The story was finished three or four months before the Russians, Nikolayev and Popovich, took off, and was in type, ready for release in *Esquire* magazine, two months before the tandem takeoff. "There's just no way," matter-of-fact Bob Considine observed, "to explain a coincidence of this kind."

Wells, Davis, Heine, Verne—none was unique. As the average person becomes aware of his intuitiveness, his psychic experiences seem to increase. It was obviously purely coincidence, but in my own case I would think of people I hadn't seen or thought of for years, and then run into them on the street. I would pick up the phone to call somebody, and they would be calling me. I began to anticipate what people were going to say—an obnoxious habit.

Little things began to fall into place. Not having a better address, I had written to Wellington, New Zealand to ask Sir Victor Goddard, Air Marshal retired of the New Zealand Air Force, about his experiences with precognition. And no answer came back. As I was wondering again where I could write, I happened to lunch one day with Professor Harlow of Smith College, who showed me the newly published book, *Beyond the Horizon*. I turned to the foreword. It was by Sir Victor Goddard. And there was his address as plain as day, Brasted, England.

A young newspaperman, Jon Bradshaw, dropped in one day with an Albert Briggs, recently of Beaumont, Texas, but now in Wall Street. Briggs talked entertainingly of himself. He had been to the University of Pennsylvania, Southern Methodist, and one other school. "My family," he said laughingly, "liked keeping me away."

"Where did you go to boarding school?" I asked politely.

"I didn't," he said, "even though my mother had been to one, and would have liked me to go."

"I suppose she went to Ward-Belmont," I said, mentioning a school in Nashville, Tennessee that I had no reason to think of at the moment.

An uneasy smile crossed my guest's face, and he looked uncertainly at the Scotch-and-water in his hand. "That was quite a coincidence," he said at last, "your guessing that school, and it has been closed for years too."

Young Bradshaw mentioned the name of a pretty model he was dating, but couldn't remember her agency.

"Would it be Foster-Ferguson?" I asked, again without stopping to think.

It was his turn to smile uncomfortably.

It was a lucky guess, I agreed, even though the agency was a relatively new one.

Many have been taken unawares by their own psychic development. Spencer Thornton, a Nashville physician, had worked his way through Wake Forest and Bowman Medical School, demonstrating his talents as a mental magician. He would read minds, achieve feats of memory, do number tricks and, of course, card tricks. He didn't pretend to be psychic himself, and like Dr. Reisenman, he had such a bag of tricks that he was skeptical of anybody who did claim to be psychic. "Early in my career," he told a friend, "I got interested in magic to better understand the trickery of phony mediums." Some of his tricks were so impressive that his audiences thought he was surely psychic, but the young doctor knew better. Yet away from the demonstration halls he was beginning to have baffling experiences. "My wife would send me a thought that she wanted me to telephone her," he said, "and I would. When she was at the store, and I was at home, I would send her a signal to buy something, and without quite realizing why, she would invariably buy it."

He began to wonder about himself. When he started to practice medicine, opening a clinic in Nashville with three other doctors, he continued his demonstrations in ESP—extrasensory perception. His first predictions publicly were a publicity stunt. One week prior to an advertised lecture, he would forecast headlines in local newspapers for the day of his lecture.

At first he had more misses than hits, but his average kept climbing. His powers seemed to grow with the demands that he put on them. But it was still "all in fun." After a few months, his predictions began to hit with regularity. He made few converts, however—the gullible continued to be astounded, the skeptics continued unbelieving. And he didn't know what to make of it himself. After he had predicted to the syllable one headline in a Texas paper, a reporter for that paper noted dryly: "Of course, such things can't happen and nobody who reads this will believe it, but what about us po' folks who were there?"

In the beginning he had concentrated on current events. Soon, he discovered, his headlines came without effort, and without depending on what was happening around him. He saw the headlines and events in snatches of words or pictures. "Somewhere in the metamorphosis of this precognitive ability," a friend explained, "he learned that the necessary ingredient for his new ability was a total empathy with the thing, person, or situation that occupied his thoughts. By empathy, he meant the total involvement in a situation, complete divestment of self, as opposed to sympathy, which is simply an understanding and deep concern. With empathy, he became the person or situation itself."

Thornton had no wish to be a psychic. He had greater standing—and more fun—as a magician and amateur trickster. Conservatives in medicine were beginning to view him with a jaundiced eye; the Baptist conference, for which he aspired to be a medical missionary, was concerned by his publicity. But the predictions kept rolling off his tongue, on the lecture platform, over the radio, and on television. He was right only half the time, even now, but still his predictions were too specific to be put down to luck or trickery. On April 3, 1959, on a Nashville television show, he said an announcement would be made within three weeks that some form of life would be placed in orbit. On April 21, the government disclosed that mice would be sent into space in a Discoverer satellite. He had also forecast a major airline crash on the West Coast in two weeks. On April 17, exactly two weeks later, a Mexican airliner crashed in lower California, killing all twenty-six aboard.

On April 22, he correctly foresaw headlines one week later concerning Mrs. Clare Booth Luce's confirmation as Ambassador to Brazil. Despite opposition she would be confirmed, but her husband, magazine publisher Henry Luce, would ask her to resign and she would do so. On May 1, this secondary prediction was also fulfilled.

In Nashville, where he was performing these prodigies, many thought the home-town boy a phony prophet. As a test, a Nashville television station, the CBS affiliate, proposed that Thornton pick the Kentucky Derby winner; the race was coming up the end of that week.

"I'll try," said Thornton. "Who's running?"

That afternoon he examined the entries in the newspaper. With the race on for May 2, a Saturday, Thornton made his prediction on April 28, four days ahead.

All the protocol of a great event was observed. There was to be no possibility of hocus-pocus. Before a group of impeccable witnesses, including pillars of the Nashville banking world, the slip with the Thornton selection was notarized and sealed, unread, in an envelope, and placed in a vault of Nashville's Third National Bank. Only a combination of three keys would open the vault, and these were held by two irreproachable vice presidents of the bank and the vault custodian. On the Monday after the race, May 4, 1959, with only Thornton knowing whom he had picked, the bankers opened the vault. Thornton was in a chamber outside, waiting with photographers and newsmen. Granville Bourne, a bank vice president, broke the envelope open. His eyes seemed to pop as he scanned the slip. Silently, he handed it to another banker standing next to him. It was his turn to blink. And no wonder. Thornton had not only picked the first three horses in order, but had called the closeness of the race precisely: "Tomy Lee in a photo finish; Sword Dancer second; First Landing Third."

Calmly, Thornton tried to explain. "Usually, the predictions come in form of thoughts, but sometimes I do see a picture. Actually, I did see some sort of horse race going on, but halfway through, the thought came to me that Tomy Lee would win. Immediately after, I got another thought—Sword Dancer. I couldn't figure out what it meant at first, but decided it would be Tomy Lee over Sword Dancer in a close one, and I made it a photo, because that's as close as they come."

In Nashville's banking circles, Thornton was a ninety-day wonder. "There was no way in the world for that slip to have been changed or altered in any way," banker Granville Bourne assured me. "I walked into the vault and, with the custodian standing there, turned one of the keys that opened the safe. The envelope was not out of my hands at any time before I opened and read it. To this day, though I have thought about it often, I don't know how he did it. But there was no chance of a trick, that I know."

Overnight, Dr. Thornton became a celebrity. He was besieged by all kinds of get-rich-quick promoters and the newspapers and television people wanting exclusive predictions. A New York newspaper woke him at three in the morning for special predictions for New Yorkers. "Alligators," he predicted, "would rise out of the sewers of New York." It was printed seriously.

Now that his forecasts were getting broad coverage, he was

concerned about their impact. Before the Derby, he had predicted an airplane crash in the New York-New Jersey area on May 8. When the prediction hit the newspapers, cancellations streamed into airplane offices. Rumors spread that the crash was predicted for Los Angeles, Denver, Dallas, and Chicago, and small panics occurred all over the country. The airlines frantically requested that he predict no more crashes.

As it turned out there was no crash in the New York-New Jersey area—a clear miss for Thornton—though eighteen months later in December 1960, two airliners did collide in a singular accident over New Jersey, with one plane crashing in the heart of Brooklyn.

Meanwhile, Thornton was hitting with a few minor predictions —a volcano eruption in Hawaii, a flood in Illinois, a stray headline here and there. But many home towners were still unimpressed. On Tuesday, June 23, 1959, the editors of the Nashville *Tennessean*, a morning newspaper, asked Thornton to predict two days ahead the front-page headline in their Thursday paper—June 25. Thornton didn't hesitate. In less than a minute, he dashed off his prediction. Again safeguards were set up to assure there would be no fraud. The prediction, to be kept under lock and key until Thursday noon, was turned over to two officers of the local Lions Club, Brainerd Kidder and Tom Dawson, both outstanding Nashville citizens. It was folded so they couldn't see it, and sealed in aluminum foil, wrapped inside two envelopes by Dawson, and placed in Kidder's safe by his secretary.

There was a big turnout at the Lions Club luncheon that Thursday, where the prediction was to be revealed. The Thursday morning *Tennessean* was very much in evidence, as a presiding officer tore open the envelopes and began to read Thornton's prediction:

"I predict the biggest news in the nation on Thursday, June 25 will be about a steel industry ultimatum to the union. This will overshadow all international news. I predict"—the speaker faltered a moment—"I predict the *Tennessean*'s main headline will read: 'Steel Threatens to Close.'"

And so it was, over eight columns.

That headline produced another front-page head in the Nashville *Tennessean*. This one announced: "Thornton Headline 100 Pct. Correct." The amazing doctor had done it again. The skeptical press was happy to pay him homage, even though still figuratively scratching their heads. The *Tennessean's* editors, as though feeling they now had to justify themselves, explained in detail that the headline had been prepared in routine fashion late the night before as the paper went to press; it had been selected after a first effort, completely different in emphasis, had been written and discarded. The first read "Sign Pact, USW Warned," and just as he had no logical way of knowing it would be written, Thornton could not have known it would be discarded. Psychically, he had cut through all the causes, and seen only the result.

And how did Thornton do it? His summary is as good as any: "The steel situation had been in the news for days, and it seemed a logical area, and predictions often come to me with a flash once I've hit a general area. But, of course, that still doesn't explain hitting it on the nose."

Concentration did seem to help. In the summer of 1959, making predictions for a Hearst syndicate, he was asked by editor Bill Levinson of New York to name the upcoming Miss America of 1960. It was hardly the sort of thing Thornton would have normally thought about. Not knowing the names of the entrants, he brooded into space. "I can't see the exact winner clearly," he told Levinson, "but I can tell you she will be from the Midwest, her talent will be in music, and her measurements will be 36-24-36. I seem to get the impression of a letter *M* very strongly, either in her name or the name of the state."

That was the way the prediction went to the syndicate's newspapers. But sometime thereafter, with the contest deadline approaching, Thornton happened to see a complete list for the Atlantic City pageant. "As his eye ran down the list," Bill Levinson recalled, "it stopped suddenly at Mississippi, and he pointed to the name Mead opposite, saying, 'That's it, that's the one.'"

But Levinson shook his head doubtfully.

"Mary Ann Mobley, the 1959 winner, was from Mississippi," he pointed out. "I'm sure they'll bend over backwards not to have her successor from the same state—and from the same college too."

But Thornton was insistent. "I see her name clearly now, Bill —Linda Mead—why don't we change my original prediction, and pick her by name since I'm so sure."

"It's too late now," Levinson said, "your selections have already gone out; it would shake the newspapers' confidence in you if we recalled any predictions."

"This is one of the times," Thornton said, "that I just know. I saw her name and something clicked."

"But Mississippi, if you recall, is hardly a Midwestern state," Levinson said.

"I was groping there," Thornton acknowledged, "but even so, if you consult the map, you will see that it is in the middle area of the country. And the *M* I saw originally was for the girl and the state."

Working closely with Thornton for months, until the doctor tore up his lucrative contract for purely professional reasons, Bill Levinson had been quietly impressed by Thornton's development in the time he knew him. "Once, I had been trying to reach the doctor by phone all day to ask him a question," Levinson said, "when the phone rang, and it was Thornton from Nashville. 'I knew you were trying to reach me, Bill,' he said, 'and I called the first chance I got.'"

On another occasion, Thornton put Levinson through a memory association test complete with questions and answers. "On that reference of yours to an azalea bush," Thornton said later, "I got more than I bargained for."

"Oh, lots of people have an azalea bush on their lawn," Levinson said.

"But I saw a whole row of azalea bushes, not one."

The editor's eyes bugged a little. "As a matter of fact," he recalled, "I had been thinking of a row down the side of my house, maybe the only row of azaleas in New Rochelle."

A scoffer himself, Thornton was to know what it was like to be scoffed at. In Toronto, Canada, in the fall of 1959, reporters asked the doctor to make a few off-the-cuff predictions concerning Princess Margaret, rumored as marrying a Canadian, and Queen

Elizabeth, reported to be carrying twins. Thornton told amused newspapermen that Margaret definitely would not marry a Canadian, and that her engagement would soon be announced to an Englishman. They demanded skeptically that he tell them the initials of the man she would marry. Hesitating only a second, Thornton came up with a set of three initials. "I answered," he recalled, "that my impression was of the initials T. R. J., in that order." And he predicted that the marriage would take place within two years. He was amused later, he said, when he saw that the initials had been reversed to fit a Canadian named John N. Turner, whom Thornton had never heard of. "I was further amused and pleasantly startled," Thornton told friends, "to read a few months later of Margaret's surprise engagement announcement to Tony Armstrong-Jones, whom I also had never heard of." He felt that he had made a precise hit, because his predictions were based on interpretations of impressions, and "R" and "Ar" give exactly the same impression, and have the same pronunciation.

At the same time, he had also predicted a tidal wave for the "West Coast," not specifying what west coast. Through hometown pride, coupled with a careless tolerance for the doctor and his gift, one reporter, Thornton recalled, assigned the tidal wave to the "west coast of Canada and Alaska." Actually, the tidal wave materialized with an earthquake on the coast of Peru; it struck part of the United States' west coast, but was "pretty washed out by the time it got to Canada."

Thornton has been making no more predictions publicy, applying himself exclusively to his medical practice. Friends, disappointed by this denial of his gift, say that he may have been born fifty years too soon. And Thornton might be inclined to agree. "Nearly everyone," he confided once, "has had some simple form of ESP experience. It is a new force, different from anything we've known up to now, and we have a long way to go before we can understand or control it. But in fifty years we may have no more awe of it than we have today of television or space travel. After all, television would have seemed fantastic too—fifty years ago."

7 ASTROLOGY, FORTUNE-TELLERS, AND PHONIES

The year 1962 was both a good and bad year for astrology. The new version of the Bible, put out by leading English scholars after years of research into ancient Greek texts, established that the wise men who heralded the coming of Christ were astrologers. From Matthew Chapter Two, Verse Two, an astrologer read aloud to me with an air of quiet triumph:

"'Jesus was born at Bethlehem in Judea during the reign of Herod. After his birth, astrologers from the east arrived in Jerusalem asking, "Where is the child who is to be born king of the Jews? We observed the rising of his star, and we have come to pay him homage."'"

But astrology also had a lot to live down in a year when Indian astrologers, moved by an unusual conjunction of seven planets, forecast the end of the world, or some equivalent catastrophe, on February 5 of that year. Not all astrologers, of course, went along with this dire prediction, but even many who didn't felt that something had to give when the seven planets converged for the first time in four hundred years.

In some parts of India business and social intercourse came to a halt while the faithful sat and prayed and waited for their day of fulfillment. Originating with the Indian astrologers, who dominate the great subculture of the occult, the word traveled from continent to continent among the *cognoscente* that a calamity was imminent. Outside India, the fear and apprehension among countless thousands was so widespread that spiritualist Manley Hall, a California prophet and soothsayer, issued a soothing pronouncement: While the conjunction might be marked by upheavals around the earth, there would be no great catastrophe; and everybody was to please remain calm.

In this country, serious-minded people, as well as the usual quota of addicts, were affected by the reports of impending disaster from the unusual planetary cluster. Two months before its scheduled appearance, as excitement mounted, an Indian exporter in this country told me that business associates in Ceylon had insisted that he leave this country before February. Only the United States and Western Europe, he assured me smugly, were to be directly affected. "I guess," he said with a doughty smile, "the Russians won't waste their H-bombs on India."

Actually, all the excitement and fear was engendered by the direst ignorance. The much-publicized conjunction of planets, astronomically, was not even a conjunction, but a mere planetary grouping of Jupiter, Venus, the Moon, Sun, Saturn, Mars, and Mercury, with no special significance for the earth or anybody else. Just after my conversation with the enraptured Indian in December of 1961. Dr. James S. Pickering, an astronomer at the world-famous Hayden Planetarium at the American Museum of Natural History, assured me that February 5 would be no different, celestially, from the day before and the day after. "It's all a lot of hokum," the plain-spoken scientist said, "just preying on these poor people's superstition and fears." The last similar clustering had occurred on February 5, 1524, without upsetting the applecarts of the times, and previously on September 9, 1186, also without the world coming to a disastrous end. The next is down for an early revival—May 5, 2005, and this is already being heralded as the dawn of a new era of peace and plenty.

Despite all the nonsense connected with astrology, some millions of Americans, three quarters of them women, have a sheepish belief in the stars, consulting astrologers personally or through correspondence, or furtively following the horoscopes in hundreds of newspapers. And as objective a scientist as Dr. Hans Bender, Europe's great psychic researcher, has acknowledged that while ninety per cent of the astrological fodder is sheer pap, the remaining ten per cent indicates that there may be something to the art itself—even if there is little to recommend its practitioners.

And in the Bible itself, basis for the astrologically skeptic Christian and Jewish faiths, astrologers have counted more than two hundred references to astrology, including the recent change in Matthew, and the Eighth Psalm, which they cite as a notable heavenly revelation of human determinism, by virtue of the stars: "When I consider thy heavens, the work of thy finger, the moon and the stars, which thou hast ordained; what is man that thou art mindful of him?"

Reflecting the popularity of the stars, one of the most successful of the country's businessmen is a publisher of astrology books and charts, known as Zolar. His down-to-earth name—Bruce King. He receives thousands of inquiries by mail, telephone, wire, and answers by mail, seeing nobody. "Astrology," says Zolar, whose name is a happy combination of zodiac and solar, "is an art, as exact or inexact as medicine, depending on the astrologer." Every one of the twelve planetary signs, he maintains, indicates a specific type of personality to begin with. "Libra's generally even-tempered, Taurus bullheaded." This zodiac sign provides a general picture. "As though," he explained, "you were told somebody was a Texan or New Yorker, and then as you get more information about the time of birth, it's like knowing whether he was from the Bronx or Brooklyn, Fort Worth or Houston."

The people who write Zolar for advice are, for the most part, women who are lonely, in trouble, getting old, or afraid of death. A woman of eighty-five writes each year, asking if she will be married that year.

But actresses, politicians, businessmen—even the Morgans and Vanderbilts—have consulted astrological charts, trying to learn the future and what they should do about it. Zolar claimed that the clique running Russia consult astrologers, as Hitler did, and that they will not engage in any imminent war because they are under a bad astrological aspect for the next few years.

But if astrology is so authoritative, why, long before he pushed into Poland, didn't Hitler's astrologers warn him off?

"They did," Zolar insisted, "but he killed his favorite astrologer when he warned him against the war and moving eventually into Russia."

It seemed rather implausible that a person's life—or an event—could be charted, just from knowing the hour of his birth.

"Why then," I asked, "do people born at the same time, under the same star, have such different lives?"

"Even twins, though born in the same circumstances, are nevertheless born minutes apart, at which time the position of the governing planet is different."

It did not quite answer the question.

Zolar did not claim to be at all psychic, but more of a mathematician. "We figure up the planetary aspects well in advance," he said. "Nostradamus correctly figured things four hundred years ahead from his horoscopes. And I have foreseen many events. For instance," he hinted darkly, "I see some things for Mr. Kennedy, but I can't talk about them because he's President."

However, he would comment, generally, on the sign of Gemini, and John Kennedy, born on May 29, was the first Gemini to ever sit in the White House. "Geminis," observed Zolar, "lack consistency of purpose, and have dual personalities. If pushed, they are impossible to handle."

In an expansive moment, he predicted with the onset of the Aquarean Age in February of 1962, a renaissance of the scientist and an end to the politicians. He foresaw mass revolutions around the world—a deduction that might have been gleaned from leafing through the newspapers, with Africa and Asia in ferment, and Latin America undergoing its customary palace revolts.

"The capitalistic system as we know it," Zolar said flatly, "is on the way out."

"Do you mean communism is taking over?"

"No, that's on the way out, too. But we're going off the gold standard, sooner than you think."

"Why," Zolar was asked, "can't you predict the stock market, if astrology is as reliable as you say?"

Zolar smiled contentedly, reviewing his own success with the market. "I've predicted the highs and lows, the new high in November of 1961, and another new high before January 10 of 1962, with a drop-off after that."

He had foreseen the spring slump, and the May market break

after the White House's ringing attack on the steel industry—one year before the big drop, recording his predictions in his astrology magazine a month before the debacle. Reading for myself, I saw where he had predicted selling waves, with new lows for May, 1962, and then the buying rally during the last days of the month. It would have been a pretty accurate report, if he had made it in Wall Street while watching the market reel under the worst selling wave since 1929: "The month [May] will start off with some profit taking and then sell off sharply. Electronics, steels, auto shares, and chemicals will follow the recent high-flying specialties down, all sections of the list will feel the pressure." And then the comment relating to the uncertainty stemming from the steel controversy: "Sharp sell-off due to outside influences. But for long term, buy blue chips on any severe break."

And the break itself, as Zolar saw it:

"Another selling wave may put the averages at new lows for the year. Reports of slowdown in many industries and profit squeeze will dampen speculative interest. Market will rally weakly from the lows. Bad news may push stocks lower at the close of this decanate." This was for the ten-day period, May 11 to May 20.

Between May 21 and May 31, "Further selling will be halted by sharp rally in old-line companies." And this is just what happened, though Zolar was a few days off in calling the turn on the break of May 28, when twenty billion dollars were slashed from market values. Even so, Zolar had not had the courage of his convictions. "I had seen the worst break since 1929," this affable tycoon of astrologers groaned, "but a broker friend of mine talked me out of sticking my chin out." Logically, he had protested to Zolar, "How can such a thing happen when the country's so prosperous?" And astrologer Zolar had deferred to businessman Zolar.

Since Zolar had been so good with May 1962, I took a look at his predictions for 1963, while they were still sticky with ink from the presses. Curiously, I noted: "A general business upswing is indicated at the start of 1963." But there would be a minor crisis at the midyear: "Around June 1963, the economy will have to bridge the gap from expansion powered by fast inventory building and government spending to expansion powered chiefly by an upsurge of business capital spending. The astrological indications are strong that the midyear bridge will be traversed successfully."

He foresaw the Negro becoming a greater economic factor, as he led the push to the cities: "The incredible restlessness of Americans continues as they wander away from the farm and depressed areas. The West will continue to boom. Hefty treks North and West by Southern Negroes will bring Negro spending on the upgrade."

Zolar had a few words for the new market: "Reviewing the business picture against the action of the New York Stock Market, it appears that business and workers' income will be better in general. But the stock market will lag considerably behind the continued rise in the over-all economy."

And how could astrology see all this? "There is an order in the universe," blandly observed Zolar, "and human affairs may very well be part of this order."

Man's birth itself, in this order, is the most important thing, astrologically, that ever happens to him. Consequently, the closer the astrologer can get to the minute and second of birth, the more accurate the forecast, Zolar said. "The timing of a prediction is off," he explained, "unless I have the exact time of the birth, though I might have the right event." The wife of a prominent publisher called him early in 1961, and wanted to know what the year held for her. He already knew her birth date, because of her prominence, but inquired after the hour. "With that additional clue," he recalled, "I told her to be careful in the middle of that month, and to make sure she was near a good doctor."

The woman was not impressed. But a few weeks later, she telephoned from a hospital. "I should have listened to you," she moaned. "I went upstate, bumped my knee in a trivial accident, and they've put my leg in traction, and I'm going to be here for weeks."

Though I had little confidence in astrology, my initial experience with an astrologer had been rather startling. I was in a business establishment in the spring of 1956, when the owner introduced me to another customer, a gray-haired, well-dressed man with a keen blue eye. As he was leaving he told the proprietor, "I won't be seeing you for a while, as I'm going to be off for Europe soon."

"Isn't it a little early for you?" the proprietor asked.

"Yes," the other agreed casually, "but I want to get there and back before the war breaks out."

"What war?" I asked.

"Oh," he said, "a war involving three continents, and I'll want to get back before October, that's when it'll break out."

With an easy smile, he bowed himself out the door.

I stared after his retreating figure with a jaundiced eye. "What's wrong with him?" I asked.

The proprietor laughed. "I guess you didn't catch his name—that's David Sturgis, the astrologist."

I was to think of Sturgis six months later when the war briefly flared over Suez. The fighting was not as extended as Sturgis had indicated; it was confined to a relatively small area in Egypt and, breaking out in the final days of October, was soon over. But I was struck by the date, which he had gotten correctly, and three continents—the French and English launching their attacks from Europe, and their Israel ally marching from Asia to join the attack on Egyptian Africa.

But actually, though he may have been letter-perfect in his forecast, the astrologer had not correctly appraised the foreshadowed event. From his precautions, I would have expected at least a major conflict or even another world war.

The stringencies of research led me to other astrologers. I telephoned Madam Hellene Paul, having heard from a fashion model friend that she had read for her with amazing accuracy. "She only charts for a year ahead," my friend said, "but she's certainly been right on everything so far. She told me I was going to the Orient in a few months, and I'm flying to Japan next week on an assignment I never dreamed I would get. She told me my son would become seriously ill but recover, and that my ex-husband would remarry. It all happened within the year, and she's told me that I would leave modeling, which I'm planning to do."

"How about romance?" I inquired.

"Not this year, anyway, but I'll go back in a few months for my next reading, and—who knows—things may pick up."

"Do you really believe in this stuff?" I asked. She had always seemed a very practical type to me, earning up to fifty dollars an hour modeling, and stashing most of it away in gilt-edged securities.

She shrugged. "All I know is that she's been very good with me." She waved her finely groomed hands airily. "Of course, she's expensive, but everybody goes to her."

Weeks later, I called Madam Paul.

"Do I know you?" she asked brightly.

"I was recommended by a friend." I mentioned the name. "A model," I said helpfully.

"Oh, the name wouldn't mean anything to me," she said. "I read for so many people."

Over the phone, she asked my name and address, my weight and height, and then age and place of birth.

"There is some difference about the time of birth," I said. "I was born about midnight, and because of daylight-saving time, or some other discrepancy, one record shows April 26, the other April 27."

"There wasn't any daylight-saving time then," she said. "Not until 1919."

I took the 27th, which made me a day younger.

"All right," she said in a hearty voice, "now that we've settled that, let me tell you how I work. I see you for an hour; it is twenty-five dollars for that hour and your chart, and five dollars additional for a chart for any other person whom you want charted."

"There's only myself," I said, economically.

"Fine, we'll only discuss your problems then."

"What problems?" I asked.

She laughed. "Well, if you don't have problems, what do you want a chart for?"

"Oh, I have problems, all right," I conceded, "but I've just grown accustomed to them."

"Well, for the next year," she said, "I'll tell you what your problems are going to be, and how to handle them." She paused. "Since I will already be working on your chart before you arrive, you might send me a check before the appointment."

"Where do I go?" I asked.

She gave me the address. "The penthouse apartment," she said.

"Naturally," I said, "close to the stars."

I inquired about another astrologer. "Oh him," she said, "he was a big fake, he spent all his time traveling between here and Europe, romancing rich women."

Madam Paul seemed more professorial than the Great Zolar. Cheerfully, she discussed with me the complicated relationship of the planets, the stars, the earth, and the person himself born under one of the twelve significant zodiacal signs, from Aquarius through Capricorn. She didn't seem to mind my not being a believer. "Most people find it difficult to believe what they don't understand."

Even before our birth, she explained, the planets were shaping and molding our natures and futures. "We are like radios," she said, "responding to vibrations coming from the stars and the ten planets nearest the earth. During the prenatal period these vibrations affect the individuals, and at birth their influence is confirmed, giving the key to our character and prospects."

I questioned how some planet millions of miles away could shape my personality.

She laughed almost pityingly. "What is so amazing about that, when every one of us, our moods and outlook, are affected each month by the aspect of the moon? Luna means moon, and that, of course, is where the word lunatic or loony comes from." Her eyebrows tilted slightly. "And certainly if it moves oceans, it can stir up man a little, too."

With a flash of memory I recalled, in police reporter days, the cops' sighing lament each month: 'The whole town seems to go crazy when that full moon comes out." And many insist that the lunar cycle has the same depressing effect on men as on women, though the physical symptoms may be different.

But, still, if the planets fixed our way of life, of what help was astrology? "If everything is set," I asked, "why consult an astrologer?"

"Oh, you have plenty of freedom of action, once you know what's coming." She paused a moment. "For instance, if you own any stocks I would tell you to dispose of them right after the first of the year." This was now late summer of 1961. "The fact that the market is going down is fixed, but not your response to a fixed situation, and therefore my foreknowledge and advice can be helpful in influencing your future action."

Consulting my notes subsequently, after the market had gone into a dramatic decline in the spring of 1962, I saw that Madam Paul had specifically stated: "Dispose of everything after January 8." Naturally, I hadn't.

She did not pretend to be psychic, like Nostradamus and some modern counterparts. "I merely interpret horoscopes, which are equivalent to architects' blueprints. Architects' plans help people build their houses; astrologers' horoscopes can guide people through their lives."

I sat there scribbling away as she prattled on, much like a professor lecturing his class. "You missed the boat two years ago," she said, "do you remember that?"

"I've missed so many boats," I said, "I can't keep them straight."

"Astrology," she said with faint reproof, "is the clock of destiny. It's not so much a matter of telling the future, but of telling you how to time your moves to your good periods for the next year or so."

She had seen only a scattered good spot here and there for me—January 1 to 15 of 1962 was one. She may have seen the disappointment in my face. "Oh, you have everything it takes to be successful," she said, "but your timing has been off." She looked up. "As a matter of fact, yours is the first chart in thousands—and I've read for many famous writers—that reveals somebody who can write, and has something to write about."

"That's very flattering," I said, "but how about all those bad periods?"

"Oh," she said, "things will turn up toward the end of 1962, and by 1964 you'll have many good spots." She laughed. "But you'll have to come back for another reading for the next year. I don't like to look too far ahead. It's difficult enough advising for twelve months."

"Do you see general events," I asked, "for countries, and governments, and things like that?"

"Oh, yes," she said, "in 1960 I saw a very bad year for our country, with many humiliations for us abroad." She laughed. "It was so bad that the newspapers wouldn't print it."

"What newspapers?" I demanded.

"Mr. Mahar, the city editor of the New York *Journal American*, called once and asked if I had any predictions for 1960, but when I started to tell him about our international embarrassments he said they wouldn't be interested in anything like that."

If one considered the U-2 incident, with Russia demanding an Eisenhower apology and rescinding its Moscow invitation to the President, and the Communist demonstrations leading to Eisenhower's cancellation of a Tokyo trip, it hadn't been a good year diplomatically for the United States.

City editor Eddie Mahar remembered the Paul prediction with a shrug. "Where would we get off taking predictions like that from an astrologer?" he smiled. And then he laughed reminiscently. "She can be good," he said, "even when she doesn't have the right date." He looked up. "Do you remember the Starr Faithful case?" I nodded, recalling the tragic young beauty, whose mysterious disappearance and death had inspired John O'Hara's *Butterfield 8.*

As a young reporter, with the man hunt in full cry for the missing girl, Mahar had been given an unusual assignment. "Find out," city editor Amster Spiro ordered, "what the stars say happened to Starr Faithful."

Having heard of Hellene Paul, the reporter bustled up to the astrologer's penthouse apartment and told her with disarming frankness that his newspaper wanted to know what had happened to Starr Faithful.

"What is her birth date?" astrologer Paul asked.

Not knowing the slightest thing about astrology at this tender stage in his career, the young reporter didn't have the least idea whether the missing beauty was a Taurus, Gemini, Pisces, Scorpio, Virgo, or whatever. "All I know," Mahar recalled, "is that I had to get a story."

So, as a resourceful reporter, Mahar gave astrologer Paul the first birth date he could think of—his own. And threw in his birthplace for good measure. Immediately the astrologer saw it all clearly.

"It was amazing what she picked out, even with my birth date and birthplace," newspaperman Mahar recalled. "She saw Starr Faithful not living beyond her twentieth year, already having lived a life of tragedy and rejection, and then saw her dying a violent death." As it turned out, Madam Paul's prediction worked out anyway, and reporter Mahar never gave away his secret. "But I was happy," he reflected, "returning to my office that day, that I was more than twenty years old, so it couldn't really be my horoscope."

There were many possible explanations. One, for instance, a flash of psychic perception; another, just plain everyday perception from diligent reading of the newspapers. Or coincidence.

Several weeks after my astrological reading, I called Madam Paul to tell her I had inadvertently given her the wrong date of birth—it should have been the 26th and not the 27th, because of the hour differential. But I discovered to my surprise that she was no longer available. In fact, she was dead. She had died suddenly on Armistice Day, November 11, 1961, in the arms of her husband, Jesse Speesman.

Had she known she was going?

"She had several premonitions," her husband said sadly.

And he himself, though no astrologer, was to have a premonition of his own. On the following May 29, he concluded all his business affairs; two days later he too was dead.

Madam Paul's custom, together with the penthouse near the stars, was taken over by astrologer Pauline Messina, who was admittedly psychic while charting planetary influences. Astrologer Messina did not believe in good or bad periods. "Astrology," she said, "should teach people to understand themselves, and then the periods will take care of themselves."

It was amazing to me how many people, disclaiming any real belief in the psychic, nevertheless put their lives trustingly into the hands of astrologers they hardly knew. And despite this passion for astrology, they still fight shy of publicity, since astrology is not a conventionally accepted way of solving one's problems. I was at lunch one day with Samuel Bronston, producer of the film spectacle *King of Kings,* and his associate, Ralph Wheelwright, discussing the wonders of Nostradamus, when Wheelwright exclaimed with a wry smile, "Do you know there are people—intelligent people—who won't make a move without an astrologer?"

He knew of a notable case. Only a few months before, Wheelwright had received a telephone call from a former aide, who was looking for a job. Wheelwright was glad to hear from him. "It's very lucky that you should call me," he said, "because I'm taking on the promotion of a new picture, and I'll be needing somebody pretty soon."

There was a pause, and then the assistant said quietly:

"Luck had nothing to do with it, Ralph."

Wheelwright was understandably puzzled. And the man explained: "I was told to call you, and that you would have something for me to do."

"Who told you this," rasped the practical Wheelwright, "when I didn't think of it until you called?"

"I was told," the assistant insisted, "that you would always have something for me."

Wheelwright found his temper rising. "Who the hell have you been talking to?" he said impatiently.

"I hope you don't think I'm kookie or anything," the assistant said.

"Never mind what I think," Wheelwright said, "what's this all about?"

The assistant tried to sound nonchalant. "It was my astrologer. He described you perfectly, and told me that my future was tied up with yours, that I should always keep in touch with you, and that you were waiting to hear from me."

Wheelwright laughed as he told me the story. "I put him on in spite of it all, because he's a good man," he said. "And the truth of the matter is, I would use him whenever I had the chance."

"Does he do everything the astrologer tells him?" I asked.

"Just about," Wheelwright said, "but why not talk to him about it?"

The assistant was not at all retiring about the astrological incident, so long as his name wasn't mentioned in connection with it. "If I were an actor, nobody'd think anything of it," he said, "but since I'm in the business end of motion pictures, a lot of those pin-striped Hollywood executives might think I was on the wacky side."

He seemed the bright junior-executive type. A constant stream of secretaries and other aides kept pouring into his office. When the last aide left, he told a secretary not to disturb him, closed the door, and turned to me. "I'm going to level with you," he said with characteristic Hollywood sincerity. "Since I found a good astrologer, life has been comparatively easy for me."

He had met astrologer Hugh MacCraig two years before, while working on a promotion project with Wheelwright. As the work came to an end, Wheelwright had suggested his aide start looking for another job. "I'm leaving now," Wheelwright said, "and I think they'll be suggesting you look around for another post, too, since there just won't be anything for you to do with our work completed."

The assistant had thought he might wait until he was told to go. "I wouldn't do that," Wheelwright cautioned, "you know, in this business you're better off in the long run if you don't force them to do something they'll hate you for."

The assistant finally agreed. But later he consulted astrologer MacCraig. "Don't make a move," the astrologer advised, "because in a couple of months, they're going to give you a new assignment, which will be better than anything you've had; the whole wide world will be your territory."

Wheelwright only shrugged when his assistant made his decision known. And then the assistant sat around and waited, wondering every day if he wasn't making a mistake. After a few weeks, he was summoned by his superior, and now thinking that he should have listened to Wheelwright, he stood passively before the movie mogul's desk, waiting for the ax to fall. "We have decided to keep you on," the executive said. "We're sending this picture on the road, around the world, and you've done so well with these road shows that we want you to handle it in a world-wide capacity."

As far as our nameless assistant was concerned, he would never doubt MacCraig again. He leaned over and said with great earnestness, tapping my knee as we sat together in his office, "And mind you, MacCraig saw it exactly—world-wide, he told me, and world-wide it was."

In charting individual horoscopes, astrologers like MacCraig often touch on national and world events that have an obvious bearing on individual destiny. For a young *Newsweek* magazine reporter, whom he read in June 1960, MacCraig reported 1961–64 as three most perilous years in world affairs. "Kennedy is a Gemini," he said, "and could aggravate things. Rockefeller and Symington are not ready." The public would not realize until October 26—a week or so before the 1960 Presidential election—how important the middle route is. "The Democratic," he said, "is too far to the labor side." Nevertheless, disregarding this astrological provender, the public elected a Democratic president, and a Gemini, at that.

Astrology has its powerful adversaries. Believing that astrology is the refuge of the cowardly, some churches, notably the Roman Catholic, have attacked "stargazing" as "foolish and dangerous," urging the faithful to let the future rest where it belongs, in God's hands. A pamphlet published by the Redemptorist Fathers of Liguori, Missouri, for instance, has charged that belief in astrology is "an insult to our own intelligence," and cites the error of St. Augustine himself, before that reformed sinner realized that he was leaning on a false crutch. "St. Augustine, in the days of his wild youth," observed the Reverend L. G. Miller, "when he oscillated from one heresy of thought to another, gave himself into the hands of the astrologers. For a time, they lulled his guilty conscience, telling him: 'The cause of thy sin is inevitably determined in heaven,' and 'Venus or Saturn or Mars was responsible for this devil action.' "

But in his *Confessions*, the great teacher of the church described his final disillusionment. The inconsistency that had troubled others decided him. Two children were born under the same star, to the very minute, and yet one was a slave, the other an aristrocrat. And so, Augustine had written: "At the time his mother was about to give birth to him, Firminius, a woman-servant was also with child, which could not escape her master, who took care with most exact diligence to know the births of his puppies. And so it was that both were delivered at the same instant; so that both were constrained to follow the same constellations even to the minutest points, the one for his son, the other for his new-born slave . . . neither of them could make out any difference in the position of the stars or any other minutest point. Yet Firminius, born in a high estate in his parent's house, ran his course through the gilded paths of life, was increased in riches, raised in honors; whereas that slave continued to serve his masters without any relaxation of the yoke."

But Isidor Oblo, a modern astrologer, had an answer. "How is it," I asked, "that people can be born at the instant—thus being in the same position or angle of the planets—and in the same city and house, and have such different lives?"

Oblo wagged his gray old head. "That's no problem," he said, "it happens all the time. It doesn't mean that both will be millionaires, or both paupers—it means only that when something good or bad is happening to one, it will also be happening to the other. Supposing one is a lawyer, the other a gangster; when the lawyer is getting a judicial appointment, the gangster may be getting a reprieve or a pardon. And if the lawyer's business fails, the gangster may be going to jail."

It was all theoretical, and certainly hypothetical. Thinking of the seventy-eight people killed in one air crash and the ninety-five in another, I asked: "If a large group of people is killed in a single accident, does that mean that their individual horoscopes would each show their deaths in an air crash?"

"It would not work out quite this way. The individual's year,"

Oblo explained, "is made up of thirty-six ten-day cycles, and would show all the people involved in a detrimental cycle."

I had met Oblo through an attractive young businesswoman, who advised that he had "been right on everything with her"—business, romance, travel. "He told me," she said, "who I was going to meet, on what day, and what would happen." She smiled. "He was never wrong."

Oblo himself acknowledged his infallibility. He worked in some intricate way not only with the stars and planets, but with the Kabala, the ancient mystical book of Jewish lore.

Besides, he was psychic, and this psychic power, he claimed, when he studied the charts, tied everything together. I had a new birth date, confirmed by a birth certificate, to submit to the stars. Hoping that the 26th would be more auspicious than the 27th, I saw the modern master in December of 1961. "You will always have money," he told me. And as I sat trying not to look too pleased, he added: "And you will attain the highest recognition."

But with every silver lining there was an inevitable cloud. "There will be many delays connected with your book, but these," he added reassuringly, "will only compel you to do a better job and come under the force of destiny." He spoke flatly. "You will be delayed, but not denied."

"But why delayed?" I inquired.

"You will have to rewrite," he said, "and other delays, too, but if you didn't go through this, you wouldn't develop."

Six months later, as I sat at my desk, long after my deadline, rewriting, I was to darkly remember the words of the master astrologer. But at the moment, looking across the table, I was not receptive. "There will be no delay," I said, "and I will have my book done in time."

He remarked dryly: "Knowledge is power, but foreknowledge is wisdom."

Like astrologer Messina, he believed astrology should first help one understand himself. "You have three weak spots in your throat," he said, "and your eyes trouble you—be careful of them." It was a lucky stroke; I had just been to the ear, nose, and throat man. I was also having difficulty with my eyes. I had just had them tested. Oblo advised patience and tolerance, good qualities both, and gave counsel that nobody could argue with: "Take everything in stride."

I had expressed some skepticism of astrology in general.

He was not the least upset. "Everything I have told you will come to pass," he said.

"But so much of the astrology is so obviously phony," I protested.

He did not disagree. "There are comparatively few astrologers who have the required knowledge," he said, "and then, even so, they may not take the trouble to map individual charts. It's a long tedious process." He looked up. "I was hours with your chart even before you got here." And then the psychic force, as with Nostradamus, helped put it all together.

It still seemed like so much abracadabra to me, with a dash of witchcraft and hypnotic suggestion thrown in. "Not at all," said Isidor Oblo, "there are some two hundred and sixteen references to astrology in the Bible, in both the Old and New Testaments." He quoted from Genesis 1:14: "Let there be lights in the firmament of the heaven to divide the day from the night; and let them be for signs, and for seasons, and for days, and years." And from Job 38:31: "Canst thou bind the sweet *influences* of Pleiades, or loose the bands of Orion?", and from Judges 5:20: "They fought from heaven; the stars in their courses fought against Sisera."

As did other astrologers, Oblo maintained that the leaders of the world from antiquity had relied on astrology. But while this lent some semblance of respectability to the art, it actually did nothing for credibility. Still it was impressive to read that Luc Gauric, favorite before Nostradamus of Catherine de Medici, had been rewarded by Pope Paul III for predicting the course of a fatal illness, and that astrologer Cosmos Ruggieri had foretold the St. Bartholomew Massacre. Nearer to our times, Hitler had astrological charts drawn not only for himself, but his enemies. He relied on astrology so much that his lieutenants secretly bent it to their service, using Berlin's well-known necromancer, Eric Hanussen, to dish up advice favorable to the Nazi cause—and their own. Before Hitler came to power, as he prepared to confer with President Hindenburg over the chancellorship, Hanussen advised him that he should demand complete power. Hitler was rebuffed, and the Nazi clique, headed by Goebbels, which had passed on this "horoscope" to Hanussen, had its bad moments. But insisting on his demands, with the conviction of the faked horoscope, Hitler subsequently got what he wanted; and Hanussen remained a power until he was eliminated for knowing too much.

For millions, the lure of the stars is strong, but still other millions of Americans, equally curious about the morrow, put their faith in fortune-tellers, to the point where fortune-telling has become a thriving business around the country. In California, South Carolina, Virginia, Illinois, etc., these hardy oracles of the future, appealing to the vanity—and the generosity—of the susceptible, line the highways and byways. In the smart supper clubs of New York City, the rich and the bored delight to hear about themselves. And the performances—if not the predictions—are far superior to those in the Gypsy tearooms and the little holes in the wall where the less pretentious hold forth, drawing hopefully on tea leaves, cards, even crystal balls—or perhaps just reading palms and sitting close, as they tune in on the patron's vibrations.

In these parlors, the poor and worried may consult their readers several times a week. In one emporium, the Gypsy Tea Kettle, in the heart of Broadway, hundreds troop in daily, women often outnumbering the men four and five to one. Dissatisfied by the readings of one fortune-teller, the fortune hunters pass to another. One nondescript woman with gray clothing and a gray face had been read by the complete corps of six mystics. But when she walked out, she was still mournfully shaking her head. Nobody, apparently, had yet told her what she wanted to hear.

Though few of the fortune-tellers are psychic, nearly all are shrewd psychologists, and listen intently for clues, with which they may later confound their subjects. Even when psychic, fortune-tellers are still under the disadvantage of having to produce for a fee, when they may see nothing but a blank. And so they patter on, guessing, speculating, to round out even a prophetic glimpse of the future. "Clairvoyance," declared Britain's popular

Maurice Woodruff, "is twenty-five per cent psychology, and twenty-five per cent padding. People expect you to keep up a string of patter in between the important things you say."

Yet with all their obvious hanky-panky, I have seen the fortune-teller brigade come through with remarkable predictions, and have checked others, equally remarkable, made over a cocktail table or tea leaves.

Even when psychic, fortune-tellers differ principally from spiritualists, seers, and soothsayers in the fact that they appeal almost exclusively to the individual's interest in himself. Even large events of international significance are delineated chiefly in respect to the subject's interest in those events.

In 1958, for instance, when it looked for a time as though the dashing, older Captain Townsend was finally to marry Princess Margaret, a correspondent for one of the wire services dropped into a little restaurant on Madison Avenue and, prodded by a lady friend, had his future read by gray-haired, plump Mary Talley, one of the favorites of the New York newspaper set, now at Armando's. She had correctly predicted the sex of two of columnist Dorothy Kilgallen's children, and foreseen the death of columnist Danton Walker. And now she was telling an amused foreign correspondent:

"I see you packing and going to Europe."

In jest, the reporter asked: "You mean for the Margaret-Townsend wedding?"

"Oh, no," Miss Talley said with a grimace. "Certainly not. They're not going to be married. Margaret is going to marry a much younger man, somebody her own age, in June of 1959, and you'll cover the wedding for your wire service."

The correspondent, whom I know well, politely concealed his disbelief. But the following year he was in London, sending back reports from London of the marriage of Margaret and Antony Armstrong-Jones.

Behind her simple little table, Miss Talley has read for Ingrid Bergman, Tyrone Power, Errol Flynn, Greta Garbo, and a host of lesser luminaries. She quietly talks to patrons about their health, careers, domestic problems, and the international situation. She says herself that she has an "extremely sensitive psychic reaction to people," and the same satisfied customers keep coming back. Constance Carpenter, the attractive blonde actress, who understudied Gertrude Lawrence in the Broadway success, *The King and I,* was one. Reading Miss Carpenter with the cards, which help her concentrate, Miss Talley foretold she would take over the Lawrence role in two months.

"But how can that be?" asked Constance. "Gertie is happy in the part and her contract goes on much beyond that."

Mary Talley shrugged, shuffled the cards, and said with a pat of the hand, "Honey, take my word for it."

Just before the two months were up, Miss Lawrence unexpectedly took ill and went out of the show, never to return. She was succeeded by Constance Carpenter.

After Gertrude Lawrence's death, Miss Talley explained that she had seen her fatal illness, but, like most readers, made a practice of not directly predicting death.

"I had no idea what was going to happen," Miss Carpenter told me, "since Miss Lawrence seemed so well, but Mary Talley told me to prepare myself for the starring role, and I did."

Miss Talley had little luck with me, but that may have been because she saw little to be cheerful about. She did see a divorce, though, but, happily, it shows no sign of materializing. She advised me to get my passport ready for an immediate trip abroad. A week later I booked passage to London, and two weeks later canceled the flight.

When a fortune-teller is good, she can be awfully good. After actress Grace Kelly had told me about her experience at Manhattan's Russian Bear, I took actress Phyllis Kirk there in connection with my research. Miss Kirk had expected the usual platitudes due one of her youth and beauty. But Rava, a small, intense woman, with dark piercing eyes, was not in a flattering mood. Looking at a professional beauty, with swarms of suitors, she saw no marriage for her in the readable future; seven years later Miss Kirk was still not married, to my knowledge, though I frequently noticed her name, romantically, in the columns. She saw the beautiful brunette in Hollywood, not surprising in view of her looks, and signing a lucrative contract, but not in motion pictures. She was quite emphatic on that—"not in motion pictures." But it would be something like that. It seemed an impossible inconsistency. Yet a few years later, I encountered Miss Kirk quite by chance in Hollywood. She was doing very well, costarring with actor Peter Lawford in a "Thin Man" series—on television.

When on the beam, as the saying goes behind the clairvoyant curtain, no psychic has been more precise than Maya Perez, the dark-haired, brooding-eyed reader now in Balboa, California, who was the first to interest me in the possibilities of the hidden past and future. She needed no cards or tea leaves to rivet her attention to her subject. Once she saw something, she flowed on effortlessly, often embarrassing couples by revelations of their innermost secrets. With many listening one night at Armando's fashionable supper club, for instance, she told young textile executive Carlo Borgia and his dancer wife, Andrea, married for several childless years: "You have been thinking of adopting children, but don't—for you will have children of your own, three or more." Later, the Borgias acknowledged that they had been quietly considering adoption. Instead, Mrs. Borgia underwent remedial surgery. And soon the children began to arrive. At last count, in mid-1962, there were three, and the proud parents were looking forward to still another.

With strangers, I noticed, Maya Perez appeared to be at her best. There was no temptation here to judge backgrounds and pasts; the subconscious had to do the work. One night, working with a roomful of strangers at a party, she did not seem to be getting much, and it was evident the party-goers were becoming bored. She read neither palms nor cards that night, but sat next to her subjects holding their hands. She was aware of the general disappointment, and explained calmly: "I can't see anything if nothing's going on."

But suddenly the vibrations in the room must have come alive. For as she looked at a lovely Southern girl with red hair, unknown to everybody but one in the assembly, she said, "I see you getting married, in the next four to six weeks. You will not expect it yourself, but it will be decided on an impulse. You will be on a Southern trip at the time."

There was nothing to perk up a party like romance. Maya Perez had regained her audience. But the girl only laughed gaily and said with a Southern drawl, "It's all news to me."

The girl, Ruth Harris, had been escorted to the party by actor John Conte, but they had been sitting apart during the readings. "Do you know an *H?*" Maya asked, using an initial when it came Conte's turn. He shook his head absently, but suddenly remembering Miss Harris, whom he had known only a few weeks, he nodded vigorously.

Maya was a good performer. She closed her eyes and her dark face became strangely impassive. "I see you making a trip soon to an *F* and a *G.*" She was still using initials, and then she gave a little gasp. "Do you know you're going to be married? You may not realize it now, but you're going to be married and soon."

Actor Conte was more concerned about a job than a wife and was obviously not impressed. He shrugged indifferently. "And what's more," Madam Perez said, "I see you going out to California to do one thing, but you will stay out there and do better than you ever did before. You will never worry about money."

Five weeks later, Miss Harris and Conte were married in Folkeston, Georgia, just across the line from Florida, where they had been visiting her parents over the Christmas holidays. "Frankly," Conte said later, "when we left for Florida, all we were thinking about was Christmas, but suddenly it seemed like a good idea, and we got married in Georgia because there was no waiting there— not because of Maya Perez."

A few weeks later, Conte flew from New York to California for a minor TV role, expecting to return shortly. But he drew a part in the motion picture *The Man With the Golden Arm,* and then picked up a lucrative spot hosting television's "Matinee Theatre," which wasn't put together until he was already on the West Coast. And five years later, he was still on the Coast—living luxuriously in a big house in Beverly Hills.

There was certain times when Madam Perez seemed more authoritative than at others. At New York's Carnegie Hall, where she once had a studio, she was reading for Natasha Boissevain, an attractive Greenwich, Connecticut socialite who was disenchanted with her retinue of suitors. "I guess I will never get married," she sighed wistfully.

Maya Perez smiled stringently. "Oh, yes, you will."

"When?" the girl shot back challengingly.

"Within two years," Madam Perez said easily. "And you will have two children, both girls."

"Then it'll have to be somebody I don't know."

Madam Perez shook her head. "It will be somebody you already know."

"Never," said Miss Boissevain airily. "I don't know anybody I'd marry."

Within twenty-three months, she was married. And the man she married, Malcolm Pray, Jr., well-known Greenwich automobile dealer, she had known from childhood. At last report they had two children, daughters.

Madam Perez gave perhaps her most impressive party performance for a group of sophisticates in the Manhattan home of Marilynn Ambrose, a New York fashion authority. It was a miscellaneous guest list drawn from the publishing, advertising, theatrical, and fashion worlds, none terribly interested in anything but what they were saying. Madam Perez had considerable competition but she plowed ahead. She turned first to a well-known Hollywood and Broadway actor, quietly separated from his wife. "I recognize you, of course," she said immediately, "so I'm not going to go into your acting career. However, I do see you directing. Have you thought of that?"

He nodded, amused.

A beautiful girl who had been talking to the party's biggest celebrity, was visibly annoyed at the interruption and stalked off angrily. The two actors—Maya and her theatrical subject—now occupied the center of the living-room stage, as a circle formed curiously around them. Maya took in the group with a practiced glance. "I don't know if it's good to have so many around." She looked sharply at the actor. "Would you like a private reading?"

"That's all right," the actor said good-naturedly, "I have nothing to hide."

Maya's jaws clicked together. "All right," she said, and proceeded with clinical detachment as she lightly held his hand. "You've been having some trouble with your wife over a child, serious trouble. This child is sick." She hesitated. "All I will say now is that the child is sick, but you understand what I mean?"

The actor's face had become grave, and he was staring at her with his mouth hanging. "Yes," he said, almost inaudibly, "I know."

She gave him another probing look. "Shall I go on?"

He nodded.

"Well," she said, "you would like this child put away somewhere, not because you don't love him, but because you think he would be better off and that it would also be better for another child, a girl. She is beginning to see young men, and is embarrassed by the home situation."

The actor's face had become ashen. He sat rigidly, trying to look composed. My hostess, sitting next to me, whispered, "I didn't think anybody in the world knew about that situation."

Madam Perez gave the actor a warm, commiserating look. "In time," she said comfortingly, "though you may not think so yourself, you will go back to your wife." She seemed to gaze over the actor's head into faraway space. Her dark brooding eyes widened with concentration and a thin glaze came over them. "I see a younger girl who would like to marry you," she said evenly. "And I feel her here tonight. She does not give off a good vibration, and she would not be good for you. Not because she is so much younger, which is what you tell her, but because she is an unhappy person and brings unhappiness to those around her." She patted his hand reassuringly. "But it will never happen. You will not marry her, not in a million years." She thought a moment, the lids folding over her eyes. "Your wife is good for you," she said. "You have been through much together. You will go back together, and you will settle your problems between you."

After the reading, the actor bowed. He looked around the circle of curious sophisticates, and said with a nervous laugh, "This woman is remarkable. I owe her this much of an acknowledgment."

In the circumstances, it was a gracious gesture, but a young, extremely beautiful girl with a sinuous body and a bold, flashing eye, pushed forward to confront Madam Perez. Hands on hips, with a disdainful leer, she demanded: "See what you can do for me, Madam."

The girl appeared to have everything—youth, beauty, and wealth. Her father was president of one of the country's largest corporations, and she was an only child. She had been drinking a little, but only enough to bring out her suppressed hostility. Maya Perez returned her burning glance with a clear eyes. She took the girl's hand in hers, and then drew back and surveyed her as though she were seeing her for the first time. "I feel sorry for you," she said simply.

There was a nervous titter among the spectators, knowing as they did that the girl had set her cap for the handsome actor twenty-five years her senior. However, Maya Perez went on unmoved. "You were married once before," she said, "and it wasn't any good." She closed her eyes. "It will never be any good." The girl grunted in disdain. "You think you would like to marry this much older man," Maya continued placidly, "but you are only thinking of his glamour, not of him. Otherwise, you would leave him alone, because you cannot give him what he needs." She looked up, squarely meeting the girl's defiant gaze. The girl's eyes were first to drop. "You are not going to marry this man," she said firmly, "He is going back to his wife." She sighed. "But don't worry, you will be married again, and again."

The girl's voice was cold, "You don't know how wrong you are," she said.

Maya rejoined dispassionately, "When I'm right, I know it here" —she pointed to her heart—"and I know I'm right." She studied the girl. "I feel sorry for you, because you can't help yourself."

The beautiful young girl did marry, somebody nearer her own age, and when last I heard, the marriage was rocking along. From my hostess, I learned subsequently that the actor went back to Hollywood and his wife. The problem child was placed in a comfortable sanatorium nearby, and the breach between the parents healed.

By no means was Maya Perez always right, but when she was right, it was often uncannily so.

I remember her once telling a friend that he would hear of his father's death within a year. "I normally don't make predictions like this," she said, "but I have a feeling that it won't affect you as it would most people." And then she added: "But you won't hear about his death until two weeks after it happens."

Brought up by his grandparents, this man recalled seeing his father only once, in childhood. He was a complete stranger. He thought no more of the prediction. But eight or nine months later, his younger brother, a New York business executive, telephoned and said, "I have just learned that our father died."

My friend asked: "What about funeral services?"

"We won't be going to any," his brother said, "he died two weeks ago."

Some fortune-tellers make no secret that they have little psychic power, but they are often strangely effective anyway. In more than twenty years at the old Versailles supper club in New York, the palmist Doris had gleaned many secrets from the lines in the thousands of palms she had pored over with her pencil searchlight. "I can often tell what people are going to do, because it is revealed in the lines of their hands almost before they have started to think about it." She did not think of herself as psychic, though she acknowledged occasional flashes. But the past, nevertheless, often revealed itself like an open book, and she read freely—if embarrassingly—from its pages. One night an older man and a young woman had invited her to their table for a reading. Scrutinizing the girl's hand, Doris observed, "You have had one child."

The girl shook her head, while the man laughed. "We haven't been married long enough," he said, "but we have hopes."

"But I see the child clearly," Doris insisted. "Perhaps you have been married before."

"This is the first marriage for both of us," the man said cheerfully.

The woman looked faint. Her husband bent over solicitously. "It's very warm," she murmured.

Doris reached for her hand again, and the woman limply gave it to her. She made another searching study. "I guess," she decided with a little laugh, "I was looking at the wrong line; I was mistaken about that child."

Three days later, the woman returned, alone. "I want to thank you for the other night," she said, "and I want you to know that you were right." She hesitated. "If he knew, it might be the end of our marriage. And I wouldn't want to do that to either of us."

For every supper-club psychic with a flair for the future, there are dozens who qualify only as skilled psychologists. "I've gone into hundreds of places, and have been told thousands of things," a lady detective told me, "but nobody ever told me I was a police-woman getting ready to arrest her."

When they stray from the future, the astrologers seem to stray farthest. Hugh MacCraig, for instance, casting a scope for a pretty model, predicted a missile war for 1962, and though the year is not quite over at this writing, it hardly seems likely. Hellene Paul saw a subject enjoying his best period in January of 1962: meanwhile, he was flat on his back with a virus. In December of 1959, while the Rockefeller-for-President aerial balloon was up, radio reporter Walter McGraw canvassed a dozen clairvoyants and astrologers on their presidential predictions. "Nine out of ten," McGraw recalled, "closed their eyes and said it would be Rockefeller, and it was the same whether they plotted horo-scopes, read cards, examined the tea leaves, or peered into the crystal ball." One seeress, Neva Del Hunter of Michigan, not only saw the Republican Rockefeller as President, but gave him a Democratic running mate, G. Mennen Williams, long-time governor of her home state. "I think," McGraw said delicately, "that she may have been motivated by the conscious intrusion of home-state pride."

One astrologer interviewed by McGraw insisted that 1961 was Rockefeller's "lucky" year. In this year, the New York governor split up with his wife after thirty-some years of marriage and lost his son Michael off New Guinea. As Rockefeller himself said, with a sigh, of 1961, "It certainly couldn't be any worse."

Making the rounds of the supper-club mystics, I learned many diverse things about myself. On the very day that I was making a trip by air to California, I was also going by sea to Spain. I was going to be married this year, next year, last year, and not at all. I was going to lose my job, get a promotion, and I was going to live to sixty, seventy-five, and eighty-four. It was almost pathetic.

But with all the bad predictions, the sly guesses, the petty scheming and guile, some apparently did catch glimpses of the future. And the fact that these tellers of fortunes were so often wrong did not explain away the times they were so unpredictably right. For, as one professional observer pointedly remarked: "All you need is one white crow to prove that all crows aren't black."

8 SHIPTON, LINCOLN, MALACHY, KRAKATOA

If Mother Shipton, England's time-honored seeress, had predicted half the things she was given credit for, she would well have deserved the epitaph:

> Here lies she who never ly'd,
> Whose skill often has been tried,
> Her prophecies shall still survive
> And even keep her name alive.

While many have questioned Mother herself, there was no questioning the prophetic nature of the final salute, for the sixteenth-century seeress' forecasts were not only maintained but actually grew with the passing years. In her time, the old crone with the misshapen bulbous nose supposedly predicted Sir Walter Raleigh's discovery of tobacco and the potato; Drake's defeat of the Spanish Armada; the downfall and death of Henry the Eighth's Cardinal Wolsey; the discovery of gold in Australia, before there was an Australia; the Black Plague; and the Great Fire of London.

New predictions kept turning up provocatively. Some were remarkably concerned with technical progress and wars in the nineteenth and twentieth centuries. However, reputed predictions of the radio, automobile, submarine, and aircraft were subsequently exploded as forgeries, even though apparently published before the actual appearance of these mechanical wonders.

Oddly enough, one early "discoverer" appeared as good a prophet as the venerable Ursula Shipton, however good that might be. In an ostensible imitation of her crabbed doggerel, this "authority" picked out the year of decision—1936—leading up to World War II, and foretold new trials toward the end of the century:

> In 1936 build houses light with straw and sticks
> For then shall mighty wars be planned
> And fire and sword shall sweep the land.
> But those who live the century through
> In fear and trembling this shall do,
> Flee for the mountains and the dens,
> To bogs and forests and wild fens
> For storms shall rage and oceans roar,
> When Gabriel stands on sea and shore,
> And as he blows his wondrous horn,
> Old worlds shall die and new be born.

But the Charles Hindley version of the prophecies, appearing first during the American Civil War, created more of a stir in England and abroad. Hindley was a reputable English editor and nobody thought that he would lend himself to anything that wasn't cricket. But eventually—in 1862—he owned up that the most remarkable of his Mother Shipton predictions—responsible for much of her latter-day fame—were forgeries:

> Carriages without horses shall go
> And accidents fill the world with woe,
> Around the earth thoughts shall fly,
> In the twinkling of an eye.
>
> Through the hills man shall ride,
> And no horse be at his side.
> Under water men shall walk,
> Shall ride, shall sleep, shall walk,
> In the air men shall be seen,
> In white in black in green.
> Iron in the water shall float,
> As easily as a wooden boat.

At first sight Hindley appeared to be a prophet himself. He seemed years ahead of the modern autocar, two generations ahead of the terrible highway toll. And the Wrights didn't make their first experimental flight until 1903 at Kitty Hawk.

But actually there was nothing psychic or intuitive about it. The English were driving around in steam-driven carriages as early as 1801, stopped only in 1836 by the Red Flag Act, which compelled every mechanically operated vehicle to be preceded by a man carrying a red flag or red light. Robert Fulton tried out the first submarine successfully in a French harbor in 1801, and it should not have been difficult to sense the increasing authority of man's efforts to fly heavier-than-air machines. For that matter, airships, or dirigibles, were already beyond the experimental stage, sent aloft for the first time in 1852.

As for floating iron, the ironclad *Monitor* and *Merrimac* had established naval history in their Civil War clash in 1862, and other iron-cladders had been previously launched, experimentally.

And so Hindley admitted his clever hoax, which included the solemn warning:

> Fire and water shall wonders do
> England shall at last admit a foe
> The world to an end shall come
> In eighteen hundred and eighty-one.

Ironically, despite the disavowals, many still take Hindley's word for Mother Shipton. He was that convincing—and they were that susceptible.

Writing with the confidence of one calmly surveying the past, because that was just what he was doing, Hindley had archly discussed Sir Walter Raleigh without batting an eye:

> Over a wild and stormy sea
> Shall noble sail,
> Who to find will not fail
> A new and far countree.
> From whence he shall bring
> A herb and root
> That all men shall suit.

And not the least wondrous of his Mother Shipton prophecies was the one excitedly hailed as predicting the Australian Gold Rush, and another the Crystal Palace, the pride of London, which was built in 1851:

> Gold shall be found, and found,
> In a land that's not now known.
> A house of glass shall come to pass
> In England, but alas!

When these verses were discredited, it was natural to discredit everything that had been credited to the old witch, and some even questioned whether she had lived at all.

Actually, though Mother was reportedly born in 1488, dying in 1561, her first batch of predictions didn't turn up until 1641, leading many to suspect that these too came after the fact.

It was the Wolsey prophecy that brought the old one posthumous fame. One version had her predicting that the all-powerful Cardinal, apparently at the peak of his political power, would never get to York seven miles away to keep an appointment with Henry the Eighth. Angered by the prophecy, the story goes, the King's first minister sent aides to get her to recant, but she looked them over calmly, smiled balefully, and said they would be brought lower than she. To illustrate her powers, she threw a linen handkerchief in a glowing fire, cackling gleefully when it wouldn't burn. There are varied versions of the identities of the gentlemen who came to call. In one version, it was Duke of Suffolk, Lord Percy, and Lord Darcy. But in 1530, when Wolsey died in accordance with the prediction, Lord Percy was only two years old, if it were the same for whom she forecast, "Your body will be buried in York pavement and your head will be stolen from the bar and carried into France." In 1572, Thomas Percy was beheaded on a scaffold erected in the pavement on the chief market place of York, and his head fixed on a pole above Michlegate Bar or gate.

In a more plausible version, Thomas Cromwell, the Earl of Essex and Wolsey's legal secretary, was sent to get her to repudiate her prediction, though heaven only knows why the Cardinal should have been disturbed by anything Mother Shipton could have said or done. She told Cromwell he was going to be laid low, and ten years later, after having succeeded his master Wolsey as the King's chief adviser, he lost his head for treason.

More of Mother's predictions, published in 1667, were immediately popular. Many people appeared ready to believe anything, including a fuzzy explanation of why their publication had been so long delayed. They had been held in trust during her lifetime by one Joanne Waller, who, as a small girl, the explanation went, had known Mother, and they were released only with Joanne's death, at ninety-four. If Mother Shipton had indeed entrusted her prophecies to Joanne Waller, the one concerning Queen Elizabeth's reign was a prodigy in itself, embracing as it did the major political events of the time, and the execution of Mary, Queen of Scots.

> The Lion being dead and gone,
> A Maiden Queen shall reign anon
> The Papal power shall bear no sway,
> Rome's trash shall hence be swept away
> The Western Monarch's Wooden Horses
> Shall be destroyed by the Drake's forces.
> More wonders yet! A Widowed Queen
> In England will be headless seen.

Right up to the great fire of London in September 1666, the predictions continued with their remarkable accuracy, and then, from 1667—the new publication date—they appeared to have lost their prophetic insight.

The prediction of the Great Fire, some say, was perhaps the only one of Mother's fulfilled prophecies that could authentically be traced back to an earlier date—and even then, it seemed to me, it was a matter of broad interpretation. For Mother, unlike Nostradamus, was not very specific. She visualized a ship sailing up the Thames, and the crew amazed because along the shore, once thronged with convenient grog shops, there was only desolation. "And now there is scarce left any house that can let us have a drink for our money."

How anybody reasonably got fire out of this I do not know.

One so-called Shipton prophecy is strangely reminiscent of various Nostradamus quatrains dealing with the Arab menace— from the land of the moon—and a spiritual renaissance.

Then shall come the Son of Man, having a fierce beast in his arms, which kingdom lies in the Land of the Moon, which is dreadful throughout the whole world; with a Number of People shall he pass many waters and shall come to the land of the Lyon [Lion]; look for help of the Beast of his country, and an Eagle shall come out of the East, spread with the Beams of the Son of Man and shall destroy castles of the Thames, and there shall be a battle among many kingdoms . . . and therewith shall be crowned the Son of Man, and the fourth year shall be many battles for the faith and the Son of Man, with the Eagles shall be preferred, and there shall be peace over the world, and there shall be plenty of fruit, and then shall he go to the land of the cross.

And so that was Mother Shipton!

Not long after Charles Hindley confessed his Shipton forgeries, Washington was astir with speculation that its most distinguished citizen was taking advice from the spirits. The death of little Willie Lincoln in the White House had been a staggering blow to the man charged with the lives of so many young men, and even while he was in the White House, rumors circulated that our mystic President was communicating with the spirits. These were later denied by his eldest son, Robert Todd Lincoln, who was away at Harvard during this period. But several distinguished Washingtonians claimed to have witnessed seances, in which the President was advised once to enforce his Emancipation Proclamation, and, again, to bolster the morale of the shattered Army of the Potomac by a tour of the front. Similarly, his re-election for a second term was predicted, and his death in the White House foreshadowed.

He assertedly saw many mediums—Charles Colchester, Lucy Hamilton, Charles Redmond—but only one, Nettie Colburn Maynard, has left an account of these singular meetings. And with her account were statements from dignitaries who claimed to know about the seances. The wife of former Congressman Daniel E. Somes of Maine, a Lincoln intimate, affirmed them. Mrs. Elvira M. Dupuy, a Washington socialite, was another to support Mrs. Maynard's account. "My husband," she stated flatly, "was a visitor to seances where Mr. Lincoln was present." And she herself attended a seance in 1862–63 at the home of a Mr. Laurie in Georgetown, with Mrs. Lincoln present and Miss Nettie Colburn (later Maynard) the medium. "She [Mrs. Lincoln] was accompanied by Mr. Newton, Commissioner of Agriculture. At this seance, remarkable statements were made by Miss Colburn, which surprised Mrs. Lincoln to such a degree that she asked that a seance might be given to Mr. Lincoln."

Mrs. Maynard gives an account of the first meeting at the Lauries' and of Mrs. Lincoln's intercession with Newton for a government job so that the spiritualist could stay in Washington. She had been visiting from Connecticut, in an effort to get sick leave for a soldier brother.

In view of Mrs. Lincoln's unstable temperament and her grief over Willie's death, her interest in spiritualism seemed plausible. But the President, according to the Maynard report, shared her interest.

Examining the controversy a hundred years later, many have been impressed by a statement from a presidential intimate who rallied to Mrs. Maynard's support. As he struggled with his portraits of the President and the historic signing of the Emancipation

Proclamation, nobody saw more of the Great Emancipator than artist Francis B. Carpenter. He sat with Lincoln during private conferences with ministers of state, attended secret cabinet meetings, roamed the streets of Washington nights with the President. But even when Lincoln's oldest friends were defending his memory, Carpenter, who thought of Lincoln as a father, did not question Mrs. Maynard's story. He even rebutted William Herndon, Lincoln's former law partner, who had joined those denying that Lincoln could have trifled with spiritualism. Carpenter disposed of Herndon's disclaimer rather neatly, vouching for Mrs. Maynard's integrity, without once referring to the controversial seances themselves. It seemed significant that he, living in the White House, should have known Mrs. Maynard well enough to be familiar with her work. "I have known Mrs. Maynard for some years," he said. "She is a talented woman. I do not believe she would tell an untruth; she is a medium of remarkable ability. I know that Mr. Herndon knew Mr. Lincoln better than any other man up to the time of his election in 1861. After his election, Mr. Herndon knew but little of him, and absolutely nothing of his mental or spiritual condition before the sickness of his son, Willie, nor after Willie's death, and I must say that Mr. Lincoln's mind underwent a vast change after that event."

Mrs. Maynard, invalided by illness, felt she had little time remaining when she finally wrote years later of her Lincoln experience. At the time, she said, she had been cautioned by Lincoln himself and by Congressman Somes not to mention the sittings. At most sittings she was accompanied by a friend, Mrs. Parthenia Colburn, who had married into her family.

After the war, Miss Colburn, whom Lincoln knew pleasantly as Nettie, married William Porter Maynard, and lived in White Plains, New York. Her three brothers and her father were with the Union Army.

During all the readings in Washington, not once did she think of exacting a fee for a gift she had known from childhood. But once, mysteriously, an envelope arrived with one hundred dollars, a great sum for those days, and Mrs. Lincoln found a government job for her friend, Parnie Colburn.

Not all the sessions were secret. Sitting for groups, which included the Lincolns, Mrs. Maynard said she usually learned later what she had said in trance, but during sittings alone for the Lincolns, she never knew what transpired, as they didn't comment in any way in front of her.

In her account she referred repeatedly to Lincoln as the greatest American, perhaps the greatest man, who ever lived. He had the saddest face she had ever seen. "Yet there was a light in those deep-sunk eyes that showed the man who was before me as perhaps the best Christian the world ever saw."

Not only his sense of the mystic, but an abiding humility drew the Great Emancipator to the spiritualist sessions. "This great and good man," Mrs. Maynard said, "did not hesitate to receive and weigh any suggestions for guidance, when given intelligently, however humble their apparent origin."

The first sitting at the White House, as she recalled, occurred shortly after she had met Mrs. Lincoln at the Lauries' in Georgetown. She was invited to the White House in December 1862, at eight one evening. The meeting took place in the Red Parlor. Lincoln came in soon after Nettie arrived. She was struck at once by his magnetic presence. The group formed the familiar circle of the seance, and she obediently went into trance. As she recovered consciousness, she sensed a suppressed excitement in the room. "I shall never forget the scene around me when I regained consciousness," she said. "I was standing in front of Mr. Lincoln, and he was sitting back in his chair, with his arms folded upon his breast, looking intently at me."

A distinguished-looking man whom she did not recognize leaned forward and whispered in Lincoln's ear. "Mr. President, did you notice anything peculiar in the method of address?"

As if shaking off a spell, Lincoln raised himself in his chair, and glanced quickly at a full-length portrait of Daniel Webster that hung over a large piano. "Yes," he replied, "and it is very singular, very."

From the conversations, the medium was able to piece together what she had said in trance. It was very much what some imagined the late Senator from Massachusetts might have said. She—or the spirit voice—had told the harassed President not to delay enforcement of the controversial Emancipation Proclamation beyond the new year. He was told to stand firm "and fearlessly perform the work and fulfill the mission for which he had been raised up by an overruling Providence."

Lincoln did not discuss the message with her, except to say gently: "My child, you possess a very singular gift; but that it is of God I have no doubt. I thank you for coming here tonight. It is more important than perhaps anyone present can understand." And then he quietly shuffled out of the room.

The Proclamation, of course, had been drawn up months before, but there had been talk that it would be put off beyond its effective date, January 1, 1863. Some opponents argued that it was unconstitutional, others that it would irrevocably turn the South from the Union, and still others, as Secretary of State Seward, felt that it obscured the main issue of the war—preservation of the Union, not slavery. But Lincoln steadfastly pursued his deepest conviction: "If I could save the Union without freeing any slave, I would do it; and if I could save it by freeing all the slaves, I would do it; and if I could do it by freeing some and leaving others alone, I would also do that."

The next meeting on February 5, 1863 was equally portentous. On an impulse, the President had accompanied Mrs. Lincoln to a seance at the Laurie house. Nobody—not Lincoln himself—knew he was coming until, filing out of a cabinet meeting, he climbed into a carriage with Mrs. Lincoln. But Nettie Maynard had told the host to expect him. "How could you be expecting me," Lincoln asked, "when I didn't think myself of coming until five minutes before?" He was told that the medium had provided the information, and he nodded, as though comprehending.

Again, Nettie had a major message for the troubled Commander-in-Chief, noted by Congressman Somes and others. The seance voice had identified itself as that of Dr. Bamford, long-time friend of the Colburn family. As though speaking only to Lincoln, the voice said "that a very precarious state of things existed at the front, where General [Joseph] Hooker had just taken command." The Army was pictured as totally demoralized, regiments stacking arms and threatening retreat, insubordination rife.

Lincoln had listened intently, his head resting in his great hands. "You seem to understand the situation," he observed mildly. "Can you point out the remedy?"

Nettie Maynard—or the spirit, if you will—replied with assurance: "Yes, if you have the courage to use it."

The President smiled. "Try me."

"Go in person to the front, taking only your wife and family, inquire into the grievances, show yourself the father of your people. . . . It will unite the soldiers as one man."

Lincoln seemed lost in thought, as though reflecting on what had been said, and then when the medium, still in trance, foretold that he would be renominated and re-elected, he smiled wanly. "It is hardly an honor to be coveted, save one could find his duty to accept it."

But his thoughts harked back to the beleaguered Army of the Potomac. "Matters are pretty serious down there," he commented softly, as though talking to himself, "and perhaps the simplest remedy is the best. I have often noticed in life that little things have greater weight than larger ones."

Before leaving, the President told Congressman Somes: "I am not prepared to describe the intelligence that controls this young girl's organism. She could certainly have no knowledge of the facts communicated to me, nor of what was transpiring in my cabinet meeting prior to my joining this circle, nor of affairs at the front, nor regarding transpiring events, which are known to me only, and which I have not imparted to anyone."

Before Nettie left that night, Somes took her aside and cautioned her to be discreetly silent, particularly with newspaper people, "until sufficient time had elapsed to remove condemnatory criticism" of the President.

Nettie was thrilled the next day to see the headlines in the Washington *Gazette:* "President is about to visit the Army of the Potomac." He was taking only his family, leaving promptly for his morale-building tour.

She was to hear again from Lincoln. Somes, sometime there-after, relayed a presidential invitation: "Please bring her to the White House at eight or nine o'clock but consider the matter confidential."

That night, she recalled, she was closeted with the President and two officers she had never seen before. Mrs. Lincoln had graciously welcomed her, but had then drawn off to a corner with Congressman Somes. There was a specific reason for the privacy. "Mr. Lincoln quietly stated," Mrs. Maynard recalled, "that he wished me to give them [the soldiers] an opportunity to witness something of my rare gift."

Promptly, she put herself into trance. An hour later, when she regained consciousness, she was standing by a large map of the Southern States. "In my hand was a lead pencil."

To the military, the President said: "It is astonishing how every line she has drawn conforms to the plan agreed upon."

"Yes," replied the older soldier, "it is very astonishing."

And then Lincoln bent over and whispered to Nettie, "It is best not to mention this meeting."

From his corner, where he had remained with Mrs. Lincoln, Somes reported he had seen the medium tracing lines on the map. But that was all.

The last meeting with the President took place after his re-election. Invited to an inaugural party, but hearing from home that her father was dangerously ill, Nettie had called at the White House to explain she could not keep the appointment; she felt the President may have wanted a sitting. The President looked at her with a quizzical smile, and observed dryly: "But cannot our friends from the upper country tell you whether his illness is likely to prove fatal or not?"

Nettie replied that she had already consulted "with our friends" and they had told her that her father's treatment was wrong, and that her presence was needed to effect a cure. The President turned to a young lady who had accompanied the spiritualist, a Miss Hannum, and said with a laugh, "I didn't catch her, did I?"

But the medium contemplated the Chief Executive gravely. "What they predicted for you has come to pass," she said. "But they also reaffirm that the shadow that they have spoken of still hangs over you."

The President made an impatient gesture. "Yes," he said, "I know. I have letters from all over the country from mediums warning me against some dreadful plot against my life. But I don't think the knife is made nor the bullet run that will reach it."

And then a melancholy expression that she would always remember fell over his face, and he said: "Well, Miss Nettie, I shall live till my work is done, and no earthly power can prevent it."

That, as she knew, was the last she would see of the great President.

It was a remarkable story that Nettie Maynard told, and students of Lincoln, aware of his mystical inclinations, could accept his interest in the field even without acknowledging that he was drawn by anything more impelling than curiosity.

But Robert Todd Lincoln's sweeping denial, nevertheless, dampened Mrs. Maynard's own sworn account of a presidential idiosyncrasy, despite the impressive array of statements from reputable witnesses. "Ex-Minister Robert T. Lincoln," one denial went, "says that there is not a word of truth in the story which has been widely published that Abraham Lincoln, his father, was a Spiritualist or that he is one himself, nor any foundation for the accompanying assertion that Mrs. Lincoln had a medium living in the White House while he was President, and that among the measures inspired by this means was the Emancipation Proclamation."

By this time, Mrs. Lincoln, who might have testified otherwise, was long dead.

Except for the summers, when it was too hot in Washington for social get-togethers, Robert Lincoln was either at college or, on graduation in 1864, with General Grant's staff at the front. Somes and Carpenter, Mrs. Somes and Mrs. Dupuy would appear better informed, less prejudicial witnesses. But, obviously, many felt a taint of spiritualism would tarnish the martyr's greatness, though he might not have thought so himself.

On the surface, the next story is obviously too good to be true. As this version would have it, Edward Samson was an editor of the old Boston *Globe* who fell asleep at his desk one night in August 1883, and dreamed of an exploding island. Though he dozed only a few minutes, the dream was so realistic that he felt compelled to write it down. The name of the dream island was Pralape, near Java. Samson described the earth-shattering explosion inside erupting volcanoes, with rivers of lava completely inundating villages. With a last tremendous explosion, the island—like some legendary Atlantis—sank into the sea.

When he went home that night, the story goes, Samson left an account of his dream on his desk. A daytime editor, assuming that the story had been rewritten from the cable reports, ran it on the front page. The story was a sensation, a complete beat, not only in Boston, but the world.

When it developed that the scoop was a dream, the story continues, Samson was fired. But soon reports of vast explosions in the Indonesian archipelago and of tidal waves in the Pacific vindicated the dreaming newsman, and he was rehired to work on consolidating the dispatches with his dream. In the very spot that he had placed his island, it appeared, a mighty subterranean explosion had shattered the volcanic island of Krakatoa, situated in Sunda Strait, between Java and Sumatra. A great part of the island was swept into the sea and an accompanying tidal wave destroyed numerous villages with heavy loss of life. The torrent of erupting ashes and lava was so great that new islands were formed nearby, and debris was scattered for thousands of miles.

As this story goes, there was only one discrepancy. Samson's island was Pralape, not Krakatoa. But this was soon happily resolved. Pralape was the old native name for Krakatoa, in disuse for a hundred years.

As it turned out, there was good reason for this story seeming too good to be true. It wasn't true. There was no Edward Samson, no dream, no Pralape.

But there was a Krakatoa story, and, by and large, it was more wonderous, some said, than the dream story. On August 28, 1883, even while Krakatoa was exploding, with a loss of thirty thousand lives, the Boston *Globe* carried a spectacular report of the disaster.

It was put together by an enterprising editor of the *Globe*—a day editor at that—named not Samson but Byron Somes. Somes, oddly, was a son of the Daniel Somes who was an intimate of Lincoln's and who figured in the White House seances. Young Somes, according to staff contemporary Florence Finch Kelly, had dreamed up the story as a hoax, getting background material from the public library and filling in with his imagination, so that he could make enough extra money from the story to pay for a trip to Washington. "The *Globe*," reporter Kelly declared, "bought it from him and ran it on the front page, where it filled several columns." Somes, Mrs. Kelly recalled, also sold his story to a New York paper, which cabled it to a London paper, and the English paper then cabled it back to other American papers that had first spurned it. Publications that had ignored the story, with its lurid details of destruction, ridiculed the Somes story, Mrs. Kelly related, until confirming word started to trickle in. "Weeks and months went by," she wrote, "and then accounts of strange happenings in far ocean waters began to drift into the news from ports on the shores of the Pacific and the islands of the south—showers of ashes, unusual waves running back and forth across the ocean—and all around the world people were wondering about the phenomenal glowing red sunsets." Not long thereafter, she recalled, there was scientific confirmation of Somes's story, with the news "flashed over all the earth of the eruption of a volcano in Sundra Strait which had blown an island over two thousand feet high out of the ocean and left in its place a basin of the sea a thousand feet deep." Looking back over the years, in her journalistic reminiscenses *Flowing Stream*, Florence Finch Kelly could only marvel at Somes's incredible reportorial feat from a distance of thousands of miles. "With his imaginary volcanic eruption," she wrote (misspelling his name), "Mr. Soames had closely hit in time and place the explosion of Krakatoa, the greatest volcanic eruption of modern times, and in his account he had included many phenomena that were parallel in the later descriptions of the actual outburst. Did the vagaries of chance ever direct the long arm of coincidence to a more amazing result?"

Offhand, it would appear that Mrs. Kelly should have been an impeccable authority on what was occurring on a newspaper with which she was closely connected. She was an outstanding reporter, later serving more than thirty years with the New York *Times,* and she had known Somes well. When he moved to Troy, New York as managing editor of the Troy *Morning Telegram,* shortly there-after—an obvious recognition of his new-found fame—she joined him as editorial writer. They were good friends, and conversed frequently about his Krakatoa story. She should have had the facts straight.

However, Boston *Globe* historians, while proudly acclaiming Somes for his handling of the Krakatoa story, claim that he had no actual beat on the disaster, but that a fertile imagination, alerted by the first meager dispatches from the disaster area, provided details later startlingly confirmed. There was no questioning Somes's ingenuity, and his grasp of the disaster's scope from the first brief flashes was clearly intuitive. Ex-*Globe* editor Willard de Lue, now the paper's historian, has pointed out that other papers, like the *Globe,* had carried the first disaster reports on August 28, 1883. "This story, under a Batavia dateline," he informed me, "was based upon one of the same date in the London *Times.* The *Globe,* which at that time was being barred from the Associated Press by a veto of the other Boston papers, has a short version of the story. As a result of past experience, the *Globe* feared that it was going to come out on the short end of what appeared to be a major disaster. Accordingly, the day editor of the *Globe,* Byron Somes (there never was an Edward Samson on the editorial staff) went to the public library, got out books on Java and on volcanic eruptions, and from the material thus gathered produced a series of major rewrites and build-ups of the original dispatch from Batavia." De Lue acknowledged the carping criticism of the *Globe's* outmaneuvered competitors. "I call his stories rewrites; others call them fakes."

For historian de Lue, there was nothing psychic about it. "The fact is that Somes sensed the magnitude of the disaster and had so soaked himself in the geography and volcanic history of the Java area that his stories proved to be amazingly accurate pictures of the actual happenings." They were so vivid, as a matter of fact, that the New York *Sun* bought all three—they ran on successive days—and correspondents on this side of the Atlantic, as Mrs. Kelly recalled, cabled them to English papers, from which they were cabled back.

Since her memoirs were published in 1939, more than fifty-five years after the event, Mrs. Kelly's memory for detail may well have grown hazy. She spelled Somes "Soames," despite their closeness, and incorrectly located the *Globe* building in Tremont Street. De Lue's version, on the other hand, was supplied, for the most part, by James Morgan, a *Globe* veteran, who was the paper's telegrapher at the time.

But all agree that Somes did a remarkable job in covering history's greatest explosion from his desk. There was so much destruction that other reporters had difficulty knowing exactly what was happening. But not Somes—he seemed to be tuned in. And the paper was proud of his achievement. "Somes was never fired," de Lue records. "In fact, in a *Globe* editorial we boasted about the wonderful news service which gave us such excellent dispatches."

And a grateful publisher, Colonel Taylor, gave his imaginative reporter enough of a bonus to make that trip to Washington possible.

Almost as controversial as the Lincoln seances have been the Malachy prophecies, handed down for more than four hundred years, and allegedly going back another five hundred years. The original Malachy, for whom the prophecies were named, was an Irish monk, a great friend of St. Bernard of Clairvaux, who vouched for Malachy's gift of prophecy, without once referring to the "prophecies of the popes" in his contemporary biography of his friend. Malachy's Gaelic name was Mael Maedoc ua Morgair. He was born in Ireland in 1095, and later became Archbishop of Armagh. In later years he visited Rome and was there said to have written his prophecies. However, so far as anyone knows, they were not published until 1595, the five-hundredth anniversary of his birth, and there are some who think that they may have been the work of the Dominican friars of that period. A Dominican, Arnold de Wion, who published them, explained that the manuscript was given to Pope Innocent II for approval, and that it then passed into the Vatican archives to gather dust for five centuries.

The Malachy prophecies consists of 111 terse Latin mottoes purporting to identify in succession all the popes from Celestine II of Malachy's time to "the time of the end."

The present Pope, John XXIII, is one hundred and seventh on the Malachy list, leaving only four to round out the total. This limitation, in the opinion of certain scholars, has led to an obvious forgery at the conclusion of the work. "During the last persecution of the Holy Roman Church," the so-called prophecy ends, "there shall sit the Roman Peter, who shall feed the sheep amid great tribulations, and when these are passed, the City of Seven Hills shall be utterly destroyed and the awful Judge will judge the people."

There was other reason for reserve. The prophetic mottoes, in one way or another foretelling who would occupy the Holy See, were suspiciously perfect from 1095 to 1595, when they were suddenly "found" and made available. But they were not nearly as effective thereafter.

However, even after publication, the mottoes frequently seemed to fit, or else have been made to fit. For instance, one of the first popes after the published prophecy was Leo XI. His identifying label—"Wave-man." "Like the wind he came, and like the water he went." He reigned only twenty-seven days. He was succeeded by Paul V, 1605–21, whose difficulties with the Protestants explains the motto: "Perverse people."

One of the most striking hits—post-1595—was the "Guardian of the hills" for Pope Alexander VII, reigning from 1655 to 1667. His family emblem was three hills with a star protectively watching over.

Down the list, through references to papal backgrounds or other activities, so many mottoes appeared predictive that regardless of disputed authorship, some felt they still had prophetic merit.

"It is what the prophecies say, not who says them, that actually makes them valid or not," observed Stewart Robb, the Nostradamus scholar, who has been similarly intrigued by the Malachy prophecies.

In the fulfillment of some mottoes there ran a vein of romance and adventure, as with Clement X, who ruled the Church from 1670 to 1676. Once the mighty Tiber, bursting its bank at floodtime, coursed into a home where a baby lay helplessly in its crib and would have swept him away had it not been for an alert nurse. The child's family coat of arms, too, was the Milky Way—in Latin, the *magnum flumen,* or literally "mighty river." The motto for Clement, eighty-fifth on the list: "Concerning the mighty river."

Innocent XIII came from a family noted for its piety, "Of good religion," and Benedict XIII, his successor, from a warrior clan: "Soldier in battle."

Still, the interpreters do more than a bit of reaching. For instance. Clement XII (1730–40), noted for an interest in architecture, designed columns for a great church in Rome. Hence, "The column is raised up." Next was "Rural animal," and the stretching appears rather obvious here. Pope Benedict XIV— number ninety-three—to whom it necessarily alluded, was a provincial and a tremendously hard worker, laboring, some commentators say, like an ox, in the cause of the Church.

Clement XIII, the ninety-fourth pope on the Malachy list, was stationed in Umbria before he became pope, and Umbria's symbol is a rose. The Irish saint previsioned him: "Rose of Umbria."

The family escutcheon of Clement XIV showed a running bear. Malachy wrote for him, *"Ursus Velox,"* or "Swift Bear."

Pius VIII's only encyclical was directed against laxity in religion. His motto: "Religious Man," which, of course, might have been applied to many of the popes.

Gregory XVI came from an order in Etruria and sponsored archeological research in the ancient baths, or balnea, of that province. Malachy's slogan: *"De Balneis Etruriae,"* or "Concerning the baths of Etruria."

Leo XIII became Pope in 1878 and reigned to 1903. His family crest was a comet of gold on an azure field; the prophetic rubric: "The light in the sky."

After a fashion, without giving them sanction, the popes themselves took cognizance of the mottoes. Clement XI was born in

Urbin; its insignia was a garland of flowers. The Malachy prophecy, "Encircled by Flowers," was adopted by Clement when he became pontiff. During the reign of a Clement predecessor, Alexander VIII, Louis XIV, Grand Monarch of France, returned Avignon to papal jurisdiction as a gesture of submission to the Church. On his coins, Alexander gratefully inscribed the motto ("Glorious penitence.") Malachy had already given it to him.

By the twentieth century, almost needless to say, there was more than idle curiosity in even ecclesiastic circles about the Malachy prophecies, even though much of the speculation was tinged with disbelief and scorn.

Certainly, there was no tendency to laugh off the motto for the one hundred and fourth Pope, as one abbe, reflecting an element of feeling within the church, asked in 1913 of the next motto, "Religion depopulated," after several previous prophecies seemed to have hit, "What does this sinister device mean?" He soon knew. Benedict XV was chosen Pope in 1914, the year that ushered in World War I and the deaths of millions of Christians on the battlefields of Europe, climaxed by the Russian Revolution in 1917 and the withdrawal of some two hundred million faithful from the Christian fold.

Benedict's successor, Pius XI, was famed for his "intrepid faith," as recorded by the motto, and well he had need for it, with Communist excursions against the Catholic Church not only in Russia, but in Catholic Spain and Mexico.

Next came a direct hit. "Angelic pastor" was the Malachy motto for the late Pius XII of the heavenly visions, whom even millions of non-Catholics looked upon as saintly.

The motto for his successor, Pope John XXIII, now baffles the Malachy proponents. Even the most fervid acknowledge that "Pastor and sailor" has no apparent reference to jovial "Papa John." However, hopefully, they look to a signal voyage of some sort to achieve fulfillment of the prophecy.

After John, four mottoes remain. "Flower of flowers" is to succeed the sailor, an augury, one interpreter suggests, of a French pope—fleur-de-lys. The next motto has an ominous ring for some —"Concerning the half moon"—the half-moon or crescent betokening perhaps an Arab or Moslem threat. "Of the labor of the sun" is the device next to the last, and could signify the age of solar energy, says scholar Robb.

"Of the glory of the olive" is the last of the mottoes. "It could mean the inception of lasting peace," Robb said, "this being the connotation of the olive branch, or since the olive is a symbol of the Holy Land, any glorification of the Holy Land might indicate a resurgence of true Christianity."

After that? There are no more Malachy prophecies. And, unless others are conveniently exhumed, the one hundred and twelfth Pope will be the first in four hundred years to take over his holy office without this traditional, if not prophetic, clue.

9 FATE OR FORTUNE

In March of 1962, an American airliner bound for Los Angeles with ninety-five aboard crashed while taking off from New York Idlewild Airport. Among the dead were W. Alton (Pete) Jones, millionaire oilman off to vacation with former President Eisenhower, and Arnold Kirkeby, millionaire hotel magnate. The dead also included a wife who had taken her husband's seat at the last moment, and seventeen unfortunates who had switched from a United flight that was canceled out at the last minute.

Through chance there were also many who did not die: the husband whose wife had taken his seat, a motion picture producer who took another flight because a star was late for an appointment, a Ridgefield, Connecticut businessman who had driven instead, and wound up in an automobile accident anyway.

So often death seemed a stroke of chance: Dag Hammarskjold's in an African plane crash, artist Emma Ench's in a Paterson fire, and the passengers on that American jetliner.

But then what is chance?

"What we consider chance may be something entirely else," observed Dr. Andreja Puharich, the brilliant researchist who has tested many psychics at his Maine laboratories.

"The fact that major events can be predicted," Puharich pointed out, "indicates that we may not have as much choice about our lives as we think. We might have enough free will to decide whether we're going to shave in the morning or night, but shaving itself is determined for us by custom."

"If the future is predictable," I asked, "to a point where Nostradamus could foresee the French Revolution, is that future then inflexible?"

Puharich shrugged. "There is a predictable pattern in the universe, and it is quite possible that man is part of this pattern; geometrically, the whole is the sum of its parts—and if the whole is predictable, the parts certainly should be."

It seemed a simple thing to change life's course by a deliberate decision. "Long before I had written a book," I observed, "Gilbert Holloway, a sensitive, told me that I would write a dozen books. Now why couldn't I upset this prediction by sitting around and letting these books write themselves?"

Puharich flashed an even-toothed smile. "From the day we're born, our individual pattern begins to emerge—our heredity, personality, and environment. Temperamentally, you could no more sit idle than fly to the moon, and anyway your obligations wouldn't permit it; you have bills to pay, a family to support, a flair for writing, and you're ambitious—all these figure in your destiny."

He studied me speculatively. "How did you happen to write your first book?"

I thought a moment. "A publishing house asked me to enlarge a newspaper series into a book."

"There you are," he said, "the opportunity to do a book fell into your lap. But your personality prepared the way, and influenced your decision to do the book."

"You could crash in a plane without it having anything to do with your personality, ambitions, or obligations," I observed.

Puharich shook his head. "In a way," he said, "the individual's personality influenced his being on that plane—his job, financial status, and need to travel. But a million things would have to happen," he conceded, "before all these passengers could be brought together to round out their common destiny pattern." His lips puckered in thought. "For a disaster to happen as predicted," he added slowly, "it obviously suggests a great independent mind shaping countless factors toward a fixed result—and the intangible called luck may be only a final fillip of the independent mind."

When a forecast didn't work out, was this because the future was changeable, or was it that even the best psychics were fallible?

Puharich had considered this problem carefully. "Some events," he said, "may be changeable, and others not, depending on their nature. And, of course"—he laughed deprecatingly—"we never know how accurate the psychic is until the event establishes his accuracy. But if things are already determined, as their predictable nature indicates, then this independent mind, with unlimited power, obviously has an interest in the flow of human events."

If there was such a thing as fate, did it do any good to know what that fate was? I recalled the case of pretty socialite Renee Dubonnet, whose father, a surgeon, had been given a life chart by a famed mystic while traveling in Tibet. It had traced not only his future, but that of everyone he loved.

In childhood, Renee could remember only vague, uneasy references to the chart, and was never encouraged to ask about it. Then, one day, she saw her father staring glumly into the fire. His own father had died that day in California.

"Are you going to the funeral?" Renee asked.

He shook his head.

"You're not going to your own father's funeral?" She was incredulous.

"No," he said.

"Why, that's not human," she said, adding brashly, "perhaps if I gave you the fare you would go."

As she looked at her father's stricken face, she would have given anything to withdraw her words. "It is not necessary that I go," he said wearily.

One night a few weeks later he left notes for his wife and children, including Renee, and retiring early, died in his sleep. Afterwards, Renee learned that the chart had listed the death chronologically of everyone in the family. "When Grandfather went," she said, "Dad knew he was not far behind."

She had no wish to see the chart. "It wouldn't have helped me," she said, "any more than it did Dad."

More than any, perhaps, the men who have gambled with their own fate, watching detached as it worked out, have given us a ringside seat at destiny's show window. On the last leg of a postwar mission from Singapore to Tokyo in January 1946, Air Marshal Sir Victor Goddard, one of the heroes of the Pacific war, had received a bizarre warning of disaster. Stopping overnight at Shanghai, the Marshal had attended a cocktail party in his honor. He was chatting with a fellow officer, Brigadier General John McConnell of the U. S. Air Force, when he happened to overhear his name mentioned by two men he had never seen before. "Too bad about Goddard being killed in that crash," one said, "but it's jolly to have the party anyway."

With a start, Goddard wondered, "Is he crazy or am I?"

One of the strangers was a Navy commander. Turning, glass in hand, he spotted the guest of honor, and began to stammer out his apologies. The Marshal graciously brushed them aside. But his curiosity was aroused. "I may be a bit moribund, Commander," he said, "but I'm not quite dead yet. What made you think I was?"

The Navy officer, considerably junior to the Marshal, hesitated nervously, but was encouraged by Goddard's easy smile. "I dreamed it," he said finally. "I had a dream last night"—he brushed a hand across his eyes—"or was it this afternoon. I could have sworn it was true. It seemed so true."

In the dream, Goddard had been in a big plane, a Dakota transport, which had crashed at night on a singularly rocky, shingly shore in a blinding snowstorm.

Goddard was flying a Dakota.

Intrigued, he asked the Commander if the dream had revealed who was with him when the plane crashed.

The plane's ordinary service crew, the Commander replied, plus three civilians, two men and a woman.

Goddard, affected by the dream in spite of himself, felt a sensation of relief. "We are carrying no one but the service crew," he said.

But in a few minutes, things had changed. The Honorable Seymour Berry, son of England's Lord Camrose, asked the Marshal if he could cadge a lift to Tokyo. Goddard could not refuse him. And then the British Consul General, George A. Ogden, asked to be taken aboard. He had been directed by the British Foreign Office to take the first transportation out for a conference in Tokyo. Goddard was becoming entranced with the way the dream was unfolding. But at least, he assured himself, there would be no woman. And then, of course, it happened. Consul General Ogden asked if he could take a stenographer abroad. She would be needed for shorthand at the conference.

Goddard philosophically agreed. It occurred to him that he might put off the flight, plead bad weather, lack of extra fuel. But how could a Marshal of the British Empire justify—even to himself—his yielding to a supernatural warning from a junior officer he had never seen before? It didn't add up.

And yet he could not dispel a sense of depression. As a soldier he was resigned to whatever came, but worried about the passengers, whose lives—or deaths—might be tied in with his. He sighed. Yet years of war had made him a fatalist. He would do nothing to alter the natural course of events. In keeping with this decision, he permitted the pilot, Squadron Leader Don Campbell, to pick the flight route for the six-hour flight and use his own judgment in any emergency. He had no way of knowing whether intervention on his part—to take an inland route away from a "rocky, shingly shore"—would prove advantageous or merely play along with destiny.

He was lounging in the plane, maintaining a cheerful aspect for the rest of the passengers, when abruptly they headed into a blinding snowstorm, unanticipated by the weather reports. And then, staring bemused out a window, Goddard saw ice form on the wings of the plane. Successively, things began to conk out.

The radio failed, interrupting communication with shore, and the de-icers wouldn't work. Looking below, through a patch of light, Sir Victor caught with a start a flash of the rocky shore that the Commander had so vividly described. It was shingly, all right. He shrugged, mentally, and looked around the plane, observing the stenographer, Dorita Breakspear. She was only twenty; it would be a pity.

The pilot Campbell had come back for instructions. Goddard had none. They couldn't make Tokyo, Campbell said, and he was already flying blind. There was no airstrip anywhere in the area. All they could do was drop down and trust to luck. The waves below were wild and ugly. Everybody dutifully put lifesavers around their necks, and prepared for the crash. It was all up to Campbell—or was it?

Grimly Goddard thought, this is it. He braced himself for the crash. It came with a sickening lurch. In his role of spectator, he saw Consul General Ogden and his seat come skipping past him, torn loose from its moorings by the impact, and looking around, he saw that Ogden had landed comfortably on a mattress. Another look, and he saw that everybody in the party, including stenographer Breakspear, had safely survived. All were shaken up, but otherwise well. Goddard felt his bones—all intact.

After congratulating himself he began to wonder why the Commander's dream had been so accurate in every detail right up to the crash, and then off in its finale. Pursuing the matter, he wrote the Commander at sea, asking him to recall whether he had actually seen him dead in the crash or had just surmised it from visualizing the crash itself. The Commander sent his regrets. With time, the dream had become vague—and so had he. "I can't say that I actually saw you dead, but I certainly thought the crash was a killer."

Reading about Goddard's adventures in an article he did for the *Saturday Evening Post* in May 1951, I wondered whether the retired officer had any secondary reflections on the course of fate. The article was titled "The Night My Number Came Up."

I wrote Goddard in New Zealand, without hearing back, and then in England, receiving a direct reply. Sir Victor had thought back often on that fateful night. "Insofar as events are the logical outcome of dispassionate action," he had decided, "they gradually integrate into a history that already exists in mental reality. Insofar as passion, fear, and negative irrationality intrude, so does distortion of the mental reality; but positive influences of love and prayer can remove negative aspects of the future events, which then integrate differently. Possibilities exist—perhaps many possibilities in the same history, any one of which can be seen." In other words, he did believe in the will changing the future. But like Puharich, Goddard felt that free will did not have broad range, though many choices did seem immediately available. "Driving in a motorcar is an experience that at first sight seems limitless," he observed. "At second sight, it is severely limited by roads, traffic, abilities. So with the fate, allotted by powers beyond our three-dimension being, within which we exercise choice; our soul in choosing life's circumstances in general, our mind in choosing actions, our body in facilitating or impeding the implementation of the mind's choosing, conscious and unconscious—our scope for life experience is limited."

It was difficult, Sir Victor felt, to discuss the infinite in finite terms. Only our own inability to shed unreal concepts of time and space, he thought, kept us from clearer understanding of the nature of a universe in which a predictable pattern of individual events is part and parcel of the over-all pattern. "Ideas, imagination, vision of the seer, the world beyond this world," said this illustrious soldier, "belong to the realm of the spirit, immediately beyond us, above us, within us. But as those words beyond, above, within, are space words, they can convey only a space concept, not a spiritual concept. How then can we write accurately about time and mind and spirit and fate?" Time, then, existed only in our minds!

At times, the hardiest skeptics have been impressed by fate's apparent inevitability. Edward Perper, road manager for impresario Sol Hurok, had been traveling with the famed Fife and Drum Corps of Scotland's Black Watch Regiment, en route to Montreal, when the group expressed a wish to visit the French-American War fortress of Ticonderoga in upper New York. It was out of the way and Perper demurred. "But," he recalled, "they said they couldn't come all this distance without seeing where Major Duncan Campbell had given up his ghost." This was the first Perper had heard of the old Scottish major.

"Is this some ghost story or legend?" he asked.

"It is all down in the annals of the Black Watch," he was told.

Near Ticonderoga, a historical marker indicated the grave of the Scottish laird who had been drawn across the sea to fulfill a haunting prophecy.

The story itself, supported by historical-society reports, was an eerie one. Sometime in the 1740s, before our own Revolution, Campbell was sitting by the fire in his Highland castle of Inverawe, when there came a furious rattling at the door. It was a wild-eyed stranger. "I have killed a man in fair fight," he cried, "for God's sake shelter me."

Quickly Campbell let the man in. As he entered the great hall the fugitive turned and said, "Swear on your dirk, Duncan Campbell, that you will not give me up."

Solemnly, the laird of Inverawe took the sacred oath, unbreakable for a Campbell. But hardly was the stranger safely concealed when there was more pounding at the door and a voice thundered, "Your cousin Donald Campbell has been murdered, and we look for the murderer."

Duncan Campbell paled, remembering his oath, and turned the men away. That night as he tossed restlessly, an apparition appeared at the foot of his bed, crying in sepulchral tones: "Inverawe, Inverawe. Blood has been shed. Shield not the murderer." It was his slain kinsman, Donald Campbell.

In the morning, Duncan told his guest he would have to go. "You have sworn on your dirk," the man said.

A compromise was reached. Campbell led the man to a cave in a nearby hill, thus hoping to preserve his oath and still not harbor his cousin's killer in his house.

But again that night, the apparition returned and repeated: "Inverawe, Inverawe, blood has been shed. Shield not the murderer."

The bedeviled Campbell, now ready to repudiate his oath, rushed that morning to the cave to take his cousin's killer. But he had gone. That night, the vision appeared with the cryptic warning, "Farewell, farewell, until we meet at Ticonderoga."

The name meant nothing to the Scot, but he had a feeling of foreboding.

Years later, now second in command of Britain's Forty-Second Regiment, the Black Watch, Campbell still remembered the warning and broodingly repeated his story to brother officers. But he had still never heard of Ticonderoga. Unpredictably, though, the Black Watch came to the colonies for the French-Indian War, and moved into battle lines north of Albany, New York. Meanwhile, Campbell had learned the Indian name for Fort Carillon, between Lake George and Lake Champlain. It was Theenderora. But the colonials pronounced it Ticonderoga. There was no doubt in the Major's mind that he would at last meet Donald Campbell there. The historian Parkman, writing of the approaching battle, took note of the Campbell prophecy: "There was Rogers with the Rangers and Gage with the light infantry . . . and the Highlanders of the Forty-Second with their Major, Duncan Campbell of Inverawe, silent and gloomy amid the general cheer, for his soul was dark with forebodings of death."

On the morning of Ticonderoga, July 8, 1758, Duncan Campbell called on his brother officers—the Frasers, Stewarts, and MacDuffs—and said wearily: "I have seen him again. He came to my tent last night saying, 'This is Ticonderoga.'" The officers laughed but the Major seemed reconciled to his fate. "I shall die today," he said.

As a prophet, Duncan Campbell was not quite on the mark. He was hit that day, but it was only a flesh wound. The regiment's Captain James Stewart, writing home after the battle, reported: "All the Captains were wounded, less or more, excepting Captains McNeil and Allen Campbell; Major Campbell got his right arm wounded, but not dangerous."

But nine days later the Major was dead. The wound had festered and gangrene had set in. His death was of enough significance for Commanding General Abercrombie to report to British Prime Minister, Robert Pitt: "Major Duncan Campbell of the Forty-

Second who was wounded in the arm at the battle on the 8th was obliged to have it cut off and die soon thereafter."

Inverawe had kept his rendezvous with fate.

At times, justifying fate, the scattered fragments of a predicted event appear to click together like a jigsaw puzzle. As a young man, Mark Twain had been told by a sensitive that, born in 1835 with Halley's comet, he would go out with its return in 1910. But long before his death, which came as the comet flared through the night sky, the American humorist had a death vision of his own—about his brother Henry. In a dream, he saw his brother, a handsome youth of twenty, lying in a metal casket supported on two chairs in a large room. On Henry's chest there was a large bouquet of white flowers with a single red rose in the center. When he awakened, the writer was so struck by the vividness of his dream that he told his sister about it. And he cautioned his brother, a riverman like himself, to proceed with care on his trip down the Mississippi that day. "If anything should happen to the boat," he said, "swim away from it." Henry laughed good-naturedly at his brother's concern. But just below Memphis, two or three days later, the boilers in the steamboat *Pennsylvania* blew up with heavy loss of life. Mark Twain hurried to the disaster scene. The victims, dead and dying, had been taken to a large building that had been converted into a makeshift morgue. Sam Clemens—Mark Twain—passed between solid rows of wooden coffins, searching for his brother. Suddenly, in the sea of crude, unpainted pine, he spotted a metal casket, similar to the one in his dream. In it lay his brother, his hands restfully folded, his eyes closed. Touched by his youth and good looks, the good women of Memphis had raised a private collection for a more imposing resting place for the unknown victim. Then, as Mark Twain stood next to the coffin sadly contemplating his brother, an old woman quietly shuffled into the big room, approached the casket, and put a white floral decoration on the dead youth's chest. In the center was a single red rose.

Being forewarned is not necessarily forearmed. No matter the warnings, people seem drawn into situations that foresight might have averted. W. T. Stead, the English editor, had enough warnings of disaster at sea to keep the average person away from any body of water larger than a bathtub. Three years before the *Titanic* went down, Stead, lecturing in New York, saw himself shipwrecked and crying for help. A year before the *Titanic* hit the iceberg, a sensitive whom Stead consulted regularly, told him that danger threatened his life "from water, and nothing else, and that travel would be hazardous for him in the month of April 1912." That was the very month, of course, that he booked passage. Still another sensitive, Monsieur W. de Kerlor, reading for Stead a year before the *Titanic's* maiden voyage, predicted the editor would embark for America on a ship not then completed. "I can see only half the ship," de Kerlor said, "meaning the ship will be completed when its whole length becomes visible." The ship was in black and that, too, foretold disaster, de Kerlor said. And if all this weren't enough, de Kerlor subsequently had a dream in which he saw himself in the middle of a sea catastrophe. "There were masses [more than a thousand] of bodies struggling in the water and I was among them. I could hear their cries for help."

The "I" in the dream he translated as editor Stead.

But Stead only smiled. "You are a very gloomy prophet," he said, as he boarded ship.

The course of predicted events often moves independently of the will—or knowledge—of the persons involved. Before World War II, Doris, the supper club palmist, was struck by the common destiny in so many young hands. And yet she could form no general pattern from the individual forecasts.

Reading one hand after another, she saw a veritable exodus from the city. Truck drivers, clerks, playboys, doctors, and stockbrokers were all voyaging to fabulously remote areas of the world. "I see them all going to the South Seas, Africa, Alaska, Burma, China," she confided wonderingly to a friend, "how can that be?" Since she was only sporadically psychic, she had missed the salient fact that there was going to be a war, with young Americans in uniform being dispatched to every corner of the world.

Skeptics, justifiably at times, attribute the fulfillment of many predictions to the power of suggestion. But obviously this has little to do with predictions that depend upon outside action. Long before I had written a book, the sensitive Maya Perez, whose predictions had launched my interest in ESP, told me quite seriously: "Your third book will be a best seller."

"I better get on with the first and second," I said rather dryly, "so I can get to the third."

When I was working on my second book, a survey of juvenile delinquency, I mentioned Madam Perez' prediction to my agent, Jean Detre, of Music Corporation of America, and I recall her saying tartly, "Maybe she should write the book."

Undertaking my third book, I was mindful of the prediction, but found it a source of amusement.

I did not work on the book with any special zeal. Indeed, I left what I thought might be the two best chapters unfinished in my drawer, because the subject—homosexuality—had begun to depress me. The book was called *The Sixth Man*. When it came out in the spring of 1961, it received indifferent reviews for the most part, and was actually attacked by one publication. It certainly didn't look like a best seller. But two weeks later it went on the New York *Times* best seller list, and stayed there for twelve weeks.

Since the Perez prediction had so inexplicably materialized, I cited the incident, as an example of precognition, to a prominent research scientist. "It is very possible," he said dubiously, "that the prediction influenced you."

I didn't quite understand.

He explained patiently. "It may have stimulated you to a point where you wrote a better book."

"You could write the best book in the world and still it might not be a best seller," I said.

"You would be influenced, nevertheless, by that prediction," he insisted.

I looked at him closely. "But who," I asked, "influenced the people who made that book a best seller?"

He regarded me with a look of pedantic triumph. "You did."

"You flatter me that I could produce a best seller at will," I said, and then laughing, added, "you have written several books—can you?"

Yet we all know that the power of suggestion can be a compelling force. It has made the well sick, and the sick strong. And it might well influence a predicted event if the subject were impressionable, and the event hinged on his actions alone. I have been intrigued, therefore, by one particularly striking example of the power of suggestion versus predicted fate, which goes back beyond the turn of the century. When he was only nineteen, the subject of this story, a quite average young man, consulted the French fortune-teller, Madam Lenormand. He wanted a frank reading, and she gave it to him. "You will lose your father a year from this day," she said—this was December 1879. "You will soon be a soldier but not for long." She frowned, studying his hand. He could hardly contain himself.

"What else?" he demanded.

"You will marry young, have two children, and . . ."

"And?"

She spoke slowly. "And you will die at twenty-six."

The young man told his friends about the forecast, but didn't seem to take it seriously. But his father's death on December 27, 1880, within a few hours of the predicted time, gave him cause to pause. When the other events began to unfold as predicted, he became successively more nervous, and finally, as he neared twenty-six, he consulted the French psychologist, Dr. Liebeault. "When M. de Ch—— became a soldier for seven months only," Liebeault reported, "married, had two children, and was approaching his twenty-sixth birthday, he became thoroughly alarmed and thought he had only a few days to live. This was why he came to consult me, hoping I might enable him to avoid his fate. For, as the first four events had taken place, he thought the last would."

Liebeault did not think it would be difficult to hypnotize youthful M. de Ch—— out of a suggestion that threatened to end his life from fright, if nothing else. "On this and the following days," the doctor reported, "I tried to send Monsieur de Ch—— into profound sleep in order to dissipate the impression that he would die on the fourth of February, his twenty-sixth birthday. Madam Lenormand had not named a date, but even so he was so agitated, I could not induce even the slightest sleep."

With his patient more panicky with each passing day, the doctor schemed to get him past the critical birth date. "As it was absolutely necessary to get rid of his conviction lest it should fulfill itself by self-suggestion," the doctor observed, "I changed my tactics and proposed that he should consult one of my somnambulists, an old man of seventy or so, nicknamed 'the prophet' because he had exactly foretold his own career of articular rheumatism of four years standing, and that of his daughter, the cure of the latter resulting from his suggestion . . ." At this point the patient would have agreed to anything. "M. de Ch—— accepted my proposal eagerly," Liebeault said. Pitting one suggestive force against another, the doctor and his associate worked together toward inducing sleep and subconsciously removing fear from the patient's mind with positive suggestion. The fear itself was corrosive. "When put into rapport with the somnambulist," the doctor said, "the patient's first question was, 'When shall I die?'"

The somnambulist concentrated on the countersuggestion: "You will die . . . you will die . . . in forty-seven years," he said slowly, thus trying to assure the young man more than normal life expectancy.

Wakening, the patient spruced up immediately; his fears were banished. "The effect was marvelous," the doctor reported, "the young man recovered his spirits, and when the fourth of February (his twenty-sixth birthday) passed, he thought himself safe."

The case was happily closed, the doctor thought. By one device or the other, he had cured M. de Ch—— of the phobia periling his sanity. But some seven or eight months later, he received an unexpected communication from the young man's family. "I had forgotten the case," the doctor recalled, "when at the beginning of October, I received an invitation to the funeral of my unfortunate patient, who had died on September 30, 1886, in his twenty-seventh year as Madam Lenormand had foretold." He was, of course, only twenty-six at the time.

The doctor kept brooding over the incident. Finally, he decided to make a report of the case while it was still fresh in his mind. "To prevent the supposition that the whole affair was an illusion on my part," he said, "I kept this letter of invitation, as well as the record made at the time of M. de Ch——'s visit to me."

As a man with little faith in psychics, the doctor had considered various possibilities. Might not fright have taken a delayed toll of the young man, affecting heart, nervous system, or glands? Had there been a recurrence of the panic which the doctor did not know about? Could not the patient have become so unbalanced by fear that he courted disaster? And so the doctor investigated, to find it was none of these. "I have since learned," he reported, "that the unfortunate man had been under treatment for biliary calculi and died of peritonitis caused by an intestinal rupture. . . ." Thus ended the sad adventure of M. de Ch——, the young man who became a classic study in vainly trying to avoid his fate.

Nearly every United States community, no matter how small, has at least one sensitive, generally a spiritualist, who doles out counsel with the future. In Long Branch, New Jersey, for instance, substantial citizens—stockbrokers, architects, engineers, business executives—flock to Mrs. Mary Reva Wood at her Church of Psychic Science. She also draws her crackpots, cranks, hypochondriacs, and lost souls, all equally welcome as they step through the portals of the tiny chapel. Many regard her as they would a doctor or lawyer, and some claim more for her than she does for herself—the supreme accolade. "You see," a sophisticated-looking interior decorator explained, "she has never missed with me."

It was rather odd, sitting around in broad daylight on a sunny veranda in fashionable Monmouth Beach, New Jersey, adjacent to Long Branch, sipping a gin and tonic and discussing this elderly, unsophisticated sensitive with a well-dressed, well-groomed group, who had a sense of humor about their own frailties. "I suppose I seem some kind of nut," said twice-wed Mrs. Claire Burnson, an interior decorator, "but Madam Wood told me I would be married three times, and I don't have the slightest doubt number three is coming up." She laughed as she dabbled at her drink, repeating a bit self-consciously, "she's never been wrong with me." She nodded at an attractive middle-aged woman sitting across from her. "Ask Dorothy," she said, "she's known me since we were kids together at the Parsons School for Design in New York." Dorothy Donley, a mild-looking woman who taught in New York, responded affirmatively. "I don't know how it works," she said with a wry smile, "but it certainly has worked for Claire."

But it did not, apparently, always work to her advantage.

Three years before, while married to government agent Lee Burnson, Claire had visited Madam Wood's little basement church. "I was just interested generally," she explained, "in what she thought my plans would be, about the children—I have three— and about my business, and things like that."

As she lit a cigarette, she explained to our host, John Rendon, a Wall Streeter, who was eyeing her rather sardonically, that she had been to Madam Wood before and had been astonished not only by her wisdom, but the reliability of her predictions.

"She must know all about you by this time," Rendon commented dryly.

"She never asked for information," Mrs. Burnson replied, "and I volunteered none. Why, she didn't even know my name until two months ago." She flicked her cigarette, ran a well-manicured hand through her blonde hair, and toyed with her drink. "Anyway, on this particular occasion, Madam Wood mentioned that I would be moving again soon. She always had me moving, and we were always moving." And then, as casually as she would have told Mrs. Burnson that she saw a moving van pulling up to the house, Madam Wood had remarked with a frown: "I see a circle of three around you—three children and three marriages."

Then in her second marriage, Mrs. Burnson said with a start of surprise, "Oh, do you see another divorce for me?"

"No," Madam Wood replied, "no divorce."

"Then what do you see?" Claire asked, puzzled.

"I see you as a widow."

"A widow," she exclaimed, "but my husband is in the best of health." She looked up. "When do you see this happening?"

"Within two years," Madam Wood said.

Mrs. Burnson scowled. "Couldn't there be some mistake?"

Madam Wood shook her head. "They tell me clearly within two years. You should prepare yourself." And she saw another circle of three—three new men in Claire's life.

That night, Claire Burnson studied her husband carefully over the dinner table. Though edgy, as he sometimes was, he never seemed healthier. But quite involuntarily, she found herself examining him thereafter for a sign of illness. It also occurred to her that he might suffer an accident; she was that sure of Madam Wood. The thought was depressing, and she tried to throw it off. She confided only in Miss Donley, her oldest friend. But consciously, and subconsciously, the prediction had its effect on her. "We were debating getting a new sofa sometime after this," she recalled, "and my husband was against it. Normally, I would have gone along with him, but I found myself thinking, 'Well, he isn't going to have to put up with it, so why don't I get what I want, since I am the one who will have to live with it.'"

Mrs. Burnson laughed nervously. "It wasn't quite as cold as it sounds; I guess even then I was trying to put a front on things, and this was a sort of nervous reaction."

For more than a year, not knowing what fate—and Madam Wood—foretold for him, Lee Burnson appeared to prosper. But then he started to complain of pain and weakness. He went to a number of doctors but they didn't help. He soon had to stop work. He lost weight rapidly and was wasting away. Eighteen months after the prediction he was dead—cancer.

One year had passed since his death and in the meantime, as predicted, Mrs. Burnson had sold her house in Deal, New Jersey, and bought a home in Miami, Florida. When I met her she had been back North only three months, and was already planning to move from an ocean-front apartment in Deal. "Mrs. Wood," she recalled, "told me I would be moving again shortly, which I hadn't intended, but I had a disagreement with the landlord."

Mrs. Burnson had a young person's zest for life. Her oldest son had recently made her a grandmother, but she was still interested in romance.

"Do the circles of three still hold?" I asked.

"Oh, yes," she said with a quick laugh. "Madam Wood mentioned my interest in two men now, and said that after October I would meet a third." She turned to Dorothy Donley. "As I have told Dorothy, Mrs. Wood even described the two men. One was rich—he's the banker from Jersey City—and the other a struggling artist, and he's just opened a dance studio." She laughed just the least self-consciously. "But I wouldn't make up my mind," she said, "until I had met the great unknown."

I thought Claire unusually frank, but she was an obvious extrovert who enjoyed talking about the most fascinating person she knew—herself.

She had several times mentioned her children. "What do they think of all this?" I asked.

Two children were at home with her: eighteen-year-old Lauralee, a lovely model, and a daughter in high school. "Oh, Lauralee kept sneering like everybody else," Claire replied, "but one day I persuaded her to go to Mrs. Wood with me. She had been a little upset over a young man; he was with a marine expedition in the Caribbean, and had just written that he was marrying somebody else in two weeks."

For Lauralee, Mrs. Wood had a promise of romantic redemption. "I see a young man in an island in the South," she said, "and this young young man is thinking of you."

Lauralee grunted under her breath.

Madam Wood regarded the girl kindly. "Even though you are skeptical, my dear, you will soon be hearing from this young man."

Within the month, Lauralee got a call from her former beau. "How's your wife?" she asked. But the wedding had been called off, and he was back courting.

From Mrs. Wood's success, Mrs. Burnson was certain now that life was pretty much a fixed pattern. "How does she know it unless it's already fated?" Her eyes traveled around the veranda, polling each face. "Doesn't everyone agree to that?"

"The prediction about the boy friend was so broad," I said, "that it might have materialized out of sheer chance. Any pretty girl, particularly one seeking out a psychic, could clearly have boyfriend trouble, and that boy friend could easily be in the South escaping the snow and sleet, and recuperating from the breakup himself." I laughed. "At eighteen, girls are always having busted romances, and the boy friends are forever coming back."

Claire looked around the company and shrugged. "All right, so that isn't a very convincing example. How about the forecast of my husband's death within two years?"

"She might have been wrong, too," one of the group said, "and then what?"

"But she wasn't wrong," Claire stressed, "she was right, and she's always been right."

"We'll see after October," I said with a smile. "That's only a few months away."

One of the women laughed. "Now, Claire, we just don't want you getting married to make the prediction come true."

Claire took it good-naturedly. "I'm very grateful to Mrs. Wood," she said, "but not that grateful."

Through virtually all of her friend's recital, Dorothy Donley had remained strangely quiet, nodding only when Claire sought some comfirmation.

A teacher, of practical, old-line American stock, dealing with reality every day, she struck me as a born skeptic.

"Have you been to Mrs. Wood?" I asked.

"No," she said, shaking her head, "I don't go to any of these people."

"Oh," I said, with a glance at Claire, "so you don't believe in it?"

She hesitated, turning to Claire. "You remember Mavis Tomlinson, don't you?" she said.

Claire nodded. "We were all at the Parsons School together."

"We were great friends," Miss Donley went on, "but after Mavis married, she went to Jamaica to live with her English husband. After her first child, she came back to visit her mother in Englewood [New Jersey] and see some of her old friends." She dropped in on Dorothy in New York, leaving the child, then only a few months old, with her mother. "On an impulse," Miss Donley said, "we stopped into one of those fortune-teller parlors." The woman read for Mavis first. "She looked at her closely," Dorothy continued, "and told her that she saw her father; he was reaching out, stretching his arms for Mavis' little boy."

In the blazing heat of a midsummer day, Dorothy Donley shivered ever so slightly. And then she recalled that she had looked quickly at Mavis, but Mavis hadn't seemed at all concerned.

"And why should she have been?" I asked.

Dorothy Donley spoke slowly. "Well, Mavis' father had died only a short time before, and the whole thing was creepy."

I could almost see her mind drifting back through the years. "And then what happened?" I prompted.

Miss Donley stirred herself. "The baby hadn't been feeling well, and two or three weeks later, despite anything anybody could do, it died. Mavis was heartbroken. As for myself, I could never again go near another fortune-teller."

What happened to Claire Burnson thereafter was quite anticlimactic. Almost a year later, when I checked with her, she still had not married again. But her younger daughter, a high school teen-ager, very surprisingly had.

"Had Madam Wood foreseen it?" I asked.

"She saw a disturbance about the household," Claire said, "and then said that my daughter would have a child and be divorced."

The girl, already separated from her teen-aged bridegroom, was an expectant mother.

But how about Claire? "Well, she told me I would change my job in two weeks, and I just did."

I was more interested in the evolution of the marital forecast. "Didn't she say you would meet your third husband in October?" I asked.

She smiled, correcting me. "It was after October that she said, not October. And it could happen at any time now."

I was glad that she was so cheerful and optimistic. With this attitude, the forecast could not but help come true—sometime after October.

10 THE DREAM WORLD

Night after night, plaguing his sleep, a vision of flames had haunted the dreams of Richard Parkinson, Sr. The dreams were so vivid and detailed that when he woke in the morning his pajamas were damp with perspiration, and he would look around nervously to make sure the fire wasn't licking away at his house. But actually his dreams had not concerned a fire in his own home in Huntington, Long Island. He had seen the flames shooting through the home of his young married son, Richard Jr., some two miles away, and he had seen his son, his wife, and their small children trapped in the flames. He wanted to warn his son, but realized the practical-minded young man would only laugh at a dream.

But as his dreams grew stronger and more vivid, his alarm grew, too, and he did everything he could to get his son to find another house.

One Sunday in February, 1962, the younger Parkinsons dropped in for their regular weekly visit with the family. As he had before, only more strenuously this time, the father pleaded with his son to move out of their ramshackle frame house. As a retired builder, he even offered to build him a new house.

But the son only smiled fondly at his father, and shook his head. "We're all right, Dad," he said.

Later that week, on a Thursday, the son stopped by with the oldest of his three children, four-and-a-half-year-old Richard III, who had fallen asleep while his father was plowing snow from the driveway next door. This grandson had been much in the grandfather's dreams. "Let him stay here," he begged, "don't wake him up. I'll take him home tomorrow." The son agreed.

With a sense of foreboding, the grandfather went to bed that night, first looking in on his peacefully slumbering grandson and namesake, to make sure that he was all right. He finally fell off to a troubled sleep. At six o'clock that morning, as he tossed restlessly, the telephone buzzed. "As soon as I heard the phone," the grandfather said, "I knew what had happened."

His son's home was ablaze.

In a few minutes, Parkinson was at the scene.

The whole family—with one exception—was trapped on the second floor of a flaming inferno. Parkinson tried to enter the building but was forcibly restrained. He stood there, sobbing, repeating over and over, "I saw it all, I saw it all. Why didn't I make them move?"

The house was destroyed by flames, just as the grandfather had dreamed. Richard's wife, Victoria, twenty-three, was found dead in the bathroom, a victim of suffocation. Two-year-old Georgia died in her crib, her dog on the floor beside her.

The father had jumped from a second-story window with his son, eleven-month-old Forest, shouting to his wife, "I'll be back."

For days he and the boy hovered near death, critically burned. Only the one grandson, detached from the flames by his grandfather's dreams, was unharmed. "I knew there would be a tragedy," the grandfather mourned, "I had so many dreams showing exactly what would happen."

Could he have done more about it? He shook his head sadly. "There doesn't seem to be much we can do about heading off things. You can warn people, but they seldom listen. I often think that whatever happens, it is God's will, though we may find it hard to understand at the time. I will always feel it was God's will that little Richard should have stayed with us that night."

Since the beginning of time, people have reported dreams of future disasters—and lesser events—but, unfortunately, only in their occurrence do dreams establish themselves as precognitive, and then, obviously, it is too late to do anything about them.

How can the dreamer tell that his dream is a warning and not just a case of overeating before bedtime, or worrying too much about some knotty personal problem? The dreamer, with an apparent precognitive dream, whether it was Abraham Lincoln or a Bronx housewife, invariably reported an overpowering sensation of vividness, distinguishing it from the usual fuzzy dream, and instead of fading during the day, it became even stronger. There was also a compulsion, noted by G. N. M. Tyrrell, of the British psychical research society, that made these dreamers feel they should do something about their dream, by word or action.

We dream, of course, even when we do not remember clearly, and the feeling that we've been there before, dismissed by many psychiatrists as the illusion of *déjà vu*, is being increasingly recognized as prevision from dreams faintly rooted in the subconscious but becoming more familiar as the event itself begins to unfold. If the dream is soon followed by the event it is more than likely that the connection will be remembered. Rudyard Kipling, in *Something About Myself*, tells of the time he attended a war memorial in Westminister Abbey. His view was obstructed by a stout man on his left, so he turned his attention to the rough slab floor, and then suddenly somebody clasped him by the arm, whispering, "I want a word with you." The scene, action, and remark were all familiar—because Kipling had dreamed it all vividly six weeks before.

Years ago, Chauncey Depew, the railroad magnate, relaxing on the porch of his country home on the Hudson River, fell to nodding, and in a matter of moments he had carried himself to the State Republican Convention in Saratoga, New York. In his dream he was introduced by the temporary chairman, a man he did not recognize, and then he saw himself making the nominating speech for Theodore Roosevelt for Governor. To thunderous applause, and a joyous triumphal march, he took his seat. When he awoke, Depew had to look around and pinch himself to make sure he was still on his veranda. His dream had been so realistic that he recalled his nominating speech word for word, and he liked what he remembered so much that he wrote it down. A week later, this was the speech he gave, in nominating Teddy Roosevelt— after being greeted by a temporary chairman he had never seen before outside his dream.

These experiences are not unusual. A student in Professor Ralph

Harlow's class at Smith College, invited to a weekend party, suddenly realized the unfolding scene was from one of her dreams. Introduced to another guest, whom she had never seen before outside her dream, she anticipated exactly what that guest was going to say. "She had a sense of detachment," Harlow recalled, "almost as though she were an innocent, though knowledgeable, bystander."

Originally, psychoanalysts, led by the first great modern interpreter of dreams, Dr. Sigmund Freud, scoffed at the notion that dreams had any sort of message that didn't smack of mother or sex. Freud himself cited the "possibilities of falsifications of memory facilitated by emotional causes and the inevitability of a few lucky shots." But the evidence soon became so overwhelming that the Viennese dream merchant was completely won over. "I am now far from willing," he said, "to repudiate without anything further all these phenomena, concerning which we possess so many minute observations even from men of intellectual prominence."

A whole new study reservoir of dreams has been built up by the psychoanalysts, carefully documented as a matter of therapy, with only an incidental interest in the psychic. A patient with a nervous problem consults a Park Avenue neurologist, and discusses a dream that has given him many a harrowing night; he sees his cousin caught in a dark railroad tunnel in Germany, and before he can turn back, the cousin is run over and killed by an onrushing train. While the doctor is seeking some reflection of the patient's mental condition in this dream, the patient, a month later, gets a letter from his family in Germany. His cousin was killed only the week before by a train as he walked through a tunnel.

However, many precognitive dreams—perhaps the majority— are going unnoticed both by patient and analyst, many experts feel, because, like other dreams, they are often symbolic. "As the ancients knew and as modern psychology has clearly shown, our ordinary dreams are often dressed up in symbols," observed Professor J. Fraser Nicol, the eminent New England researcher, "It would be surprising if the only exceptions to those laws were cases of precognition and telepathy. Yet, according to the current methods of psychical research and the attitude of mind rather guilelessly brought to the investigation of spontaneous phenomena, that is exactly what we profess to believe. Perhaps that is the reason why cases of spontaneous precognition [in dreams] are so hard to find. The fault may lie not with the dreamer but with the investigator."

Symbolism, of course, was no problem for the mystic. Troubled by dreams which frightened without enlightening them, hundreds turned to Edgar Cayce for help.

A dreamer himself, Edgar Cayce had no trouble deciphering dreams. Once, a stockbroker, who was Jewish, came to him with a curious dream. Three weeks before, he had dreamed that he had attended a Catholic funeral, where everybody was having an incongruously gay time. "I was crossing myself as though I were a Catholic and not a Jew, and dancing gaily around the coffin."

The interpretation was rather obvious to the sage of Virginia Beach. The stockbroker was dubious. But years later, marrying a Catholic, he was to change his faith, and, when he died, was buried with the last rites of the Church.

Cayce, in trance, had his own idea of what dreams were made of, indicating that when the mind was in this slumbering state the subconscious was most receptive to telepathic images. Cayce put dreams in three classifications—those brought on by unfortunate combinations of food, fatigue, etc.; visions stemming from continuation of thought containing warnings and premonitions; and superconscious experiences relating to soul development—as the visions of St. Paul or Daniel.

The most intricate dream seemed to present no problem to the dreaming Cayce. Frightful incongruities were explained while he was himself asleep. Invariably, as with the "stock market dream," he would indicate why they had developed and what they foretold. In May of 1927, for instance, a middle-aged Florida realtor, married and with three children, sent Cayce a report of a vivid dream—known as the Spider Dream. Unlike his other dreams, it wouldn't fade away.

It was indeed an unusual dream.

"I was standing in the back yard of my home," the man reported. "I had my coat on. I felt something inside the cloth on the cuff of my left-hand coat sleeve. I worked it out, but it was fastened in the cloth and broke off as it came out, leaving part in. It proved to be a cocoon and where it broke a small black spider came out. The cocoon was black and left a great number of eggs—small ones —on my coat sleeve, which I began to pull off. The spider grew fast and ran away, speaking plain English as it ran, but what it said I do not remember except that it was saying something about its mother. The next time I saw it, it was a large black spider, which I seemed to know was the same one grown up, almost as large as my fist. It had a red spot on it, but was otherwise a deep black. At this time it had gotten into my house and had built a web all the way across the back inside the house and was comfortably watching me. I took a broom, knocked it down and out of the house, thinking I'd killed it, but it did more talking at that time. I remember putting my foot on it, and thought it was dead. The next time I saw it, it had built a long web from the ground on the outside of the house in the back yard, near where I first got it out of my sleeve, and it was running up toward the eave fast when it saw me. I couldn't reach it, but threw my straw hat in front of it and cut the web and the spider fell to the ground, talking again, and that time I hacked it to pieces with my knife."

Scanning the dream myself, my only reaction was one of repulsion and bewilderment. Even Cayce seemed to hesitate when asked to give an "interpretation and a lesson to be gained from this dream." He launched instead into a general discourse on the meaning of dreams. "Dreams are the action of the subconscious forces of the body, manifested through that state when the conscious forces of the physical body are subjugated."

And then with a little more on dreams generally, he began his interpretation. It was a warning, Cayce said, and not a particularly complex one, about a situation as familiar as Adam and Eve.

Cayce's prose rambled, but his meaning was plain. The dream was a warning of the breakup not only of the real-estate man's home, but of his business: "Both the spider and the character of same," Cayce said, "are warnings to the body as respecting the needs of the body taking a definite stand respecting the relations of others who would in this underhanded manner take away from the body those surroundings of the home that are in the manner of being taken—unless such a stand is made."

Then, Cayce got down to the heart of the matter—the other woman. She was associated with the subject in business, though Cayce had no hint of this and did not know the man. "The conditions of the relations of the entity, the body, with another," Cayce said, "are of the nature as is emblematically shown by the relations of this body with this other body; that its relations at first meant only what might be turned to an account of good in a social and financial manner; yet, as has been seen, there has come the constant drain on the entity, not only in the pocket but in the affections of the heart, and now such threaten the very foundations of the home—and threaten to separate the body from the home and its surroundings; and unless the entity [the realtor] attacks this condition, cutting same out of mind, the body, the relations, the condition, will come as seen."

Still in trance, Cayce, the good husband and family man, did his best to keep the threatened marriage together. "Take the warning then," he said. "Meet the condition as a man, not as the weakling—and remember those duties that the body owes to those to whom the sacred vows were given, and to whom the entity and body owes its position in every sense, and to whom the entity should act in the sense of the defender, rather than bringing through such relations those dark, underhanded ways, as said by that one who would undermine. Yet these relations have grown to such extent as may present a menace to the very heart and soul of the body of this entity. Beware! Beware!"

As it developed, the realtor didn't heed the warning. He continued his association with the woman, who had ingratiated herself by helping him financially, got tied up with some shady associates of hers, lost his business, separated from his wife and children, and went broke. After it had all transpired as Cayce had warned, he visited Virginia Beach with his new wife—and former business associate—and stayed on to live, so impressed was he, after the fact, with the Cayce analysis of his dream.

It was difficult obviously for the ordinary layman like myself to perceive the symbolism of the dream. I wondered how a brilliant psychoanalyst would have interpreted the Spider Dream had the realtor come to him. In quest of an answer, I consulted Dr. Joost A. M. Meerloo, Dutch-born psychoanalyst, who was a friend and disciple of dream-expert Freud.

Dr. Meerloo was a short, stocky, good-natured man with a benign look. He smiled tolerantly when I told him I would like him to analyze a dream that had already been interpreted by a mystic. "I would like," I explained, "to see how close he was to a scientifically accepted pattern of dream interpretation."

He shrugged, and with a disclaiming gesture of the hands said, "Of course, I can only give my interpretation."

He listened impassively as I read the Spider Dream itself aloud without reference to Cayce's interpretation, and without even mentioning that it was Cayce who had interpreted it.

When I had finished, the analyst smiled comfortably. "Actually," he said, "it is not a very difficult dream to interpret. The symbolism is quite obvious." He paused. "Here is a man obviously trying to break out of the web. Originally, he wanted to get away from his mother"—ah, I thought, the inevitable mother—"and then this feeling was transferred to the wife. He is determined to break out of the nest. That, of course, is the significance of the web."

I could not help smiling. The uneducated Cayce, in trance, and the scholarly disciple of Freud had arrived at virtually the same conclusion.

"You and Edgar Cayce," I said dryly, "gave the same diagnosis."

He lightly dismissed the comparison. "It was not a difficult interpretation."

But Cayce, in his warning, had virtually indicated that he knew his warning would not be followed. The two "Bewares" were quite eloquent, even after thirty years. No psychoanalyst could have ventured so far.

Symbolism in dreams, of course, was as old as antiquity, as Professor Nicol had pointed out. Calpurnia had tried to keep Julius Caesar from going to his death at the Senate House, having dreamed that she saw the gable, suggestive of his position as Chief of State, fall from their house. Also, more aptly perhaps, she saw him lying bleeding in her arms.

The Biblical dream of Joseph is well known. Flung into a dungeon, he interpreted the dreams of Pharaoh's butler and baker, correctly telling one that he would be freed in three days, and the other that he would be hanged. Summoned by Pharaoh himself, he explained that the seven fat kine swallowed in Pharaoh's dream by seven lean kine meant that seven years of famine would follow seven of plenty. In this instance, the dream, with Joseph's help, had apparently done some good.

But, of course, this is only a Bible story, and few psychic researchers—or laymen—take it literally.

Richard Parkinson, Sr., thought it God's will that he should have a dream that spared his grandson. Others have contended equally eloquently that warning dreams, if heeded, will avert disaster. Dr. Ian Stevenson, head of neurology at the University of Virginia Medical School, has reported that a dream, remembered in time, apparently decisively altered an event. In September 1958, as reported by Stevenson in the *Journal of the American Society for Psychical Research*, Mrs. Roger H. Fellom of New Orleans, dreamed her twenty-month-old daughter Vivian was sitting on the window sill of their home, dangling her legs. Suddenly the child started to lose her balance and was about to fall. The mother awakened in a terrible fright and rushed into the child's room. She was sleeping peacefully.

The dream stayed with Mrs. Fellom. Three weeks later, missing the child, thinking of her dream, she again rushed into her room. "And there she [the child] was in exactly the same position as I had seen her in my dream." She caught her up and lifted her to safety. She was grateful for the dream. "Without its warning, Vivian's journey would have ended in disaster."

The dream world is boundless. When asleep, the individual is always dreaming, some authorities say, and the dream world may have many pointers for him if he can only understand his dreams.

Apparently it is not difficult to cultivate dreams, with a disciplined effort. Instructions from one expert close to Edgar Cayce are elementary. "Place a pad and pencil within arm's reach of your bed," he suggested. "Immediately upon awakening pick up the pencil and put down the fragments of the dreams." For the first few days, he advised, these records may be sketchy and incomplete. "There may be days when the individual cannot remember a single shred of a dream experience." But the force of suggestion can be helpful. "As the individual is about to fall asleep," the authority said, "he should repeat to himself several times: 'I will remember my dreams.'" But pencil and pad must be within reach. "Only this act of expectancy," he said, "repeated day after day, will convince the subconscious. Gradually, memory of dreams will increase, until there is a regular, constant flow of thoughts and mental images." These can be studied and sorted out later. "Within a few weeks," he declared, "the dreamer will have a journal of dream experiences that can be used to his own advantage."

But the professionals, listening to countless dream experiences every day, are opening a broad new vista for the scientific researcher. As Dr. Jule Eisenbud of Denver has pointed out, the parapsychology and psychoanalysis files are bulging with prophetic dream evidence of train wrecks, plane crashes, fires, and other catastrophes. Eisenbud himself, in contemplating patients' dreams, has been primarily concerned with the "psychoanalytic dynamics" of the dream, as he puts it. Still, increasingly, the precognitive aspects of some of these dreams have stared him provocatively in the face, demanding to be investigated. In fact, Eisenbud, intrigued by the precognitive material, has conducted experiments of his own. And one of the most dramatic cases in his file evolved out of his own curiosity.

This particular dream occurred during the night of April 28, 1944, when Eisenbud was practicing in New York City. In this dream, one of his patients, who was having trouble with his own family in real life, saw himself arguing with his mother-in-law, who, with the incongruity typical of dreams, was trying to persuade him not to go swimming. The next thing he knew he found himself in bathing trunks and a robe in the lobby of a hotel that was either the Pennsylvania or the Wellington in New York. He took an elevator to the top floor and was then let out into a service hall.

The patient, as Eisenbud described it in the *Psychoanalytic Quarterly*, awakened at seven-thirty in the morning, startled by his unusual dream. His family had lived at the Wellington, so there was some association there, but there was no accounting for the Pennsylvania.

At ten that morning, visiting Eisenbud in his New York office, the patient reported his dream. Meanwhile, without his knowing it, one hour after he had wakened, at 8:30 A.M., there had been an explosion on the top floor of the Pennsylvania (now the Statler Hilton Hotel) when a drum of cleaning fluid blew up. Cascades of water under heavy pressure came tumbling down the stairs into the lobby, which was soon flooded with five inches of water. The blast had burst a water main.

There had been no reports of an explosion over the radio, and the news did not reach any of the newspapers until the afternoon editions. Indeed, news photographers did not arrive on the scene until eleven in the morning, an hour or so after the psychiatrist had listened to his patient's dream.

The New York *Times*, Eisenbud pointed out, carried a picture of the flooded hotel lobby, and a large clock in the picture showed the time to be 11:05 A.M.

The newspaper accounts were particularly striking in view of the "swimming" phase of the dream. One young group of hotel guests seemed to find the flood particularly amusing, shaking hands with the hotel employees and imitating their favorite strokes. They were the Cornell University swimming team.

What made the incident especially interesting to the doctor was that he had tried an unusual experiment in precognition on the very night of the patient's dream. While the patient was home, Eisenbud worked in his office with a trained hypnotic subject, trying to plant the suggestion that he anticipate headlines in the New York *Times* two days hence. "I suggested to the subject in deep hypnosis," Dr. Eisenbud recalled, "that our concept of time was artificial and that he could just as easily go forward as backward, if he wanted to."

The doctor had never conducted an experiment of this nature before and consequently was not disappointed when the hypnotic subject could not see anything. Yet he was apparently to get what he sought from an unlooked-for quarter. "But two days later I was confronted with data that strongly suggested the possibility that my patient had hijacked the task given my subject." To the doctor, not only was this an amazing development in itself but, if true, it reflected the importance of motivation in hypnotic suggestion—and in precognition. The hypnotic subject had no motivation, except perhaps his fee, while the patient, emotionally identified with his analyst, had perhaps picked up the signal telepathically in an unconscious effort to please his mentor. At any rate, this was a working theory. "I had given my experiment subject an impossible task for him," the doctor said. "He had failed. But my patient, looking for reassurance from me, had said in effect, 'I can succeed where your subject has failed. You want headlines two days from now. I'll give them to you, but give me the encouragement I need to go ahead and do what I want.'"

There was a good deal of apparent symbolism about the dream. The mother-in-law's own son, pursuing his career against the wishes of his family, as the patient had, had suffered a fatal tumor of the brain—developing, so to speak, an explosion on the top floor. "The patient, in similar circumstances," Eisenbud concluded, "was apparently fearful of a similar explosion."

Obviously, as a psychoanalyst, Eisenbud was more concerned about the psychological aspects of the dream, but even so, if there was a precognitive aspect, it had little to do with the patient's own future, applying to a flooded lobby in which he had no interest. The simple hypnotic suggestion given one man, that he was holding in his hands a copy of the New York *Times* two days hence, may incredibly have worked on another man. There seemed no other explanation, except coincidence.

The dreams of another Eisenbud patient presented a somewhat clearer case of precognition. Twice she foretold plane crashes. In one dream, the patient, a young woman, had heard that a plane out of New England, which a vacationing roommate was taking to join her fiancé, had crashed, and the roommate had been killed. "The plane that the roommate took the next day did not crash, but a later one, out of the same airport, did, with a heavy loss of life," Eisenbud reported.

The actual crash, as Eisenbud figured it, was precognitive. But the introduction of the roommate onto the plane was the result of a death wish arising out of jealousy, and so the dream got mixed up in symbolism. "There was little question of the girl's destructive, though unconscious, wish against her roommate, based not only on the fact that Nora got the man," Eisenbud said, "but that she was leaving her to go to him."

A year later, now 1955, Ethel, the patient, had another dream. Nora had married months before, and the remaining roommate was dating a young man seriously. Ethel appeared to be taking the situation well. The roommate, Polly, had gone East on vacation, and three days before her expected return her young man invited Ethel to a concert. She thought it a mere friendly gesture and accepted. "But as the evening wore on," the doctor noted, "the young man became open in his advances toward the patient. She became annoyed, and dismissed him curtly at the door."

That night, troubled, she had her second airplane dream. "At an airport, I was standing by myself watching a big plane I was supposed to take somewhere. People were getting off at two exits, one at the front, one at the rear. I thought to myself that the plane looked bigger than any I had ever been on before, sort of like the one my sister had taken to Europe. I saw TWA in big letters. I felt a sense of danger and had a premonition that the plane was going to have an accident, but kept telling myself that I'd been scared before and nothing awful had happened. I couldn't decide whether to get on or not."

The patient was up at seven-fifteen that morning, getting herself ready to leave for work. She turned on the radio for the news at seven-thirty, when an announcer broke in suddenly with a special bulletin: An airliner had just crashed with a heavy loss of life. The crash had occurred at 7:10 A.M., when the liner collided with a private plane two minutes after taking off from the Cincinnati airport. Even before his announcement, the patient knew the name of the airline. It was TWA. "Oh no, not again," she cried.

To many it has become evident that fear, tension, and neuroses, the gristmill of the analyst, tend to bring on prophetic dreams. So many patients are so fear-ridden about the past, one psychiatrist suggests, that they strive to concentrate on the future rather than the past, and this may lead to precognition. It seems highly conjectural.

Dr. J. H. Rush of Boulder, Colorado, has pointed out that a single dream may weave together its material from the subject's own recollected experience "and from the past and the future" of which he has no conscious knowledge. Hence, it does not surprise some that a single dream is often a combination of events, past or future.

In this connection, Dr. Jan Ehrenwald, well-known psychiatrist and psychic researcher, tells of a thirty-eight-year-old floorwalker for a department store who suffered from an anxiety hysteria whenever he got in crowds—in buses, subways, movies, restaurants. To the psychiatrist, this hysteria was an obvious defense mechanism against homosexuality, and by no means unusual. After months of psychotherapy, the patient reported a dream apparently springing out of his latent fears. In this dream, a rough-looking man came into the store and began opening and closing a large pocketknife. There was something menacing about the action and the dreamer felt alarmed. He hurried off to fetch help. Suddenly this dream situation dissolved, and he was sitting next to the same man, and they were conversing in friendly fashion. He took out a knife and flipped it open, but it was no longer a large blade; it was only an inch long, and he felt reassured.

The phallic symbolism of a knife in a homosexual situation was, of course, obvious to the psychiatrist.

The original dream had occurred on November 5, 1947. Two days later, the patient sat down in a bus, Dr. Ehrenwald recalled, and alongside him was a man who suddenly pulled out a knife with a small blade and began peeling an apple with it. He was not afraid of the man and talked to him pleasantly.

On November 16, nine days later, the remaining portion of the dream seemed to come together. A wild-eyed man, dressed like a tramp, came into the store, walked up to the cutlery counter, and as the floorwalker watched him uneasily, he balefully returned his glance and raised a knife across his throat in a menacing gesture. Frightened, the floorwalker ran to call police. When he returned, the man was gone but the counter girl was visibly shaken. Before leaving, the stranger had muttered: "When that guy bothers me, I will cut his throat open."

This was enough to send the floorwalker back to his psychiatrist. By putting the two events together, and reversing their order, Dr. Ehrenwald was able to recognize virtual fulfillment of the dream. "In this way," he said, "we see the patient alarmed by the brandishing of a large knife in the store, and then as on the bus he sat alongside somebody and discovered that the knife was smaller and meant him no harm."

He had apparently not only foreseen the future, but allayed his fears of homosexuality.

To a cautious observer like Ehrenwald, this dream is only suggestive of precognition. "But it offers enough, together with other precognitive dreams and visions," he declared, "to indicate that we should try to study events from a new frame of reference from which time, space, and causality have been removed."

Like Jeane Dixon, many dreamers have reported seeing numbers that had no significance for them after they wakened. On November 9, 1947, Archibald Jarman, an appraiser for an English real estate concern, had an unusual dream, which he considered prophetic because it stayed with him. Jarman took the unusual scientific precaution of writing down the dream and telling a person of substance about it. His dream, as he wrote it down and narrated it to M. B. Campbell, director of a large contracting firm in a London suburb, was fundamentally this:

The dreamer, Jarman, found himself in his dream standing between the sea and a grassy race track that spun off into infinity. Scattered over the sandy beach and the green track was a great throng, all intently gazing down at the track.

In the distance he saw tiny dark pinpoints, which he realized were the horses beating down on the track in a spirited race. Soon he could distinguish the silks of the horses, and then, as they neared the crowd, all but one veered off and galloped toward the sea. As the one horse passed, incongruously ridden by a man wearing a business suit, the big crowd cheered, and four numbers were posted on an enormous long white board, similar to a tote board. The numerals, consecutively, were 2-0-2-0.

In his dream, Jarmen sensed the horse had won the race, and it was a popular victory. He shared in this general elation, and it was with a feeling of satisfaction that he awakened and began rubbing his eyes. He had had dreams that he considered precognitive before, and they had left him with the same vivid impression of reality. Ten minutes after he woke up, twenty minutes, and an hour later, his mind still dwelt on the race. He told Campbell about it in the course of making a business call, he knew nothing about the races, having never seen a race or made a bet. Campbell didn't know much more, but together they pored over the London *Daily Telegraph*, checking on the racing program at Leicester, a nearby track. In his unfamiliarity with racing parlance, Jarman first thought it possible that the four numerals suggested the recent efforts of the horse—two second place finishes and two out of the money. The two men then tried putting the numerals together and came up with 20-20 or Twenty-Twenty but this didn't apply to age, weight, or any other statistic they could think of.

As the day wore on, Jarman put the dream out of his mind. But in the evening, he bought his customary *Evening News* on the way home, glanced at the headlines, then the late news. Suddenly, he saw something that gave him a start. At the top of the Late column was the result of the 3:45 post-time race at Leicester. It had been won by a horse with the improbable name of Twenty-Twenty, with world-famed jockey Gordon Richards aboard. It was a flat race, the Stoughton Plate, and Twenty-Twenty paid a good price, this being only the second race the bay gelding had won in a long career.

Jarman felt depressed by the turn of events. In going over the racing program with Campbell, he had turned his attention exclusively to the figures and ratings, not thinking the names of the entries could possibly be relevant. He had achieved the horseplayer's Valhalla, a winning long shot in a dream, and he had bungled it. "Although I don't approve of betting," Jarman said forlornly, "had I seen that name in the entries I would have risked a handsome wager."

Campbell, intrigued by Twenty-Twenty's victory, signed a state-

ment confirming that Jarman had told him of his 20-20 dream
the night before. "We had not considered the names of the
runners," he testified ruefully, "when trying to allocate the figure
2-0-2-0."

11   FORD, FODOR, AND SURVIVAL

While investigating the late Edgar Cayce, I heard the perfectly
astonishing report that a lovely Princess, well known to Americans,
had predicted the Allied invasion of the Suez two months before
it occurred. And even more amazing, she had reportedly received
her information from the mystic Cayce, who had died more than
ten years before.

Despite the bizarreness of the report, there had been a reliable
eyewitness to the proceedings, a prominent American who was
visiting the royal palace when Cayce's spirit dropped in after
dinner.

Since Eisenhower and the State Department, as I recalled, had
been caught napping by the Franco-British maneuver when it happened, it seemed rather intriguing that the Princess should have
known about it even before it happened.

Having had a mild acquaintance with the Princess before she
became a princess, I wrote inquiring about the incident. "As it
happened," she wrote back, "we were three people sitting around a
small table. I had just finished reading the biography of Edgar
Cayce entitled *There is a River*. I was very familiar with his life
and work. It was for that reason that we tried to call him one night
in August of 1956. The book was placed under the table as we
began the seance. Two of us were very aware of a peculiar odor
in the room. The seance began and after a while we were led to
believe that we had contacted Edgar Cayce. We asked many ques-

tions regarding the world situation and were given answers that amounted to the fact that there would be an armed dispute over Suez with England and France taking part, but without the participation of the United States. There were a few other minor questions asked to which we were given answers that later developed to be true. The seance lasted about two hours. Mr. Cayce seemed reluctant to leave us, but we said we would try to contact him another time, which we did two nights later."

They thought no more of the message until the invasion occurred—weeks later in the last days of October. More impressed than she may have cared to admit, the Princess decided to stop invoking spirits, Cayce's or anybody else's. "I would like to say that in recent years I no longer participate in seances, as I feel very strongly that it is tampering with a world and with powers that we know little about, and thus can become very dangerous. For this reason, I would appreciate that you not use my name."

Like the Princess, I had been at seances, but I had not been terribly impressed. I had also been at seances where Cayce ostensibly came through, but curiously his predictions or advice invariably concerned the topics under discussion earlier that same evening. I had been further disillusioned when I observed a medium apparently in rapt communication with the spirits sneak a look at his watch. In the midst of all these wonders, he wondered what time it was.

Nevertheless, I have ample evidence where psychics claiming a spirit source have made remarkable predictions, regardless of how they did it. In upstate New York, a spiritualist, consulting the dead father of Taylor Caldwell, then an unknown and frustrated writer, predicted the precise date that a rejected manuscript of hers would be published, and forecast, minutely, the successes to follow.

Invoking similar spirits in the California home of actress Mae West, spiritualist Thomas Jack Kelly of Buffalo, New York, forecast the bombing of Pearl Harbor by the Japanese almost to the week, foresaw the length of the war, and predicted the death of President Roosevelt in a fourth term, though he was then only beginning his third.

In another seance, Melvin L. Sutley, a Philadelphia hospital administrator, was "greeted" by his wife, who had supposedly come through to influence the sitting, and then, for the first time, heard the names of two of her infant sisters; one he had never even known of before.

Touring the country with his communications from the dead, medium Arthur Ford predicted to a skeptical newspaperwoman that a missing federal judge from her home town would turn up a drowning victim—and he quoted the judge, who was only later revealed to be dead.

But while many of the spiritualists have been able to convince the deceased's relatives and friends of the authenticity of these messages, they have not had similar luck with the research scientists. Even granting the validity of the prediction, some say, the spiritualist or medium only thinks he's getting his information from an outside source. "In reality," observed Dr. Nandor Fodor, friend of Freud and author of *The Haunted Mind*, "it's a dramatization of their own subconscious."

Regardless of its source, the doctor believed in precognition because he had seen it work. "Just before the outbreak of the war," he said, "my wife and I were planning to buy a house in London, but a clairvoyant friend of ours had a premonition of disaster the moment he stepped into the house. In the German air blitz a year or so later the house suffered a direct hit, and everyone in it was killed."

The psychic could see ahead, the doctor thought, because his mind is in tune with actual time—a sort of continuous and co-existing past, present, and future, which the psychic observes much as a flier looks down and sees all the bends and twists of a river.

There was some evidence for Fodor's dramatization of the subconscious. The English researcher, Dr. Samuel Soal, had once reported a medium, Mrs. Blanche Cooper, picking up the spirit of an old acquaintance, a Gordon Davis, whom Soal had not seen or thought of in years. "Spirit" Davis, in renewing acquaintanceship, had talked about nothing more important than his old house at Southend, giving a detailed description of it. Soal was reasonably impressed by the unlikely name plucked out of thin air by the medium, but three years later he learned that Gordon Davis was very much alive. To confound things further, Davis, subsequent to the seance, had taken a house in Southend, corresponding in every detail with the one described by the medium years before. There was one intriguing explanation for it all. "Perhaps," one observer noted, "the medium was being precognitive without knowing it, and had anticipated Davis' death while living in this house."

Some researchers have tried to explain away the psychic as a purely physical process, completely eliminating any spiritual considerations. "I have seen photographs of mediums at work," said Henry Belk, founder of the Belk Psychic Research Foundation, "where rods of light not discernible to the naked eye have extended from their solar plexus across the room."

But Dr. Hans Bender of the University of Freiburg, Europe's renowned psychic researcher, to whom Belk was making his point, only murmured politely: "Even so, how would that explain people predicting in curious detail events that will not occur for weeks, months, even years?"

"It might be explained," Belk had said, "by some form of creative energy produced by the mind."

"Within small distances," the Professor said, "I could conceive of a magnetic force influencing some events, but not the larger distances." He smiled serenely. "There is something else." He turned to me. "Have you heard about the Russian experiments behind the Iron Curtain?"

I shook my head. "In their Leningrad laboratories," Bender continued, "the Russians have been making tests with cards similar to those used by Rhine at Duke and Soal in London."

"I have heard of those experiments," Belk said.

"But did you know," the Professor said, "that by using a Faraday shutoff cage, which eliminates the possibility of magnetic waves affecting the transfer of thought impulses, they have also eliminated the possibility of physical causation?"

"But all this has nothing to do with precognition," I said. "Merely telepathy and mind reading."

His face became strangely solemn. "In Russia," he said, "my colleagues are not permitted to investigate precognition."

"And why not?" I asked.

"Because if they confirm it, they must then try to account for it." The Professor looked significantly heavenward. "If events can be predicted before they occur, it may mean they already have their niche in the universe, and if there is such an order, atheistic Russia might not want to explain how that order got there."

Many skeptics have wondered why, if they go to all the trouble to come back, the spirits should confine themselves to inconsequential messages. But many messages, precognitive and otherwise, have been of major import to the people receiving them, dealing not only with intensely personal problems but with the great issues of the day. They have not been exclusively received, either, by wishful thinkers, or dolts, but have made many new believers. In January 1938, the English-born novelist Taylor Caldwell chanced into a spiritualist demonstration one night and had an experience that not only cast her out of the throes of depression, but revamped her thinking for the rest of her life. The future looked bleak for author Caldwell then. She had recently finished up a thousand-page manuscript that a New York publisher had tentatively agreed to publish and then had rejected. She saw the work of years going up the flue. On the trip back from New York, her husband, Marcus Reback, a Government worker, had vainly tried to comfort her. She was inconsolable. And he, privately, felt no better. Back in their Buffalo home, a day or two later, they were walking past the city's Statler Hotel, when they saw an announcement of a spiritualist meeting inside. On the spur of the moment they decided to go in. The crowd was so thick they had to push their way through to the hall and then only standing room was available. Suddenly, however, as though by magic, two seats were made for them. "I saw two people in front getting up," Reback recalled, "and I rushed with my wife down the aisle. We sat down just as the demonstration began."

They had never before seen or heard of the spiritualist, Dr. Charles Nicholson of England, and the spiritualist did not know the obscure struggling writer and her equally obscure husband.

The couple sat there tensely, waiting for the demonstration to begin, half-wondering why they had come, congratulating themselves that nobody in the assemblage recognized them. On the platform, listening intently, Nicholson appeared to be getting a few tentative messages. Suddenly, he stood stock-still, and looked out over the audience. "I get a message from an Arthur," he announced. His eyes ranged over the front rows. "Has anybody here a father named Arthur?"

Miss Caldwell raised a timorous hand. "My father's name was Arthur," she said.

The Englishman regarded her with interest, struck by the English accent in an upstate New York community. "Your father," he said, "is trying to tell you not to be discouraged. He knows you have just had a bitter disappointment, but he wants you to know that the manuscript you have written"—this was the first mention of a manuscript—"will be published, and it will be quite successful."

The Rebacks were now on the edge of their seats, listening intently. Nicholson, looking directly at Taylor Caldwell, continued: "Your father wants you to know the manuscript will be sold on April 2 of this year to another publisher, and"—he paused dramatically—"it will become a great success, and establish you as a writer."

There was still more. "A year from now, after the book has been published and is successful, you will be in California, working on a motion picture version of the book."

Spiritual communication, subconscious dramatization, or what, it all turned out as medium Nicholson had said. "On April 2," Reback told me, as his wife nodded agreement, "we signed a contract with Scribner's to publish my wife's novel, *The Dynasty of Death*. It became an instant best seller around the world, and a year later we were in Hollywood working on the movie."

There are, of course, phony mediums who do not even try to convince themselves that they are communing with the spirits. Actress Mae West, experimenting with spiritualism in the hope that it would give her a key to the riddle of life, had about lost faith in the spirits when she met the Reverend Thomas Jack

Kelly, Welsh-born head of Buffalo's nondenominational Universalist Church. Knowing she was a conspicuous target for phonies of all sorts, the actress had sent a business associate, James A. Timony, to observe Kelly when he demonstrated one night in a Los Angeles hall.

Timony was with a friend, Joe Stanley, an ex-fighter, when Kelly, blindfolded, turned toward them and said:

"I get the name of S——." He rattled off a long, unpronounceable Polish name. Stanley, whom Timony had thought to be Italian, went pale, and his hand trembled. "That's my real name, my family name," he whispered hoarsely.

Kelly was now ready with the message. "The father of this man," he said, "is here with information for his son. He wants him to know that he was killed, and his body thrown into the water. It was not an accident."

The effect on Joe was remarkable. The blood drained from his face and he started to perspire. He turned to Timony and observed that his father's body had indeed been found in the water, but the family had always thought he had drowned naturally.

Timony was impressed, and so was Miss West when she got his report.

Kelly was summoned to the performer's home in Santa Monica for a seance. Many others were there, friends and relatives. Kelly asked to be blindfolded, as he preferred to work this way, both to block out extraneous impressions and to lessen the suspicion of trickery. His spirits were not long in tuning in. Kelly himself spoke quietly, but with great resonance, as the messages seemed to come from every part of the big room. He was responsive to questions, encouraging the members of the group to ask anything they liked. Since the time was October 1941, the war was very much in everyone's thoughts and Miss West spoke for the majority when she inquired: "Will we get into the war?"

Kelly hesitated only a moment, as though listening to a buzzing in his ear, and then replied crisply:

"There will be a surprise attack on Honolulu within three months by Japan."

There was a slight rustle in the room, nothing more. It seemed a ridiculously provocative statement, designed to capture the attention of the moment.

The next question was:

"How long will the war last?"

"From five to six years."

It was hard for anyone to conceive at that time how beleaguered England would hold out that long. And then Kelly calmly added, without being asked:

"President Roosevelt will not live out his fourth term."

He had impressed at least one person—Mae West. The blonde actress, more renowned for worldly than unworldly attributes, found herself yielding to the Welshman's cool confidence. "Will we win the war if we get into it?" she asked.

The spiritualist held his head to one side, as though better to hear the voices that supposedly hovered around him. "Yes," he said finally, "America and England together will win the war."

In a few weeks, Japanese bombs over Pearl Harbor had made Kelly a man of destiny in the Mae West household. The performer whose throaty "Come up and see me sometime" had become an American byword, considered his performance far more suggestive than any of hers, though on an entirely different level. "The assertion by Reverend Kelly that President Roosevelt would not live out his fourth term had a double impact," she observed to me, "because at that time there had been no indication that F.D.R. would even seek a fourth term."

She consulted Kelly repeatedly and remained impressed. "He used absolutely no gimmicks," she said, "no gadgets, and no assistants." As a theatrical expert herself, she had studied his technique. "Sometimes he would say before beginning, 'If you hear any voices or whisperings around me, pay no attention to them.'"

She had many talks with spiritualist Kelly about his spiritual pipeline and his belief in survival. "Whisperings are often heard about his head when he is demonstrating extrasensory perception," she said, "and he has told me that the voices are the source of his information." And having studied him for many intent hours, she was able to state flatly: "And he is definitely not a ventriloquist. The source had to come from outside the room."

Blindfolds didn't seem to obscure Kelly's vision, mentally or otherwise. "With six brand-new linen handkerchiefs tightly folded around his eyes," Miss West said, "the Reverend Kelly could answer questions in sealed envelopes without opening them, and then crumple up the envelopes and unerringly throw them into a wastebasket five or six feet away."

The West-Kelly association has continued happily for more than twenty years, and she would often show him off to confound the unbelievers. "In 1945," she related, "while I was in Chicago with my play *Catherine Was Great,* I brought Reverend Kelly from Buffalo; and before a select crowd of judges, police officials, a state's attorney, and their wives, Kelly solved three murder cases to the amazement, satisfaction, and appreciation of the law-enforcement officials there."

But the Wests were to have more direct evidence of the Reverend Kelly's remarkable powers. After Mae's sister, Beverly, had been briefly visited by a stranger indentifying himself as a friend of her parents in Brooklyn, the Los Angeles police came looking for the man. They said he was wanted by police back East for killing his wife. All poor Beverly could do was tell the detectives that he had been there and left.

Distressed by this innocent involvement, Mae West decided to ask Kelly if he knew where the fugitive could be found. "Do you mind if I call a friend in Buffalo?" she said to detectives. "He might be able to help us."

The detectives shrugged, and Miss West picked up the phone and put through a long-distance call to her spiritualist adviser. As Kelly came to the phone, she started to explain why she was calling. But Kelly quickly interrupted, "The man the police are looking for was arrested twenty minutes ago."

Limply hanging up the receiver, Miss West turned weakly to the detectives and repeated what Kelly had said. "He says we can stop looking."

Shrugging again, a detective called police headquarters. As he stood there coolly, waiting for a report, a curious expression of disbelief, and then wonder, stole over his face. Slowly, he returned the phone to its cradle. "They say our man was arrested in San Diego a half hour ago; it just came in."

Mae West had felt an irresistible impulse to call Kelly that day, and put it down to the power of mental suggestion. Some eighteen months after the death of his doctor wife, Melvin L. Sutley, president of the American College of Hospital Administration and retired head of Philadelphia's Eye and Ear Hospital, reported a similar force of suggestion. He had been home reading, his mind wandering absently over the pages, when the thought suddenly struck him that he should try to contact his wife, Margaret. Before her death, they had talked speculatively about life after death, without, of course, coming to any conclusion. The impulse to reach her became overwhelming. He knew of no mediums, but remembered that a nurse at Women's Hospital in Philadelphia, where his wife had been a surgeon, had frequently invited them to seances.

He did not recall the nurse's name, but calling the hospital, was told it was "Miss Hoffman." That night he telephoned her. "Miss Hoffman," he said, "this is Melvin Sutley, I trust you remember me."

"Of course, Mr. Sutley," she replied, "I've been expecting your call." And then she elaborated. "Your wife has been coming through to us, and she told a few of us at a seance the other night that she was trying to impress upon you to call me. She asked that I not call you, even though she wanted us to get together, since she wanted you to have a sign."

A seance was quickly arranged. As Sutley sat rather rigidly, not knowing what to expect next, the amateur medium, a hairdresser named Catherine Shive, reported a message from his father's side of the family. "It comes through as Wils," she said, "so I suppose it's Wilson." With a bit of a tingle up his spine, Sutley recalled that his father's brother, dead for thirty-five years, bore this unusual first name.

The medium's face grew a little more intent now. Important messages seemed in the air, perhaps even the one Sutley was waiting for. "Your wife Margaret is here," the medium said, "she is with her two sisters who died in infancy before she was born.

Their names are Laura and Perley. They also send greetings."

This was about all there was. But Sutley was greatly stirred. He remembered vaguely his wife having one sister who had died in infancy, but she had never mentioned her name. He began to inquire about the sisters, writing to the only living member of her family, Mrs. Mary Charlesworth, in Oklahoma. The reply soon came back. "There had been only one child," Sutley said, "and the name was Perley. She had died at the age of three months."

That seemed to settle the matter. But then his wife's former secretary, with whom he had discussed the matter, suggested that he check the urn in which his father-in-law's ashes had been placed after his cremation many years before. Sutley had never seen the urn. Sent on from Boulder, Colorado, where the father had died, it had reposed since in a Philadelphia mortuary. "The thought of the ashes had been distasteful to me," Sutley said, "and I never even had the package unwrapped."

Sutley had it unpacked. It was in the form of a bronze book. Inside, engraved on a flyleaf, were the names of his wife's family, beginning with her parents. Then he saw his wife's name, with only the date of birth, since she had died after the father. And Perley—"died at three months," and then still another name caught his eye: "Laura—died at birth."

As a practical man, Sutley realized that the name Laura might have been invoked by the medium's subconscious. But how had it gotten there? "As far as I could determine," Sutley said, "the only living person who could have known that name would be the engraver in Colorado: he had filled in the information years before, and he was probably dead too after all this time."

The "dead" were often more loquacious—and psychic—than the living. The eighteenth-century mystic, Emanuel Swedenborg, who apparently could describe mundane events at a distance as though hovering over them, once confided that he had talked with the dead and they had told him that they lived pleasantly in a vast world of planets that were as mighty cities compared to the earth villages they had left. Swedenborg got an audience because once, surrounded by many witnesses, he had described, as it was going on, a terrible fire in Stockholm, three hundred miles away, announcing finally—and correctly—with a sigh of relief that it had been conquered three doors from his own house. He also forecast his own death to the day in advising the ecclesiast Charles Wesley that he would not be able to meet him after Wesley had finished a tour.

Introduced into everyday affairs, the spirit element can be disconcerting to nonbelievers. When his son disappeared mysteriously, a Long Island businessman consulted a medium to learn whether the youth was dead or alive. After some concentration, the medium advised: "Your son is in spirit."

The youth had committed suicide by throwing himself off a bridge but he did not want his father to fret. He was happy about things just as they were. Knowing his son's interest in the stock market while alive, the father decided to put the medium to a test. Each visit, he would ask searching questions about the market, and soon his son was telling him what he should buy and sell. Following the medium's advice, he had spectacular success. Everything he bought went up, everything he sold, down. His broker, curious, said one day, "You must be getting good information."

The businessman nodded casually.

"Any special market service?"

The businessman shook his head.

But the broker persisted. "What have you been using?"

"My son has been helping me," the businessman responded.

The broker expressed surprise. "Oh, I didn't know you had a son; is he in the Army?"

"Oh, no," the businessman said pleasantly, "he's dead."

Many spirit stories were truly out of this world. Told of a woman picking up a phone, to warn of a suicide in Brooklyn, my only response was, "Who paid for the call?" But there have been even more curious cases. Mrs. Claire Blauvelt, a New York society woman, widow of millionaire sportsman Hiram Demarest Blauvelt, reported a singular message from her dead husband, which a psychic already had predicted. "In October of 1960," Mrs. Blauvelt related, "shortly before the third anniversary of my husband's death, I went to Carolyn Chapman, the sensitive, whom I had seen many times before. She knew I had been recently seeing a certain man and that we were planning to be married." Yet, the psychic told her, "You are not going to marry that man. But your husband does have a message as to what you are going to do. On October 16, the anniversary of his death, if you look at your wedding picture, you will see that message plainly written there."

Even for Mrs. Blauvelt, who had come to believe in the psychic over the years, this was too much. She put the message out of her head the moment she left Mrs. Chapman's studio near Manhattan's Gramercy Park. But a week later, on October 16, which was also her husband's birthday, she was in her bathroom applying the finishing touches to her make-up when she heard a pinging noise, and saw spangles floating across her vision. Suddenly, she recalled the prediction about the writing on the picture. She hurried into the bedroom, where the full-length wedding picture hung, and there, she said, as though etched by a dull knife, she saw a message in her late husband's familiar, slanted handwriting. "The words were on the trouser leg in the picture," she said, "and they seemed to be fading, but I could make out the initials of the man I was going with—'Love-Wife-November.'"

In all fairness to herself, Mrs. Blauvelt did wonder whether she was having a hallucination, until the following month, November, when the man she was to marry announced he loved somebody else and was going to marry her directly. "I guess," Mrs. Blauvelt said wryly, "that made her a wife."

She has often thought about the experience. "I know a lot of people will say I was seeing things," said this darkly attractive matron, "and I was, but it was as real as anything that ever happened to me." She laughed. "And even if I only saw it in my mind, which I doubt, who put it there?"

Every spiritualist, like a good performer, has her own way of doing things, and the Reverend Mary Reva Wood of Long Branch, New Jersey was no exception. The spirits swirled around Mrs. Wood's head and spoke to her from every corner of the room. She had become a spiritualist reluctantly, after the death of her daughter, Josephine. Her mother, who had been psychic, had often urged her to put her own psychic gift to work. And Mrs.

Wood had observed with a grimace that the field was so full of peculiar people, that it seemed no place for her. Her mother replied, "If you are thirsty on the desert, you will drink out of even a rusty cup."

She lived with her husband in a large corner house, in a tree-shaded pleasant little town that had been the summer refuge for presidents and their families. Hearing of several experiences, I had decided to visit the Church of Psychic Science myself. A stockbroker friend, who had driven my wife and myself from his nearby home to the church, had agreed to come in with us since there was no place else to wait.

We proceeded downstairs into a small chapel, where a red light gave off a rather eerie glow. There were a few bare wooden seats facing an altar. The Reverend Wood, a small, plump woman with a tired haggard face and sorrowful eyes, sat facing us on a slightly raised platform. "I do not have to touch you or be close to you," she announced in a tired voice. "I establish contact through the vibration of your voice. When I ask a question, merely say yes or no."

My wife was on the edge of her chair when the spiritualist, shading her eyes with a gnarled hand, said impersonally, "Shall I read you first, my dear?"

She sat there a moment, eyes closed, a study in contemplation, and then outstretched an arm as though summoning the spirits. Finally, she turned to my wife. "I see some trouble around you," she said, again shading her eyes with her hand. "It involves some older people, like your parents."

She looked up. "Do you know what I mean, my dear?"

My wife's father had recently suffered a heart attack, and her mother had been hospitalized for another complaint. She nodded, and then quickly remembering the injunction about voice vibrations, said swiftly, "Yes, I do."

The Reverend Wood had noticed a small gold disk dangling from my wife's neck. "I see that pendant swinging on its chain," she said in a dull voice, "and it tells me that you are going to make a lot of money, and very soon. For as it swings, it seems to become a gold coin."

Being of practical Scottish ancestry, my wife asked: "How soon?"

Madam Wood closed her eyes. I thought she might become vague at this point. But she couldn't have been more specific. "In ten days," she said, "I see things picking up."

My fashion-model wife, who had done well before our rather recent marriage, had been caught up by domesticity, and had gone into a slump. But only that week she had been ambitiously planning to relaunch her career.

While my wife was meditating pleasantly on this turn of events, Madam Wood frowned. "You will be making more money soon, but there will also be additional burdens on you, beginning in October, due to the demands of others."

This was the summer of 1961, and my wife would not have long to wait to learn what these new demands would be.

The spiritualist turned next to me. Shielding her eyes, she said, "They"—in an apparent reference to the spirits—"see you excavating, digging, digging, always digging. . . . Does that make any sense to you?"

"I have been a newspaperman for twenty-five years."

She seemed delighted by the analogy. "Can you place an old woman near you, older than a mother but whom you knew as a mother? She seems to be coming through now, and she is pleased with the work you are doing. Can you place who I mean?"

"My grandmother brought me up," I said.

The Reverend Wood's hands were folded in her lap, and her head was bowed. "What is this I get about a ring?" she asked with a frown. "There's been some disturbance about a gold ring. Can you place that?"

"My wife," I said, "just lost her gold wedding ring."

She straightened out her dress with a prim movement. "Well, don't worry about that, it'll turn up, but not for a while."

I had been doing considerable research in the psychic field but had not yet signed a book contract. "I see you signing contracts for not one but two books this year," Madam Wood said. She did not seem at all surprised by the nature of my project. "You will draw deeply for your inspiration," she said, "and it will be a best seller. It will be praised and criticized; for every word of praise there will be another knocking it. But it will win acceptance."

She thought a moment. "The other book will not be as important, but it will do well." She seemed to be listening, her attention drawn to a corner of a room. "I get a four," she said, "that may be four weeks or four months or August 4 for your book." She turned to my stockbroker friend then, who was itching to get out of the small, dank room. She concentrated, her head slumped on her chest, and said almost soothingly: "You are upset because you cannot get what you deserve out of your work." She held out an arm and her voice throbbed with sudden vigor. "But you will, mark my words, after the first of the year, you will get the recognition you deserve. So hold on."

As we got into the car, the stockbroker looked abstracted.

"Thinking of that promotion?" I said.

He laughed. "As a matter of fact," he said grudgingly, "she did get my situation. But it must have been luck."

We had seen Madam Wood in July of 1961. Actually she had not told us very much, but I thought I would check out the few things that she had forecast. In the week of August 4 I received a publisher's contract for my book, and then three months later, unexpectedly, I signed a contract for a second book.

In October, time for my wife's added burden, we had an unexpected addition to our family—a close relative whose problems were of concern to my wife, coming to live with us.

My wife, resuming her career, was immediately successful.

Months later, at the Christmas holidays, I saw my stockbroker friend again. "And how about you," I asked with a grin, "how's your situation?"

"No change," he said shortly, his face clouding a little. "Nothing will happen there."

His wife had joined us. "Oh, they'll never give him anything," she said, "he should get out."

Shortly after the turn of the year, I got a telephone call from the broker. His voice was rather sheepish. "In all honesty," he said, "I had to call you." He paused. "They have given me what I wanted—a partnership in the firm."

I thought for a moment. "Isn't that about what Madam Wood told you?"

"Yes," he said, "but it was certainly unexpected."

"She seems to be doing well so far," I said.

"Yes," he agreed, "she was right somehow, but"—and he laughed—"I still don't believe it."

Good mediums are often like telephones—instruments that understand neither what is said nor where the voices come from. In Cleveland, once, a young man approached spiritualist Arthur Ford after a demonstration and thanked him for a message he had received that night. "You made only one mistake," he said, "the spirit who sent that message was not my father." He turned to an older man standing nervously next to him. "My father is here with me tonight." At this, the older man gulped and then said with sudden resolve, "Son, I should have told you this long ago. You are my adopted son." As it was the son's turn to blanch, the older man added, "That could very well have been your father tonight."

Clergymen, collaborating with the ordained Ford in a spiritual movement, have found Ford a remarkable "telephone." After a seance with Ford, the Reverend Roy A. Burkhart of Columbus, Ohio, reported that several spirits, coming through, had brought up confidential matters that he had discussed during their lifetimes only with them. One businessman, for whom the Columbus airport is named, was in a grateful mood: "I will always meet you at the airport, and see to it that you have protection wherever you go." He appreciated what Burkhart had done for him in life. "If I had not had that time with you when I passed over, I would have been in complete darkness," Ford had quoted him as saying in spirit. And then, still protective, he predicted: "There will be no atomic war; you have nothing to fear."

After forty-five years as a psychic, Ford acknowledges that he never knows what he will get in trance. In the spring of 1960, he offered to read for syndicated Washington columnist Ruth Montgomery after she mentioned casually that she had recently written a series of articles in which she exposed certain mediums who seemed to be duping the gullible.

She agreed rather skeptically when Ford offered to go into trance and see what would develop. But her indifference soon vanished. Presently, closing his eyes, Ford was bringing her messages from people she hadn't heard of in twenty years. "There seemed little chance," she said, "that Ford could have known their identities."

There was a message from a man named Tucker, who claimed that he used to write stories directly on a linotype machine at the Waco *News Tribune,* where she had worked as a cub reporter many years before. There was another message from Pat Neff, president of her alma mater, Baylor University, which had given her an honorary degree, and from Walter Moursund, dimly recalled as dean of Baylor's medical school. They were pleased the reporter was doing so well.

While Miss Montgomery's interest had been captured, actually nothing much had been said. Then Ford introduced the name of Clyde Wildman, from Lafayette, Indiana, where Miss Montgomery had lived in her late teens. Wildman seemed to have something to say. "He says," Ford's voice droned, "that someone who lived near you in Lafayette has mysteriously disappeared, and wants you to know he has drowned; he's over here now." There was an effort to further identify the man who had drowned. "He appears to have been an official of some sort—a judge."

As a reporter, Miss Montgomery was conditioned to checking things. First, she checked on Tucker. "Don't you remember Jinx Tucker?" her former Waco editor said. "He's the only newspaperman I ever knew who put his stories directly on the linotype machine. He passed away a few years ago." Moursund and Neff were also dead.

Then the reporter telephoned George Lamb, editor of the Lafayette *Journal Courier,* to check what Wildman had apparently told her. "I don't remember living near any judge," she told the editor. Lamb promptly identified the missing official. "That would have been Judge Lynn Parkinson," he told the reporter. "He lived in Lafayette, when you lived here, and he was sitting on the United States Court of Appeals when he disappeared in Chicago last fall."

The search for the jurist had turned up few clues, and many believed he was still alive. He had not been replaced on the bench, and his pay checks, issued regularly, were piling up. A hat and an umbrella, identified as the Judge's, had been found on the shore of Lake Michigan. But a few weeks after the Ford sitting, a decomposed body was dragged out of Lake Michigan. It was the missing Judge Parkinson.

Although his predictions are usually incidental, Ford once started off each new year with a round of forecasts. One of the most remarkable came in the last year of World War II. In January of 1945, even though the Allies were then clearly winning the war, Ford forecast that two of the Allied Powers' three great leaders would not finish the year in office. The prediction was recalled years later by Gertrude Tubby, a long-time aide to Dr. James Hyslop, for years the guiding light of the American Society for Psychical Research. "I remembered it," Miss Tubby said, "because it seemed so incongruous at the time, with the Allied leaders everywhere prospering. And yet Roosevelt died in April, Churchill was turned out of office; a few months later only Stalin remained."

More dramatically, later that year, Ford was to pinpoint the end of the war with Japan, at a time when few knew of the atom bomb and a long island-hopping war appeared inevitable. The prediction came at the medium camp in Ephrata, Pennsylvania in August of 1945, when Ford, going into trance, said that Japan would lay down its arms within the month. Lesser mediums eagerly wrote down the prediction for subsequent checking, and prevailing opinion was that the dean of American mediums had overreached himself. "Arthur, I hope you haven't made a fool of yourself," said a medium who had respected him for years. "If I were you," she added, "I'd get out of camp." Ford himself decided it might be better to pack up. "When they read my prediction back to me," he said, "I couldn't believe it myself."

But the atom bomb, within the month, was to make him a better prophet than he thought.

Like most psychics, Ford was not impressive looking. He was short and dumpy, with a round, red face. He spoke with a nervous lisp, his movements were quick and jerky, the muscles in his face occasionally twitching. However, on a platform, getting his messages, he was an entirely different personality. Years before, I had encountered him for the first time at Carnegie Hall, as I sat in a front press row and watched skeptically while he fascinated an overflowing auditorium with messages from the dearly departed. He called off names rapidly, and people in the audience would rise instantly, sometimes gasping, even sobbing, other times nodding understandingly as he passed along the message. "What a spot for a plant," I could not resist whispering to a friend next to me. And then, even as my friend nodded agreement, Ford called off a spirit name he knew, and another skeptic was lost.

As a young man, Ford had often been front-page news. Once he claimed to have cracked the Houdini code, bringing a coded message back from the great escape artist who had promised his wife that he would get a message back to her if there was survival after death. Another time, in a plane with sneering newsmen, he assertedly got a message from Arthur Conan Doyle, the spiritualist father of Sherlock Holmes, and from the son of Dr. Henry Webster, head of Manhattan Eye and Ear Hospital, who was in the plane and apparently acknowledged the message.

In a painfully frank biography, *Nothing So Strange,* the medium had revealed the torments of drug addiction and alcoholism—the addiction induced by medical injections after a car smashup, the alcoholism following his successful fight to kick the drug.

His account of how he first realized he was psychic carried a certain amount of conviction. During the World War I influenza epidemic, he was a second lieutenant at Camp Grant. One night, retiring early, he dreamed that he saw the names of all those who had died that night in camp. The names stayed with him all the next day. Consulting the camp casualty lists, he found the same names as had appeared in his dream. Then his dreams began to broaden. He began to see the rosters of men dying at the front, and their faces. Subsequently, checking the newspapers, he found these names in the casualty lists. One night the face of his brother flashed through his dreams with the others. And the next day, brother George was dead. Depressed and disturbed, Ford went to a minister for advice. The minister told him to pray.

He wrote home to Titusville, Florida asking if there was any insanity in the family. Only an aunt, he was told, and she was just "tetched." She was a medium in Jacksonville.

At Transylvania College in Kentucky, preparing for the ministry, he was encouraged to develop his powers by a professor who was a pioneer researcher in psychic phenomena. After he left school, he permitted his gift to express itself naturally. Along the route, he picked up a spirit guide, or control—Fletcher—who helped him get his messages. And while to Dr. Fodor Fletcher would only be at best a subconscious dramatization, to Ford he was very real. Checking on Fletcher's credentials, when the guide first whispered in his ear, Ford had learned that Fletcher, killed accidentally, had at one time lived in Florida, not far from the Ford family, and had then moved to Canada with his parents. He was a Catholic, Ford said, using his middle name so as not to embarrass his family, and he spoke with a French-Canadian inflection—Ford's voice in trance from this time on.

Luckily, perhaps, Ford takes no responsibility for what Fletcher says. In February of 1962, at the home of Mr. and Mrs. Harry Stanley of Avon, Ohio, Fletcher brought a message from Judge Edward Blythin, presiding magistrate at Ohio's spectacular murder trial—the Sheppard case. The judge, dying in 1958, had learned in his new home that Sheppard was unjustly convicted of his wife's murder. "Tell them," he said through Fletcher, "that the crime was actually committed by a person who had already confessed, but whose confession had been ignored."

Waking from trance, Ford was considerably intrigued by the Stanleys' report on what Fletcher had said. But he was not nearly as impressed as Mrs. Stanley, whose own private convictions of the Sheppard case were now dramatically confirmed. "I called Sam Sheppard's brother," she said, "thinking he might appreciate the lead." The brother listened politely and murmured, "Thank you for calling; we have always thought our brother innocent."

Many of Ford's messages conveyed specific warnings, but, as with Jeane Dixon's, these warnings didn't seem to head off the dire event. In trance, Ford had warned the cashier of a Newark, New Jersey, brewery that he would be pounced upon and robbed if he weren't more careful in going to the bank. Two weeks later, the cashier was robbed on a Newark street. He was so impressed that he not only doubled his safeguards, but took up the study of psychic phenomena.

Not all of Ford's predictions are momentous, or even important, except perhaps as they manifest his belief in spirit survival. Reading for Dr. F. W. G. Swan, director of the Bartol Research Foundation of Swarthmore, Pennsylvania, before his death, Ford predicted that Swan would soon be honored with a degree by a London university. Six months later, the invitation was extended, and within the year, before an applauding audience at Prince Albert Hall, Swan received the distinction that Ford—or Fletcher—had foreseen.

In his long career, Ford has often been accused of fraud. When he claimed receipt of the Houdini message, correctly naming the Houdini code word, he was accused of collusion with Houdini's wife, Beatrice, who, in turn, had been suspicious of the medium until he gave the word that she and Houdini had secretly agreed upon.

Once, a radio interviewer pointedly asked Ford: "How can anyone believe anything in a field where there are so many charlatans?"

Ford smiled equably. "How about all these exposés of crooked disc jockeys and television quiz shows—does that mean that all radio and TV performers are dishonest?"

He has made a good living as a psychic, but is not interested in money. Repeatedly, he turns down requests for sittings from the wealthy, who could substantially help his Spiritual Frontiers, a predominantly clerical group dedicated to reviving the psychic messages of the Bible. "What we need more of," he observed laconically, "is not money but faith."

But he still gives private sittings as he travels the country, interesting ministers in his new interest. He no longer gives the demonstrations from the platforms, which brought him his fame. "At times I wondered," he explained, "whether some of the messages were coming from the spirits, or from the subconscious of particularly sensitive people in the audience." In private readings, of course, this may also be possible. But very often he has told people what they did not know themselves, but which they verified on inquiry.

Ford has not always been right. Reading for a Michigan businessman in April of 1961, he told him his father had a heart condition—which he had—and that he would "pass over in three months," but six months later he was still alive, and Ford merely said then that the father "would not live too much longer." "He also said I will live one heluva long life," the businessman reported, "but that we can't prove for some years to come."

Whatever the source of his communications, Ford increasingly feels that the people he reads for are a necessary link to his messages. "When I got the judge who had drowned," he said, "the link was reporter Ruth Montgomery, even though she didn't recall any such person. In the Houdini message, the link was John Stafford of the *Scientific American*, who was concerned with Houdini's promise to get word back to his wife if there was survival."

Cayce, too, Ford pointed out, had generally required some link —the written request for a reading, the name and address of the subject, the desire to be helped. But Cayce had not required a guide, and had shown a remarkable facility for cutting across time and space.

Had Ford ever wondered what made the Cayces—and the Fords —tick? Though we had talked long, I had one last question for him. "Why," I asked, "if there are spirits, should those spirits see any better now than they could on earth?"

He smiled, and scratched at his thinning hair. "Einstein once mentioned that many apparently unexplainable things might be explained in terms of the fourth dimension—a sort of timeless time, in which everything is presumably happening at once. But for myself"—he grinned broadly—"I have to go along with all the thousands of people who over the years have told me that I had delivered a message that nobody on earth could have given them."

12 THE CRIME-BUSTERS

In time there may be no crime because the criminal won't have a chance. And there may be no political coups or surprise attacks on frontiers because surprise will be impossible. Even now psychics are solving crimes that baffle our greatest sleuths. In Holland, the clairvoyant Croiset described the disappearance, step by step, of a girl mysteriously missing in Kansas, and correctly predicted a break in the case. In Virginia, Peter Hurkos, merely going over the scene of a crime, successfully identified a man sought for the murder of a family of four, and foretold the day he would be arrested. He also predicted, accurately, that the man would be held for other murders. In Georgia, an elderly fortune-teller, scoffed at by police, foretold when and where the body of a missing woman would turn up—and by her vision gave police their first inkling of foul play.

In Washington, Jeane Dixon, merely looking at a trusted officer of a business house, was able to predict that he would one day betray his trust, though her warning to that effect was blandly ignored by his employers.

In New Jersey, police have turned so often to a psychic for help in murders and missing person cases that she has taken the professional name Florence Psychic, and is so listed in the New York City telephone directory.

On the diplomatic front, Mrs. Dixon had been able to foresee the Korean War, and its stalemate, after meeting an American foreign service officer who could not himself have logically foreseen both developments.

In performing these wonders, the psychics displayed no powers of deduction, and intellectually were often several cuts below the sleuths who appealed to them for aid. But still, given the slimmest clues, or none at all, they would often break cases without stirring from their chairs.

Even in the laboratory experiments, dear to the hearts of parapsychologists, these crime detectors have been amazing. Holland's Gerard Croiset, for instance, ten days before a meeting, was asked to describe the person who would occupy each chair at the conference. One chair stumped him. He could only shake his head over it, and repeat, "I see nothing." Dr. W. H. C. Tenhaeff of the University of Utrecht, supervising the experiment pointed to another chair. Croiset's face immediately brightened. "I see a woman, her face scarred in a recent auto accident."

Thirty persons had been expected for the conference, and only twenty-nine showed up. The empty chair? The one Croiset could find nothing for. And the lady with the scarred face? "How," she asked Croiset, "did you know about my road crash in Italy two months ago?"

Croiset excels in missing person cases. Once he was consulted by telephone about a four-year-old child living fifty miles away, who had vanished twenty-four hours before. He said that the child's body would be found three days later in a canal near a bridge in its home town in Eindhoven.

And that was exactly where it was found three days later.

Croiset is also a psychometrist, getting impressions of the past, present, and future by merely touching an object. Once he was asked to feel a hammer, which a pretty girl had wrenched from the hand of a man who had battered her with it, and run off. He described her assailant, whom she could not identify in the darkness, as a "tall dark man with a disfigured left ear." And when a man fitting this description was picked up for another crime, police taxed him with the hammer attack, and he confessed.

Time and distance made little difference to Croiset. When his twenty-four-year-old daughter disappeared from a Topeka, Kansas hospital, Dr. Walter Sandelius, professor of political science at the University of Kansas and a Rhodes scholar, picked up a phone to ask Croiset about it. Six weeks had passed since the girl had been reported missing on October 18, 1959, and the police had been getting nowhere.

"Can you help me?" Sandelius asked Tenhaeff.

Croiset was put on an extension. "Is there a river near the hospital?" he asked.

"The Kansas River," Sandelius replied.

Croiset nodded, closed his eyes, and began tracing the girl's movements on leaving the hospital. "I can see her running over a broad lawn," he said, "and crossing a viaduct." On the other end of the line, Sandelius excitedly affirmed the description of the landscape.

Then Croiset saw the girl riding in a truck and a large car and arriving at a city on a body of water, with many small boats dotting its surface.

"Do not worry," he assured the father, "she is alive and well, and you will have more definite news in six days."

He asked for photographs and maps of the area to pinpoint the girl's location.

Exactly six days later, as he came down the stairs of his Kansas home to make a second call to Tenhaeff in Holland, Professor Sandelius got a jolt—there was his daughter, sitting comfortably on a sofa, as though she had never left. There was a tearful reunion, and then the father asked his questions. Carol had hitched two rides after fleeing across the hospital lawn, one in a truck, the other in a big sports car. And at the very time that her father was engaged in his three-way conversation with Tenhaeff and Croiset, she was in Corpus Christi, Texas, near a large body of water, with many small boats.

In the meantime, Sandelius had sent on the maps, and received a letter from Tenhaeff reminding him "that there would be news in six days, a little plus or minus."

The forecast had made little impression on the distracted father. "I did not have this prediction in mind," Professor Sandelius told me, "when I wired to arrange for another session on the telephone, as soon as I thought Dr. Tenhaeff would have received my letter for Croiset. Only when I got up on the morning of the second telephone conversation to Tenhaeff, and found that Carol had come in an hour before, did I realize that she had come in precisely an hour and a half less than six days after Croiset's statement to this effect."

From another psychic Sandelius had received more definite assurance of Carol's return. Consulting a sensitive closer to home, he had been told that she would return unharmed "before Christmas." On December 17, she strolled into her home.

To fretful relatives, routine police methods often seem painfully slow and unavailing. When her sister, Mrs. Jane Coats, disappeared suddenly from her home in suburban Atlanta, Miss Evelyn Stowers, an Atlanta saleswoman, couldn't banish an uneasy sense of disaster. She had spoken to her sister only the day before, when they had discussed Christmas presents for the three Coats children. But Jane's husband told police that his wife had merely grown tired of their marriage and had taken two thousand dollars and cleared out. Miss Stowers was openly skeptical. "My sister," she said, "would never leave the children."

Miss Stowers reported her sister's disappearance to De Kalb County police in November 1958. The disappearance was duly noted, and men were routinely assigned to the case. But the sister was not satisfied with the way things were going. When she wasn't checking police, she was bringing pictures and descriptions of the missing housewife to the Atlanta newspapers, talking to reporters, and knocking on doors in the Coatses' neighborhood in the slim hope that somebody might have a clue.

She eagerly agreed when her aunt, Mrs. Edna Farmer, suggested they consult a fortune-teller, a Mrs. Josephine Pittman, who had a reputation for locating misplaced jewelry and people. But when they drew up to the seer's ramshackle house in Stone Mountain, fifteen miles north of Atlanta, Miss Stowers felt her first misgivings when an elderly, unkempt woman with an unhealthy pallor came to the door.

But Mrs. Pittman became more impressive as the sitting proceeded. She peered into a crystal ball and then looked off into space broodingly. Everything that she said was etched forever into the mind of the sister, listening entranced.

"She said that my sister was dead," Miss Stowers recalled shortly thereafter, "and that she had been strangled with a cord and buried in a shallow grave. She said the grave was beside a new road not far from where my sister lived, and she described a bridge under construction nearby."

There was a more singular prediction, inexplicable at the time: "A little animal with a sharp nose and pointed ears would lead the way to her." There were more details of the grave scene, water that did not appear to be a lake or river, and a grove of trees. There was even a description of the missing woman's attire. "She saw my sister dressed in night clothes with a bedcover wrapped around her."

Continuing her own investigation, Miss Stowers began searching for terrain that fitted Mrs. Pittman's description. Meanwhile, police had received reports of the Pittman revelations, and had decided this sort of thing must stop. "We knew that what she had told the family had upset them terribly," said De Kalb County Detective B. S. Ivey, "and we went out there to tell Mrs. Pittman to cut it out."

Mrs. Pittman calmly listened to Ivey and his superior, Detective Captain T. L. Wayne, and then said quietly, "I told them the truth."

The officers dryly asked when the body would be found. "If not in January," Mrs. Pittman said, "it will be in mid-March."

Three months later, on March 17, 1959, construction work was resumed on a section of highway in north De Kalb County after a long winter layoff. During the noon break, workmen observed two opossums fighting with each other on the dirt ramp of a bridge they were building. As the possums fled, the men noticed an object jutting out of the loose dirt. This was what the "little animal with a sharp nose and pointed ears" had been fighting over. It was a human hand.

As Mrs. Pittman had foreseen, there were pools of water around the shallow grave, from recent rains, and grove-like clumps of trees lined the right of way. Though the remains were unrecognizable, an autopsy revealed that the victim—a woman—had been strangled with a cord. "In my opinion," testified Dr. Herman Jones of the Georgia Crime Laboratory, "she died from strangulation or suffocation from this cord being wrapped around her neck."

The body was in night clothing, as Mrs. Pittman had foreseen —shreds of green pajamas, a blue housecoat. And it was wrapped in a plaid bedspread. There was little Mrs. Pittman had missed.

Coats denied that the undistinguishable remains were those of his missing wife. But Miss Stowers identified the engagement and wedding rings found near the body. She had given her sister the blue housecoat only the year before.

Three months later, Coats was convicted of murder and sentenced to life imprisonment. During his trial, it developed that he had been seeing another woman, a divorcee, just before his wife disappeared.

To the psychic, in a very literal sense, murder does—sometimes —out. With his theory of the odic force, Dr. Reisenman feels that the murderer leaves a trail of emotion—anger, fear, resentment, appendages of the crime—that the psychic can latch onto years after the incident. In the same way, the psychic can enter a room where diplomats have sat, and penetrate their plans better than any spy. "Give a psychometrist like Hurkos a scrap of Khrushchev's clothing, or"—he laughed—"a wisp of his hair and he might be able to tell you everything Khrushchev had done and was planning to do."

But Jeane Dixon needed no such clue. Reading a State Department career officer in the spring of 1950, she foresaw not only his own future cloak-and-dagger activities, of which he knew nothing at the time, but the imminent "police action" in Korea. She also predicted to this aide, Frank Schuler, now a Washington executive, that the Korean War would end in a stalemate. "If we had all known that at the time," Schuler observed later, "there wouldn't have been any point in getting involved."

He remembered the prediction well because he had thought it so harebrained at the time. "She said the war would end with neither the United States nor the Communists getting what they desired because of factors introduced after the conflict. It was a pretty good hit. The Chinese threat of intervention at the Alu, subsequent to hostilities, was an outside factor that checked our drive for complete victory, while we were still strong enough to deny the Communists their victory."

She also told the incredulous Schuler of Stalin's death, hastened by associates, and pictured his replacement. "He will be succeeded by a fat man with a round, pasty face and a hair style similar to Napoleon's, a hank of hair slapped down over his forehead." When Malenkov succeeded Stalin three years later, Schuler felt he already knew him. And reports of Stalin's demise being expedited by frightened subalterns came as no surprise.

Although Schuler was then moving in top-secret levels, Mrs. Dixon, meeting him for the first time, seemed to know more about his plans than his superiors did.

"She told me I would be leaving for Europe in two weeks on a special mission," Schuler recalled, "and that while it was designed originally to take me only to West Germany, it would broaden unexpectedly and carry me all over Europe, the Middle East, and North Africa in a most delicate operation."

Shortly thereafter, as predicted, Schuler was sent to Frankfurt as an aide to High Commissioner John McCloy. "The mission was designed to keep me in West Germany," he said, "but within a couple of weeks, the whole nature of my job changed, and I became a roving emissary with headquarters in Paris." His mission was so hush-hush that in many capitals of Europe he was known only as Mr. X. "And I covered all the areas that Mrs. Dixon had said I would, before leaving the foreign service in two years." This departure had also been predicted.

In the crime field, Mrs. Dixon has done better than the detectors, anticipating felonies before they occur. She warned one of the country's wealthiest widows that she would be blackmailed if she were not more discreet. The following day, the woman— whom I have met—telephoned frantically. She had just received a blackmail note from a young man she had made the mistake of being kind to.

In 1957, Mrs. Dixon was closing a real estate deal in the offices of the Realty Title Insurance Company in Washington, when an executive, Charles Mitchell, suggested she give his concern more of her business. "Not while this man is with you," she said, referring to a company vice president whom she had just met. "I won't trust him with any of my money and you should watch out for yours."

Mitchell was flabbergasted. "Why, he's one of our most trusted officials."

"Well," Mrs. Dixon repeated, "you'd better watch out."

Three weeks later, the trusted vice president, as reported in the Washington *Post*, fled the city, while his associates counted a forty-thousand-dollar shortage.

"Yes, she told us about him," Mitchell confirmed, "but how could anybody pay any attention to it—the man had been with us for twelve years, and we had implicit confidence in him."

The most publicized of the psychic detectives is Peter Hurkos, the Dutchman who has claimed solving twenty-seven murders in seventeen countries. He had also received considerable publicity for recovering the Stone of Scone, taken from Westminister Abbey before Elizabeth's coronation. But Scotland Yard said otherwise. While the search for the Coronation Stone was making the headlines, Hurkos had traveled to England at his own expense. In London, he was permitted to go over the Abbey ground and handle objects presumably touched by the bandits. He had then given a press conference, at which he described the thieves, said they were in England but would soon be leaving for Scotland, and predicted: "The Stone will be returned in three weeks."

On a tip, Scotland Yard traced the fugitives to Glasgow. Then, in the belief they were Scottish nationalists trying to draw attention to their dream of partition, the Yard promised to look away if the Stone was returned intact.

As mysteriously as it had disappeared, the Stone returned—three weeks later. But Hurkos, Scotland Yard insisted, had nothing to do with it, even if he had accurately predicted its return.

Still, Hurkos got so much of the credit that in the House of Commons Her Majesty's Government felt compelled to publicly deny that his intervention had been helpful.

In this country, Hurkos has become a regular crime consultant. In Miami, police put him on the faded trail of the killer of five-year-old Judy Roberts. After eight years the case is still unsolved, but Miami police say that Hurkos accurately described how the child was slain, revealed gruesome details of the attack that only they and the killer supposedly knew, and indicated a suspect. "We can't say he was wrong," a police official observed, "but we weren't able to prove he was right."

He is remembered favorably in Miami for his work in the Smith case. It opened in October 1958 when Navy Commander John T. Stewart, fifty-three, retired, was shot to death in his Key Largo apartment, and his car stolen. A few hours later, Edward Sentnor, sixty-three, a cab driver, was shot and killed in his cab in downtown Miami, a short drive from Key Largo. Both men were killed by bullets from a .22 automatic, and later, as the cases were connected, police theorized that the killer might be the same man, without having the slightest idea who that man might be. In their quandary, they asked Hurkos if he would sit in the dead man's cab and tell them what impressions he got, if any. After a few minutes of intense concentration, the psychic clambered out of the taxi and began his report in his peculiar full-throated guttural voice. As police listened amazed, he described not only one murder but two. Lieutenant Tom Lipe, head of the Miami homicide squad, directing the investigation, disclosed that Hurkos not only drew a word portrait of the killer, describing even his stance, but went into his past, and actually named him. "It was also the first real intimation," Lipe said, "that the same man was responsible for both murders. Hurkos said he had killed a man in the Keys, which we didn't know at that point, and had been in trouble before. He said he was tall and thin, with a tattoo on his right arm, walked with a slow ambling gait, like a sailor, but could move like lightning when he had to. He was well known in Havana and Detroit, and his name was Smitty."

Actually, Hurkos was off a bit on the name. The fugitive, as it developed, was not Smitty, but Smith, Charles Smith. He was a merchant seaman who had shipped into Cuba, and he had served time in Michigan. At the request of Miami police, a rogues' gallery picture of Smitty was obtained from Michigan authorities. It was identified by a Miami waitress who told police of a customer—tall and slim, with the rolling walk of a sailor—who had boasted one night of killing two men. Convinced "Smitty" was their man, Miami police sent a "wanted" flyer with his picture and description to police around the country. Less than a month later, after pulling a stickup in New Orleans, Smith was picked up there, and returned to Miami to face trial. Found guilty of the cabbie's murder, he went to prison for life.

In some published reports of the case, Hurkos didn't rate a mention. While Lipe was ready to give the Dutchman his due, many of his colleagues were not. "Some police," the homicide chief observed, "aren't able constitutionally to accept the sort of thing Hurkos is doing any more than they could have accepted a flight to the moon twenty-five or thirty years ago." He smiled. "I don't understand it myself, but I'm willing to use anything that works, and accordingly give credit. Twenty to thirty years from now, what Hurkos is doing may be accepted as commonplace, and it may even be understood. Who knows?"

Lipe had found Hurkos trustworthy. "In our work with him," the policeman said, "I have never known him to claim anything that wasn't so, nor did he ever ask leading questions. When he gets into a case, he isn't so much concerned with what the police are telling him as with what he sees himself. If anybody breaks in on him when he's talking, he asks them not to interrupt. He just isn't interested in knowing what the police know."

Hurkos has agreed with this conception of himself. "All I ask the police to do," he said with characteristic modesty, "is to take me to the scene, and then let me alone." On the scene, as he concentrates on the crime, flashes of newsreels unfold before his eyes. "It's like a film being played only for me," he said. "I can see things in great detail, and I can describe what I see."

In the case of missing Florida Judge Curtis Chillingworth and his wife, Hurkos told Florida authorities long before the case was cracked that Chillingworth and his wife had been abducted, their bodies tossed into the ocean, and that Mrs. Chillingworth had been slain only because she was a witness. He named as instigator former Judge Joseph Peel of West Palm Beach and said, as a tape recorder spun, that while Peel didn't do the actual slaying, he knew all about it. At Peel's trial, subsequently, all developed as

Hurkos had said, and the former Florida magistrate is now serving time for masterminding the murders.

Hurkos' greatest triumph came in a case for which he was publicly ridiculed. In June 1960, he burst onto the scene of a Virginia murder probe in a bright blaze of publicity. Three days after he hit Falls Church, Virginia, center of the investigation, he was taking credit for solving four murders—the eighteen-month-old slaying of motorist Carroll Jackson, his wife, and their two small daughters. With the apprehension of a thirty-four-year-old trash collector, who had supposedly confessed the crimes, Hurkos was quoted by the newspapers as saying: "I've done a good job here. I worked three days and cracked the case." And then came an elaboration, vainglorious even for Hurkos: "With Dr. Reisenman [the psychiatrist and criminologist who had brought him into the case] I went to the churchyard where Carroll Jackson and his wife, Mildred, and their two daughters were buried. I went later to the scene of the crime and to the Jacksons' former home, where I was able to handle some of their clothing and personal possessions." At the contact, he had felt a series of strong vibrations, which had translated themselves into revealing mental pictures. He even saw the suspect's wife—she had "two missing upper teeth and a pointed nose."

Yet ten days later it all looked like a grim fiasco on Hurkos' part, with the arrest in Arkansas of another man for the murders and the release of the suspect Hurkos had apparently fingered.

The new suspect, Melvin Davis Rees, thirty-one, a jazz musician from Hyattsville, Maryland, had been arrested by the FBI, and a diary found in his old home seemed to settle his guilt. The excerpts told the story. "Caught on lonely road, then after pulling them over, leveled pistol, and ordered them out . . . car trunk was open for husband and both bound. Now the mother and daughter were all mine."

Rees was also implicated in the earlier murder of Mrs. Margaret Harold, thirty-six, a clerk at nearby Fort Meade. Her body had been found not far from the shallow grave near Annapolis, Maryland, where the bodies of Mrs. Jackson and six-year-old Susan Ann were to be exhumed three years later. Jackson and eighteen-month-old Janet were found under a brush pile in woods near Fredericksburg, Virginia.

After Rees's arrest, the Washington newspapers cried out against crystal-ball justice, bitterly attacking Hurkos and the Virginia police, who had co-operated with him. In New York, newspapers that had been planning features on the three-day psychic wonder canceled their plans. The Hurkos bubble had burst.

A year or so later, as the Rees trial was making headlines in Washington, I mentioned Hurkos' failure to Dr. Reisenman. The doctor looked puzzled. "What failure?" he said. "He was fantastically successful."

It was my turn to appear surprised. "He picked out the trash man from Falls Church, Virginia, and it was Rees who committed the murders."

Reisenman smiled. "You've been reading the papers. Actually, though the papers never got hold of it, Hurkos also got Rees, and described him down to the last detail."

"Then why was the first man arrested?"

"Peter got both men—the trash man and Rees, and he described both. The difficulty was that he got one through telepathy and the other through psychometry. He read the minds of the police officers who thought the Virginia man guilty, and he got Rees through his contact with the dead people's belongings—the odic force."

"Did he tell the police about Rees?"

"He was quite specific. After touching Jackson's shoes and the little girl's dress, he closed his eyes and began to describe the killer. He got Rees's height correctly—slightly over six feet—said he was left-handed with a tattoo on his arm, and added that he walked like a duck and stood like an ape. That description fit the long-armed, muscular Rees, and had no application at all to the other man. There was no question whom he meant."

"Then why didn't they pick Rees up?"

"Oh, they were going to, and they sent two men out to West Memphis, Arkansas, to get him, but the FBI got there first."

I was surprised that the police had shown this much confidence. "He impressed them right off," Reisenman said. "Standing where the bodies had been found months before, he described the positions in which they had lain, told how each of the four had been killed, and in what order. Although only the police knew it then, he said that Mrs. Jackson had been sexually assaulted. On the Harold murder scene, he went to a grove a mile from where the body had been found and plucked the woman's skirt off a bush, where it had hung unnoticed for three years. He said that Mrs. Harold had been killed unintentionally, and that coincided with police information, and then he said that the Jacksons and Mrs. Harold were killed by the same man."

Along with the trash man, the musician Rees had been one of many suspects, and so Hurkos had actually pinpointed things for the police in describing the killer as an artist, which the trash man certainly was not.

But I still wasn't sold on Hurkos' role.

"From the papers," I said, "I gathered that Hurkos thought the case ended with the trash man's arrest."

"Not at all," Reisenman said, "because this man really wasn't even arrested, but was committed for observation at his wife's request. But even so, his being picked up in three days didn't conform with Hurkos' prediction . . ."

I hadn't realized Hurkos had made any predictions.

"Oh, yes, that was the most remarkable thing of all. The day Hurkos arrived, appearing on television he said the case would be cleared up in fourteen days with the arrest of the murderer. Rees was picked up two weeks afterward to the day."

He had also predicted the killer would eventually be indicted for nine murders. "He has already been officially tied to five—the Jacksons and Mrs. Harold," Reisenman said, "and police say they have information tying him with two more, and they may yet get to nine. But they could tell you more about that."

"How about his announcement that he had solved the case in three days?" I persisted.

"Actually he had; it only remained for Rees to be picked up."

"But he described the 'killer's' wife, and Rees had no wife."

"This was telepathy intruding again, but obviously Hurkos' prediction excluded anybody picked up before the two weeks were up."

As a newspaperman, I was still baffled. "If all this is true and Hurkos helped solve the murders, how did the wrong stories get out without ever being corrected?"

Reisenman shrugged. "Obviously, the police weren't going to talk their heads off about bringing in a sensitive to help them solve a murder. The reporters found out about the trash man because that happened right within the area, but Hurkos' connection with the Rees pickup didn't come out since reporters hadn't stumbled on it and the police had no interest in blowing up Hurkos."

He looked at me frankly. "However, if you have any doubts about Hurkos' role in the case, you can check with Inspector Jack Hall of the Virginia State Police, who handled the investigation." He laughed. "Peter certainly impressed him before he got through."

"In what way?" I asked.

"In every way, personally and professionally."

It had been a meeting, apparently, that Hall wouldn't soon forget. "When he first met Hall," Reisenman related, "he told him, 'Don't worry, your wife is all right,' and then as Hall looked up with a start, he said, 'She's going to the doctor's office to keep a noon appointment and she's going to be annoyed when she gets there because he's going to have to see three emergency cases before he gets to her, and she'll have to wait.'"

And so it happened, as a phone call by Hall soon determined.

As Hall looked at him wide-eyed, Hurkos continued, "You haven't had any children in eighteen years, and you don't expect any anymore, but you're going to have another child, a girl, and she will be born on June 24, 1961, just about a year from today."

At this, Hall smiled, but was impressed in spite of himself.

"Did it all come true?" I asked.

"Ask Hall," Reisenman said, "he'll tell you."

I got back to the murders. "How did you happen to call in Hurkos?" I asked Reisenman.

"The police had picked up and questioned more than fifteen hundred suspects, and still had one hundred and sixty-five suspects under consideration, including two of my private patients. I was concerned with clearing these two, since I felt they were innocent, and the knowledge they were under suspicion for so heinous a crime was certainly not conducive to mental health."

"But weren't the police a little reluctant to put up the money for Hurkos? I understand he's expensive."

"I footed the bill," the doctor said. "It cost me three thousand dollars, and it was worth it, in more ways than one."

He looked up with a smile. "Actually, Hurkos was more amazing with people around him—like Inspector Hall—than even in putting police onto Rees. Some of his predictions were remarkable; there were at least twelve instances of precognition on his part that have already come true."

"Were they things he might have known about or learned through judicious inquiry?" I asked.

"I don't know how he would go about schooling himself, since he didn't know anybody he met here, we didn't know him, and he flew in from Miami right after I put through a phone call for him."

"He may have sensed trends or probabilities from the attitudes of the people around him, guessed at things, and told them what they wanted to hear."

He laughed. "Okay, dissect this one from the analytical point of view. I met Hurkos at the airport in Washington and, recognizing him from his pictures, went over to greet him." As Reisenman reached into his wallet for an identifying card, the picture of an elderly man dropped out. Hurkos bent down and picked it up. As he handed it back to Reisenman, the words catapulted out of him. "That man is eighty-two years old," he said, "he has had four accidents in the last two years, and his condition is going to gradually deteriorate, with the blood vessels shrinking in his head. He will live from six to twelve months."

The picture was of Reisenman's father, who lived in Meadville, Pennsylvania, with a son, Joseph.

"Except for the forecast of death, everything Hurkos said was right," Reisenman said, "but the doctors had said my father was improving and as a doctor myself I thought they were right."

This was on June 10, 1960.

Brother Joseph still reported that the men of medicine gave the elder Reisenman another five to ten years, but on February 8, 1961, eight months later, he passed away.

Hurkos seemed to enjoy his performance and its impact. At the airport, in the presence of police, he made a weather prediction. "For the next three and a half days," he said, "all the time I am here, the weather will be perfect—sunny and mild, and then, as I leave, you will have a terrible storm."

And how had it happened?

"Just as he predicted; the moment he stepped on the plane, it started to pour," the doctor said, "—the worst cloudburst in five years, with the cellar in my home flooded for the first time."

In Reisenman's home Hurkos continued to perform. "He looked at a picture of my mother on the wall, not knowing it was my mother, and said: 'That woman died on May 8, 1959, at three in the morning, and nobody was with her at the time.'"

But Hurkos had made a mistake. The death had occurred on July 8 of that year. "May 8 was my mother's birthday," Reisenman said, "and I suppose this date flashed through his mind and he confused it with the other mental picture he had."

Introduced to the doctor's eighteen-year-old son, Robert, he blurted out: "You know, your girl friend looked better before she dyed her hair." And then as Robert's eyes bugged, he having previously given the girl this bit of information himself, Hurkos said: "Another thing, her father died eighteen years ago while reading the funny papers."

Meeting Robert later, I asked about Hurkos. "My girl friend had dyed her hair," he said, "but she didn't know about her father dying like that. So she asked her mother, and her mother looked at her a little strangely and said, 'Yes, but who told you?'"

But Hurkos' greatest prodigy around the Reisenman home was reserved for a small child. Little Mary Alice, then about two and a half years old and the youngest of seven children, had been ill almost from birth, and could not walk or toddle. The doctors said she suffered from cerebral palsy and would never walk. "Hurkos put his hand on little Mary Alice's back as she sat on the porch,"

Dr. Reisenman said, "—this was on June 11—and said: 'She'll walk on her birthday, December 21, for the first time, and then four days later, on Christmas, she'll walk to the tree and pick up her presents, and will continue to walk.'"

I interrupted. "Did you tell him the child's birth date?"

"No, he apparently picked that up, like he did the other dates, through that universal newsreel of his."

And how right had he been on Mary Alice?

"When December 21 came around," Reisenman said, "we deliberately made no effort, my wife or I, to encourage her to stand up, toddle, or walk. If anything was going to happen, it was not going to be induced through any coaxing or urging on our part and I had no wish to implant the idea in the child's mind—though we had repeatedly tried to get her to walk before this."

Without urging, as her parents half-averted their eyes, the child miraculously took her first few tentative steps. She fell down, but got up and started over again. During the next few days, she made a few more exploratory steps, without showing any real progress, and then on Christmas Day—as Hurkos had forecast—she toddled triumphantly to the tree and stood there, smiling, as her parents' moist eyes reflected their emotion on this anniversary of Him who said: "Suffer little children to come unto me."

I had caught a glimpse of Mary Alice. She was then almost four, and she skipped and romped about like any healthy normal girl her age. Her legs were sturdy and strong.

Knowing how skeptically doctors regarded the laying on of hands, I still felt bound to ask, "Do you think Hurkos has healing powers?"

"I can only accept the evidence. He predicted she would walk after five doctors said otherwise, and he predicted the date. That, to me, is evidence of precognition and Hurkos only foresaw the event."

I was still intrigued by the murders. In the Jackson case, Hurkos had been like a bloodhound picking up scents all over the place, and his difficulty in separating the scents struck me as rather unfair. "Doesn't this make it awkward for an innocent man who happens to confuse the bloodhound's trail?" I asked.

"There shouldn't have been all that confusion," the doctor said, "after all, Hurkos did tell them that the killer was out West, and they went out West for him."

"Then how," I asked, "did the FBI get there first if the Virginia police had all this information?"

Reisenman gently tilted his eyebrows. "Why not ask the police," he said, "that's their department."

Just outside the drowsy little town of Culpeper, Virginia, at State Police Headquarters, I looked up the man who could answer my questions—Inspector Jack Hall.

Hall was a dark, handsome Virginian with graying hair and a soft drawl. "Hurkos," he said, with a shake of the head and a quizzical smile, "we won't forget that name for a long time."

"Did he really help break that case?"

"Everything Dr. Reisenman told you was true, and then some."

"How about Rees being indicted for nine murders?"

"We've already got him tied in for seven, and we know of two more."

"How do you account for the newspaper stories saying that Hurkos had failed?"

"They were right about Hurkos having put the finger on one suspect, but they didn't know about the other, and we certainly weren't letting out anything at the time that would have warned the man we were trying to pick up. But he did put his finger on Rees, and he told us pretty much how it was done." He shook his head. "That man could pick up the strangest things. For instance, he told us that Mrs. Jackson had only thirty-one teeth, and checking the autopsy report we discovered that he was right."

"How do you think he got two men?"

"Dr. Reisenman's theory about reading our minds on one and getting the other through touching things might be right—I don't know. But the two suspects had lots in common. What the public doesn't know is that they even lived in the same house, an abandoned shack, for a while, though not at the same time, and Hurkos might have confused the pair there."

"Did Hurkos actually put the finger on Rees or the other man?"

"From what he told us of the way the crimes were committed,

and from his description, it became obvious that Rees was our man."

I thought again about the mix-up in the newspaper accounts. "Did Hurkos meet any of the reporters himself?" I asked.

"Yes, they were all skeptical, as was to be expected, but he converted one or two."

"How was that?"

"As I recall it, we were at Dr. Reisenman's office in Falls Church, and one of the reporters from a local newspaper was passing disparaging remarks about Hurkos' powers, and Hurkos suddenly turned on him and said, 'You know, you're a nice fellow, and all that, but you're a married man, and you shouldn't be going out and doing what you do with Helen, because she's a married woman.'"

Hall laughed as he recalled the scene.

"You know," he said, "that reporter turned white and slunk out of the room, and from that time on he started writing favorable stories about Hurkos."

"How come, with all that Hurkos did, the Virginia police didn't pick Rees up?"

"Oh, well, Rees was a hot suspect, and the FBI had him under surveillance too; and then when our boys went out there to pick him up, as the doctor mentioned, they grabbed him first."

Studying Hall's saturnine countenance, I wondered how a veteran police officer with his hardheaded experience could have seriously listened to a psychic. "Wasn't there any resentment or opposition by the police toward bringing in a man like Hurkos?"

"Captain Lindsay at the State Police Headquarters in Richmond decided that it couldn't do any harm since we didn't seem to be getting anywhere."

"What was your own reaction?"

"Oh, I thought it might be interesting, but policemen, as you probably know, are pretty dubious about this sort of thing."

But Hall's skepticism had soon turned to wonder.

"When Hurkos met me, he started telling me things about myself and my family that no outsiders knew. He told me that I had hurt my back years before and that it was bothering me; he said

I had a brother who was a cripple and that I had a son who had died of Leukemia several years ago, and he gave the date; and he told me my wife and I were going to have another child, a girl."

After eighteen years the Halls had given up hope of another child.

"And did you have that child?" I asked.

"Yes, we had a girl, born one year later on June 24, 1961, the very day he predicted." He shook his head marvelingly. "I meant to send him an announcement, but I didn't have his new address handy"—Hall's dark face broke into another smile—"and I figured he probably knew he was right anyway."

"You're sold on Hurkos then?"

The inspector turned the toe of his boot thoughtfully as we stood there talking on the steps of the police station on a warm, sunny day. "Put it this way," he said, "he's got something that I don't understand and that nobody else seems to understand, and I don't know if he understands it himself. But when he starts telling you things about yourself that even you never knew before, you've got to wonder."

"Like what, for instance?"

"Five or six years ago I had been set down, suspended a few days, by my superiors for an infraction of the rules. I had forgotten all about it. But when Hurkos came here I took him inside and introduced him to my superior, the lieutenant. He shook hands, looked at the lieutenant, and then spoke out. 'This is very unsual,' he said. 'You two men are friends, but five or six years ago, you'—and he pointed to the lieutenant—'recommended the dismissal of the inspector for breaking the rules.'"

There was a dead silence for several moments, with the lieutenant turning beet red. "You know," the inspector said casually, "I had never known of that recommendation before."

"Well, was Hurkos right?" I asked.

"Oh, yes, looking at the lieutenant I could tell that—not that it really matters now, as we all have a pretty good working relationship here."

"Would you bring Hurkos in again if you had another difficult case on your hands?"

"If it were up to me," the inspector said, "I wouldn't hesitate. As I said before, I don't know how he does it, but he certainly knows things that no ordinary thinking man could ever know." His face broke into a half-sheepish smile. "Once when we were riding along on the highway, Hurkos turned to me and said, 'Your wife is not far from us, she's in a car a few hundred yards ahead of our car.' We were in a little hollow at the time. I picked up speed and rode over the crest of a small hill, and there I saw my car with my wife in it."

"Could somebody have told him?"

"He had never seen my wife before, and besides, he had been with me in the police car long before she even thought of taking the car out."

"How do you think he does it?" I asked.

He shrugged. "I haven't got the slightest idea, but he must have something working for him."

"What is that?" I asked.

He turned his face to the sky, without answering directly. "It's enough," he said softly, "to make you believe in the Almighty God."

13 THE PSYCHIC MACHINE

A fall on his head made a great psychic out of Peter Hurkos.

Before that he was only a Dutch house painter, crude and un-lettered, hardly knowing what the word psychic meant. But since then, in the subconscious state in which he does his most remark-able work, he has been observed to speak out in Polish, Latin, Spanish, and other languages he knew nothing about in his wak-ing moments. And waking, he has drawn precise pictures of buildings a thousand miles away that he had never seen.

Long before he came to this country, the durable Dutchman, who looks like a bulky, good-natured Andrei Gromyko, was billed as The Man With the Radar Brain.

He appears to have been aptly titled, for Hurkos, more than any of the well-known psychics, is like a psychic machine. In a crime he may pick up a hundred remarkable clues without being able to weave them into a satisfactory solution. Like a machine, his services are available to the highest bidder, hunting for oil wells, tracking criminals, policing the personnel of stores. He has had two or three managers since arriving in this country, and at one time a whole foundation was built around him with money a major pursuit.

Many of his claims are so extravagant as to be immediately questioned. Yet, according to researchists who observed him for two years, his predictions for the future and perceptions of the past have been right nearly ninety per cent of the time.

On television he has performed astonishingly, on screen and backstage, fascinating audiences on the Jack Paar Show and later confounding the skeptics who had cynically put him on without believing in him.

Perhaps more than other psychics he is confused about his powers because his gift was thrust on him when he was already an adult. Fixed in his concept of living, he was abruptly faced with a strange new world that opened wonderfully. His confusion is reflected in his own attempts to explain the fall some twenty years ago that changed his life overnight. He had been painting a house in Zuidwal in his native Holland when he slipped and fell off a scaffold, dropping thirty feet and suffering a concussion. "When I woke up," he said, "I began to tell the doctors and nurses secret things about themselves, things that only they knew. That's how it started, and it's kept on like that since. I cannot understand it, and I cannot explain, though I often think I would like to know how it works."

During his two-month hospitalization, it was often a tossup as to whether Hurkos had a sixth sense or was a mental case. "I told my nurse not to bother about me but to take care of a valise that I knew she would lose," he recalled. "The nurse was dumbstruck.

She told me that she had just returned from Amsterdam and left the valise on the train." Not an important manifestation of psychic power, but the machine was beginning to function. Hurkos was finally discharged from the ward, he said, after astounding the hospital's staff psychiatrist, a Dr. Pieters, with revelations of his personal life. The doctor was glad to see him go.

It had been uncomfortable having him around. Shaking hands with a departing patient he had cried out to hospital attachés: "Don't let that man go—he'll be shot outside." That man, an Allied agent, was shot to death in the street a few hours later.

He was thirty-two years old when he entered the hospital, thirty-two when he left it, but in those few weeks he had grown into an entirely new dimension.

Life was never again to be the same for the man born Peter Van der Hurk. He was able to look at men and tell them things about themselves they had not known, and he was often able to predict events that he could not possibly have drained out of them or their subconscious.

Yet, with all his incredible achievements, he has still made extravagant claims. Holland's Dr. Tenhaeff has charged, for instance, that Hurkos wrongly claimed to have "received a statement from me by which I declare him to be one of the world's best clairvoyants." And yet Tenhaeff acknowledged that Hurkos "possessed a certain degree of clairvoyant talent."

Since Hurkos was obviously not born psychic, many have wondered what role the fall had in his becoming an extrasensory marvel—whether it actually knocked something loose or unlocked a latent power with its traumatic shock. He had first noticed the change himself after recovering from a two-day coma.

There is no evidence that Hurkos felt spiritually motivated or that such motivation had anything to do with the genesis of his gift. To some, Hurkos was an obvious gland case, a fluke brought on by an accident. They took no account of the fact that others have had similar accidents without being similarly affected. "Today," said Henry Belk, the man who put up the money to bring Hurkos to this country, "we know Hurkos' injury was in the midbrain, disturbing the medulla and upsetting the pineal or pituitary glands. His gift was not a mysteriously divine bestowal, but purely a biologic physical brain injury that can be repeated upon any human."

But there are not many Hurkoses.

His fall took place in 1943, and before the end of the war he was thrown into a concentration camp by the German invaders. However, he was not disheartened, he said, because he foresaw D-Day and the German defeat. He could predict, for the edification of other inmates, the day and hour of new Allied bombing raids, but then almost any astute observer could have done the same.

After the war, his visions continuing, he developed a local reputation for locating missing people or describing how they had met death. When a small girl disappeared from home, the people of the village took up a collection and sent for him. He told them she had been strangled, but he couldn't find the body or the killer. There were too many distracting images. Later, her body turned up, strangled.

He worked for a while in Paris, in a sitting room that served as an office, handling objects and staring at photographs, or occasionally he would go to the scene. He thought of himself as a crime specialist.

Vacationing in his native Holland from a crime-detecting career in Paris, he matter-of-factly told two companions: "Tonight a farm near here is going to burn. Janson is the farmer's name, and his place is over by the small canal. It will happen at nine o'clock."

This was but a half hour or so away. After inquiring where it was, the three men drove hastily to Janson's farm, but as they approached they could already see the red glow from the flaming wooden buildings. On the scene, Peter retrieved a padlock from the shed where the fire had started. "Peter, you could help the police on this thing," one friend said. Hurkos was willing, and the police, plagued by a rash of fires, reluctantly went along. Hurkos held up the scorched padlock. "I already have this," he said, "and I would like photographs of everybody in the district. Identification photos, school pictures, snapshots—whatever you can get me."

Next morning at police headquarters, he pored over scores of photographs face down. On each he placed the padlock, and concentrated. Perspiration rolled down his face from the effort. After watching him for an hour, the police went off to lunch. Upon their return, Hurkos turned up a photograph and exclaimed: "This is the one."

The police chief and his aides grinned. "That boy," the chief said, "is one of the brightest, best boys in the neighborhood, and his father is one of the richest and most respected men in the country."

But Hurkos was adamant. "Take this boy in and there'll be no more fires. I promise you."

Grudgingly, the chief complied. Questioned closely, the boy tripped himself up and finally admitted everything. People suddenly recalled seeing him in the neighborhood of the fires.

Hurkos was not a great social success in Holland. Invited to perform at swank parties, he often disclosed—convincingly—extramarital affairs, skulduggery, even treason. In one session, reading the distinguished husband of his hostess, who watched with a polite sneer, he soon removed that sneer, informing the astounded audience that the man whom they honored as a great patriot had actually been in league with the Germans. Subsequently, the patriot was revealed as a traitor and a family's life ruined through a simple party. "Never invite Hurkos," one party-goer noted dryly, "if you have anything to hide."

In 1956 Hurkos was brought to this country by Belk and tested by Andreja Puharich at the Round Table Foundation laboratories at Glen Cove, Maine. After some study, Puharich was not so sure that a physical injury had made Hurkos psychic. "Peter," Puharich decided, "had an emotional shock that triggered his psychic faculty." The fall might only have precipitated that shock.

In the laboratory he was equally remarkable. Four times out of five, when researchers handed Hurkos a concealed object—a butterfly, a safety pin, a button, sometimes even a blank sheet of paper—in a sealed envelope, he was able to tell what was inside by merely touching the envelope. When he only looked at the envelope, without touching it, his average dropped to two out of five. And when he neither looked nor touched, but sat with eyes closed, he failed completely.

But under the influence of a photographer's Strobe light, which Puharich felt reduced the distinction between the conscious and the subconscious, Hurkos often correctly identified five out of five objects without seeing or touching the envelopes.

In one experiment, illustrating the possibilities of psychic communication, a Dutch telepathist named Harry Stole would hold an object, whose identity he did not know, while some forty miles away, Hurkos would correctly identify the objects forty-three times out of fifty—a formidable eighty-six per cent average.

In a wooden compartment, known as the Faraday cage, Hurkos was at times ninety-five per cent correct, convincing Puharich that Hurkos' power lay within himself. "The cage," the psychiatrist observed, "prevented electrical impulses from penetrating the walls, establishing that Peter's ESP was not due to electromagnetic radiation."

But even at Glen Cove, Hurkos' most dramatic successes came outside the laboratory. Working best under the stimulation of real-life situations, he made remarkable predictions for Puharich and his friends. After meeting a widely-known personality at the Maine laboratory, Hurkos got a vision of this man's brother attempting his life, this without having ever heard about the brother, who was a student living in California. In his vision, he saw a man's wrists slashed and bleeding. Puharich was startled—and impressed. "Almost immediately," an observer said, "Puharich got on the phone and called his friend in New York. The line was busy for some time. When Puharich finally did reach him, the New Yorker was doubly flabbergasted, because he had just been talking to his brother's psychiatrist cross-country, and had been advised that his brother's condition had deteriorated, and there were fears he might hurt himself."

The New Yorker flew out to California, and had his brother removed to another institution where it would be easier to watch him. "Everything of potential danger was taken from him," the observer noted, "belt, shoelaces, silverware, even a water tumbler, all but his eye-glasses which he needed for normal vision. Three weeks later, when nobody was looking, he smashed his glasses, and slashed his wrists with the jagged edges of the lenses. He was caught in time, and rushed off to a hospital ward, his wrists dripping with blood, just as Hurkos had foreseen."*

Hurkos had tremendous impact on Henry Belk, even though Belk has never been quite sure that his importing Hurkos was a providential step. "I have seen him do many remarkable things," the department-store magnate said, "but I have also seen him erratic and confused."

At first, Belk was completely captivated by his protégé. Finding him more effective than a business machine, he used him successfully to spot dishonest employees. "In many cases," an observer said, "Hurkos put the finger on workers who had been trusted for years." In the Belk store in Charlotte, North Carolina, touching pictures of employees in the personnel files, Hurkos soon knew more about them than their bosses did. "Hurkos said whether they were married, how many children they had, what their aptitudes were," Belk said. "He amazed John Mark, the personnel manager, by telling him what kind of jobs they held and how they performed them. He was uncanny."

At parties, Hurkos still displayed the embarrassing candor that characterized his first psychic years in Holland. "In October 1956, in my home in Charlotte," Belk said, "he told Martha Warrington, a friend of mine, about a recent trip of hers to Mexico, describing what she had done with such detail that she was convinced the Mexicans had sent up a report."

Hurkos thought nothing of reciting a husband's infidelities in front of a wife. "I know of at least one case," Belk reminisced sadly, "where Peter's outspokenness had a lot to do with breaking up a marriage—there are some things that should be sacred, even to a psychic."

This foible of Hurkos' is well known. Even his wife, greeting him at the airport, has jested wryly: "Are you kissing me, or just checking?"

*The names of the persons involved were deleted when it was considered that the revival of this incident might have an adverse effect, emotionally, on the brother, who has been showing signs of recovery.

In time, with discipline, Hurkos learned to control this tendency to blurt out whatever he saw. He now hesitates periodically during his readings, often weighing the impact of his words before he churns them out. Some feel that this self-imposed curb on his spontaneity has somewhat impaired his effectiveness. "His images come so fast," an interested observer noted, "that when he hesitates, they pile up in his mind, often overlapping and resulting in a confused over-all pattern, and this can be doubly confusing because he does not necessarily picture events or incidents in any order, but may jump from one period to another, repeating images as he sees them."

In Dr. Reisenman's home in Falls Church, Virginia, he flit effortlessly, but often confusingly, from one person and period to another. Even when he rattled off his impressions without hesitating he could still be bewildering. But those watching him work have never doubted his sincerity any more than they would doubt an IBM machine.

Could he heal, too, in the same way as a short-wave diathermy machine or an infrared lamp, just through the sheer impact or pulsation of his energy force?

In the case of the Reisenman child, there have been suggestions that Hurkos, like Edgar Cayce, may have practiced healing as well as precognition. If he could heal nobody else, according to witnesses, Hurkos could heal himself. One evening in Belk's New York apartment, as a half-dozen of Belk's friends and business associates sat around talking, Hurkos suffered a bad fall. "He twisted his leg so that one of the bones broke clear out of his skin," Belk said. "Blood was all over the place." As a former serviceman, Belk felt he had seen enough broken bones during the war to tell a break when he saw one.

As Hurkos cried in pain, the men lifted him onto a bed. He bowed his head, as though in prayer, "and before our very eyes," Belk said, "the bone went back into place and the torn skin healed and became smooth."

Belk wouldn't have believed it himself if the other witnesses had not been there to confirm what he saw. To give the incident a semblance of credibility he asked the witnesses, all men of substance, none addicted to psychic phenomena, to record what they had seen that memorable night, May 17, 1958. This tape he played for me, giving me the names and the addresses of the men who had been with him that night. They made an impressive array and all told the same story. But it was still hard to believe.

"Now," said Belk, turning off the tape recorder, "do you believe it?"

I shook my head. "I'd not only have to see it for myself," I said, "but I'd have to have a couple of doctors there whose diagnosis I could trust, and I still wouldn't believe it."

But Hurkos had other testimonials. A few months thereafter in Orlando, Florida, he voluntarily gave a reading for music-shop proprietor Bill Baer, who had experienced pains in the left side of his body—the arm and the chest area—and thought it might be heart trouble. Hurkos promptly advised Baer of severe pain in two areas. "I was astonished that Hurkos knew about my pain," Baer said later, "as I had not mentioned it to any living soul—including my wife."

Upon Baer acknowledging the pain, Hurkos inquired if he would like it removed. "Naturally," Baer related, "I replied in the affirmative, whereupon Hurkos had me remove my coat. He then ran his hands a number of times over the two painful areas, as well as down my back. In a very brief time a miracle had occurred, for the pain vanished. Immediately I could pound my fist over the heart area, whereas shortly before I could not touch this area with the ends of my fingers without causing the pain to be aggravated."

While grateful, Baer was understandably baffled. How had it been done? He was sure that he had not been hypnotized. "Hurkos would not permit me to look into his eyes. And there was a re-assuring word, too. He told me that I did not have heart trouble but that the pain was due to nerves." Some two weeks later, when Baer discussed his case, the pain had not recurred.

As he has so often, Hurkos glibly credited his achievement to one greater than himself. The music man was ready to agree. "Hurkos," said Baer, "freely admits that he has the Divine gift, and I am convinced that there is no other explanation."

But others are not so easily convinced of the dauntless Dutchman's ethereal connections. "Many people," a fellow psychic observed, "confuse psychic powers with spirituality. It is quite possible to be psychic and worldly and to misuse a power that is not always understood. We all know psychics who, instead of dedicating themselves to good works, have virtually made corporations of themselves, and are in business looking for oil, picking the horses, trying almost anything that anybody will pay them to do."

Belk's disenchantment with Hurkos appears to have stemmed from the extraordinary confidence he reposed in the psychic in the first place—both personally and in business. A family tragedy helped to sour Belk. "In June of 1957," he recalled once, "my ten-year-old daughter disappeared from our home in North Carolina while playing, and we searched the area for her for hours down by the Catawba River near the house and around the grounds." Distraught, the father telephoned Hurkos at his Miami home in the hope that the psychic could tell what had happened to the child. Hurkos thought awhile silently. Nothing came to him, he said finally, but he would concentrate and call back. Five minutes later he phoned Belk in Charlotte.

"Have you found her yet?" he asked.

"No," the agitated father said.

Hurkos hesitated a moment, and then blurted out:

"Henry, I don't know how to tell you this, but her body is in the river near your house. She's drowned."

The room seemed to reel around Belk for a moment, but he quickly recovered himself. "I asked Hurkos where she was, and he told me that I would find her near a certain clump of bushes at the edge of the river. I went directly to that spot and she was there just as he had said in the position he had said."

There is no sadder lot than a father burying his child. Belk could not easily reconcile himself to his loss. His mind traveled morosely to Hurkos, and Hurkos' gift. "If he could see ahead," he said bitterly, "why couldn't he have told me what was going to happen to my child in time to save her?"

In business ventures, relying extraordinarily on Hurkos, Belk reported little success. "I dropped twenty thousand dollars looking for uranium in Utah," he said, "and considerably more opening stores in Miami and Atlanta that Hurkos had predicted would be successful." Belk eventually gave up both stores, but less prejudiced observers report that both properties later did well under different auspices. "Hurkos," one observer said, "might have had the long view."

In recent years Hurkos has been earning a very good living, charging for private consulations just as a doctor, lawyer, or any professional man would do, although his fees are often stiffer than any doctor's or lawyer's. "He wanted $150 just for one reading," a Michigan man told me, "and I figured no reading could do me that much good."

Even though they are impressed by his powers, customers often bridle at the prices. In the summer of 1961 his agent in Milwaukee, Wisconsin, his newest headquarters, had asked oilman Russell Maguire, who was interested in psychic research, if he would care to retain Hurkos to find oil for him.

Both Maguire and his wife had been struck by Hurkos' ability. Shaking hands with the attractive middle-aged Mrs. Maguire, whom he had never seen before, Hurkos had spouted out:

"You have arthritis."

"Since I was twenty-four," she replied.

He stood off and surveyed her a moment, then commanded: "Write out something and let me hold it."

As he fondled the slip of paper his brow knit into a frown. "Your mother is ill," he said. He drew his hands across his belt and down to his pelvic area. "Through here," he said, "she is having trouble in this area, but I can't quite see it clearly."

"She fractured her hip and is convalescing," Mrs. Maguire said.

"She will get better," he assured, "though she is a very old woman."

Discussing the performance that night in their Greenwich, Connecticut home, the Maguires were favorably impressed. But Hurkos was still too rich for the wealthy oilman. "After they wrote me," Maguire said, "I wrote back and said that I would be willing to give Hurkos a small percentage of all the oil my company turned up through him."

But the Hurkos group wasn't interested in small percentages.

"They wanted expenses, a fee for looking around, and a big percentage of the oil well," oilman Maguire reported. "If they didn't find anything, they still got paid."

The oilman declined the offer. "I preferred the services of geological engineers whose records for oil discoveries were certainly better-tested by time. And they weren't as expensive."

Unlike Edgar Cayce, the psychic machine has no aversion to participating in stunts. And in at least one notable instance he outdid an electronic brain, which had been spoon-fed a barrelful of statistics without arriving at the right answers. After the brain failed to come up with the pennant winners in the 1959 major league baseball race, *This Week Magazine*, a weekly supplement, asked Hurkos to see what he could do about picking the winners. The Dutchman made a series of visits to the teams' spring-training camps in Florida before the '59 season got under way. He knew nothing about baseball, had never seen a game, and couldn't tell a home run from a base on balls. But he ran his fingers over bats, balls, gloves, even the wooden splinters in players' dugouts. This was psychometry. But he also concentrated on taking his magic newsreels off the universal film. He walked into the Milwaukee Braves dressing room after an exhibition game at Al Lang Field in St. Petersburg and concentrated on catcher Del Crandall who was dressing. After a few minutes of this bird-watching, leaving him limp from perspiration and strain, he walked out into the sunshine and said of the previous year's National League champs:

"This is a magic team. Perfectionist. I get a terrific feeling. Milwaukee will be at the top most of the year. But in the last days they will lose the flag to the Los Angeles Dodgers."

A team that nobody gave a chance was his choice.

For some reason unknown to the experts, who had picked the Dodgers to bring up the National League cellar, Hurkos liked the Dodgers.

And so it turned out. "Milwaukee," a sports prognosticator said, "looked like the class of the league. But the National League race finished just as Hurkos had predicted, with Los Angeles coming through in the fading days of the season to edge out Milwaukee, which led for a good part of the season."

In the American League Hurkos had trouble with the perennial champions, the New York Yankees. He was chased by Casey Stengel, who didn't want him "whammying" his players, and sneaked back a second time when the manager wasn't around to concentrate on the tobacco spewings of such Yankee luminaries as Moose Skowron and Whitey Ford. This was a team so sure of itself, so supremely confident, that their sublime arrogance conveyed itself to the psychic. "They do not think they can lose," he said. And fretting more over this choice than he had over the unlikely Dodgers, he finally picked the Yanks to beat out the Chicago White Sox. "New York," he said, "will win the American League pennant, and then beat the Los Angeles Dodgers for the World Championship."

As the baseball world knows, the Yanks were beaten out by the White Sox, one of the few times in Stengel's long reign that they didn't carry off the pennant.

Psychometry—and telepathy—working simultaneously, had apparently again upset the psychic machinery as it had in the Jackson murder case. "While the White Sox kept coming up psychometrically, Hurkos was evidently swayed to the Yankees," an observer noted, "by their own overpowering confidence, which communicated itself to him."

He is one celebrity who delights in turning the tables on his interviewers. During the Hollywood movie strike two or three years ago, syndicated film columnist Joe Hyams asked Hurkos about the strike. The machine digressed a moment observing that it was right "only eighty-seven per cent" of the time. "If I was one hundred per cent right, I would be God." And then, the prediction:

"After the strike is settled—regardless of when—the movie industry will never regain its status. The major studios will be destroyed. The independent people will get ahead and most of the pictures will be switched to Europe."

There was nothing startling about the prediction. Hurkos was only confirming a noticeable trend. Hyams was not particularly impressed. But then, as the writer sat there placidly reviewing his notes, Hurkos bent over and whispered hoarsely. "There are times when your arms are so heavy you can hardly raise them. Go to a chiropractor. Have him work here on your spine"—Hurkos tapped a ridge on Hyams' back—"and you will be well."

Hurkos had other news for the newsman. "Have a watchmaker look at your watch. The mainspring needs to be replaced. Also your son has a tendency to ear trouble. Isn't that so?"

The psychic machine—like a good radio—had tuned in beautifully on the writer. "Hurkos was right on all counts," Hyams reported. "The chiropractor straightened me out. The watchmakers said the watch needed a new mainspring, and my son does have ear trouble."

There was static at times and the set was not always up to par. Kay Gardella, television editor of the New York *Daily News,* interviewing the machine, could not give Hurkos as good a report. As their interview proceeded, Miss Gardella took from her wallet a picture of a baby and placed it in an envelope. Hurkos didn't see the picture, nor did he look at the envelope. He simply rubbed his hand over it. "I see a dog. Yes, there's a dog in this family. He has long ears. There are three in the family. I see a dog and a man. The dog has something wrong with his right side. Is that not right?"

He wasn't exactly right, or maybe he was. "The baby's father did own a dog with long ears, but he died," editor Gardella said. "However, not from an injury to the right side, but from a heart attack. As for the number in the family, four would be more correct. However, there was a separation in the family; the man moved out, and soon there were three."

Miss Gardella gave Hurkos a ring to work on. "Fingering it," she said, "he made some unusual medical prognostication that to our knowledge and our doctor's was absolutely untrue." Then he said that Miss Gardella would receive a letter from Germany with bad news in it. "We're still waiting for that letter," she reported months later. But as she was leaving the restaurant, wondering who she knew in Germany, the editor overheard a couple at the next table talking in German. "It occurred to me," she said, "that Hurkos might have tuned in on them. I felt like telling them they should enjoy themselves while they could, for a letter with bad news was coming—maybe."

Television has no terrors for the psychic machine. On TV the impressions seem to shoot at him with the same frequency from all over the room—or the globe. When he appeared on the Paar show in January of 1962, he was so convincing that many viewers wondered whether the performance had been staged. But Paar's producers were even more suspicious than the audience. "In choosing subjects from the studio audience," production aide Larry Kantrowitz said, "we tried to avoid anybody who appeared anxious to be called."

The first subject was an obvious stranger to the show. She stood up uncertainly, and looked as though she would have gladly scooted for the nearest exit. Rubbing a calling card produced with a self-conscious smile by the young lady, Hurkos announced with assurance: "You had better go to your dentist—I see you going next week."

The girl broke into a nervous laugh. "I broke my tooth last week," she said, "and I've already made an appointment."

There was a sprinkling of applause.

Vic Parry, one of the guest comedians, was noticeably skeptical. Hurkos touched his wallet and said, "Your father died on a Friday. He had something wrong here"—and he put his hands to his throat—"and that's what he died from."

The comic said quietly, "My father did die on Friday—he had cancer of the throat."

There was no applause—only a few scattered gasps.

The machine then handled a personal article belonging to comedienne Pat Carroll, also a guest on the show, without knowing whose it was. "I don't see your mother and father together. . . . Your mother was operated on." He ran his fingers over the article again. "This person almost drowned when young." With an effort Miss Carroll restrained a gasp. "She saw a bad accident in a car when she was between five and six." He paused. "She's had a rough time, a hard worker, started from scratch. She has a birthday in December, and she has swollen glands."

All told, it didn't add up to much, and was rather sketchy and disjointed, but it was all correct and perhaps all it required was an evaluating brain to bring that person's life into focus.

Next was a heavy-set, good-looking man with a serious aspect. "This man," Hurkos announced, "has stomach trouble, and he just had a child." He thought a moment. "The child weighed eight pounds three ounces." The man laughed outright. "That's right," he said in sheer surprise. "Eight pounds, four ounces." As somebody whispered that the scale was probably off, Hurkos added, "And the child has been having trouble with its mouth." He was right again.

Although the machine had performed beautifully, Hugh Downs, the Paar moderator, was still dubious after the show. "Let me draw a picture of your house," said Hurkos.

"He drew a perfect replica of Hugh's house in Connecticut," Kantrowitz recalled. "Showed the dead-end street, with the house the third from the corner, and a dead tree in its precise position on the lawn." Downs was impressed.

Kantrowitz had already been treated to an exhibition of the machine's artistic faculty. "He copied perfectly a Japanese wall design that I had created for myself, a sort of wall tree, with one branch looking as though it were poking through a window. I don't think there was another design like it in New York. And then he described my bedroom, declaring correctly that the rug on the floor was shaped like an artist's palette."

Earlier, before the show, Hurkos had told Kantrowitz that his wife had hurt an ankle in a skiing accident, and then, said, "You had an accident when you were twelve; you were hit by a bat, playing baseball."

"No," said Kantrowitz, "I was thirteen."

"You were twelve," Peter repeated with authority.

That night Kantrowitz checked with his mother on the telephone. She thought awhile. "No, Larry," she said, "you were twelve."

The machine is not a very good mirror. Even in trance, in the subconscious, it can see nothing clearly for itself. But being a human machine, it still tries. In 1957, in a reading that was recorded, and which I subsequently heard, the psychic machine made a singular prediction. It predicted its own death. It even picked the date—November 17, 1961.

But in the fall of 1962, approximately a year later, Peter Hurkos was still very much alive and in business. The machine was run down. It needed a little rest. That was all.

14 FATIMA—FACT AND FANCY

In the early part of 1960, Catholic information centers were flooded with calls from the curious—Catholic and non-Catholic alike. In New York City alone, St. Patrick's Information Center received thousands of inquiries.

And nearly all asked the same thing: Was the Fatima prophecy going to be opened, and when would it be revealed?

The prophecy was opened and by report sent on to Rome, but the information itself, now the subject of great speculation, has not been revealed. It may never be revealed, or it may be revealed at any time, depending on the wishes of the Pope.

In the absence of an announcement, wild rumors circulated, feeding on ignorance, superstition, and malice. One rumor swept Italy that the Holy Father had opened the Fatima prophecy in the presence of a Bishop and both were shocked speechless by what they read. There were reports that the prophecy had foreseen the destruction of the Church because warnings of penance and devotion had gone unheeded by the Western world. At a meeting in New York, an anti-Catholic "reverend" of a naturalist church "disclosed" confidentially that the Church had been ordered to redistribute its wealth to the poor, regardless of denomination.

In some areas of the Catholic clergy, where the prophecies were never seriously considered, there was even lighthearted humor, intended to dismiss the prophecies or at least put them in proper perspective. At the height of the presidential campaign in 1960, with the Catholic Kennedy pitted against the Protestant Nixon, the joke went:

"Do you know why the Holy Father hasn't made the last Fatima prophecy known?"

"Why?" came the response.

"Because when he opened it, it said, 'Don't vote for Kennedy.'"

Back of this jest lay a serious feeling that altogether too much had been made of the prophecy at the expense of the penance and devotions, which had been the original message when the vision of the Holy Mother first appeared to the three children of Fatima in 1917.

In fact, responsible Catholic sources now denied there was even a prophecy. It was only a message, a recommendation, or a suggestion made by the surviving child of Fatima, Sister Lucy, who had reported the first visions, together with the warning that Russia would "chastise" the West if it did not mend its ways.

In this spirit of de-emphasis, there was even a report that far from being top secret, the prophecy had been placed unsealed in an envelope in 1939, and turned over to Sister Lucy's Bishop in Portugal for safekeeping until it was to be opened in 1960. "Sister Lucy had been ill," a church dignitary close to the scene told me, "and the Bishop thought it might be a good idea to take down any further recollections she might have of the visions. There was nothing significant about his request or her compliance, or even the date. The whole thing was exaggerated out of all relation to reality."

It would be a simple matter, I thought, to squelch all these rumors for once and all.

"Then why not reveal it," I asked, "and put an end to all the controversy?"

"Because it is time to discourage those who have tried to make a cult out of the prophecies instead of the worship," he replied evenly.

But there was still a message, regardless of its nature, and since it came from the nun whose original visions had inspired this worship, it was of interest to those who were interested in Fatima. Monsignor Harold Colgan of Plainfield, New Jersey, spiritual founder of the Blue Army, a Catholic group dedicated to the devotions of Fatima, was in Portugal when the prophecy, which he styled a recommendation, was opened in 1960, and he had heard that the Bishop of Leiria, governing the diocese embracing Fatima, had sent it on to the Pope.

"Of course, there was a lot of speculation about it," the Monsignor said, "but there is nothing unusual about the contents of the envelope not being revealed. It could be revealed tomorrow, in five years, two hundred, or never. The Church itself is eternal, and time itself is unimportant."

But what did it say?

"I have an idea," another Catholic source said, "that the message may have concerned Russia in some way, and that it might have added to present world tensions to have made it publicly known. However, it is only surmise on my part."

Despite the sentiment in the Church, many Catholics, devoted to the Fatima story, found it hard to suddenly recast their thinking and detach themselves from a mystical fascination with the Fatima prophecies. "All those other predictions coming true is what made me feel that the Lady actually made an appearance," said a devout Catholic woman employed by the Church. "I don't see how the two things can be separated."

She was as curious as ever about the nature of the last of the so-called prophecies.

But the Church was significantly silent all through 1960. And then toward the close of 1961, the Church, semiofficially at least, took cognizance that the period for revealing the new "prophecy" had come and gone without the long-anticipated revelation. On October 6 of that year, on the eve of the annual worldwide pilgrimage to Fatima, the official news service of the National Catholic Welfare Council published a statement by a Catholic authority in canon law amounting to a virtual disclaimer of the prophecy.

"I do not reject the whole Fatima story," Monsignor J. D. Conway said, "though I am not personally deeply impressed by it.

I have no serious questions about the credibility of the apparitions —that was declared by the Bishop of Leiria after seven years of investigation and careful study by theologians. I am not opposed to the Fatima devotions—they involve penance, sacrifice, the Rosary, and devotion to the Mother of Jesus. But I think it [Fatima] has been often misused for purposes bordering on superstition: as a threat to inspire fear, as a goal to hatred and superstition, as a club with which to fight political enemies—and I don't mean Russian."

Much of the prophetic message, he claimed, had been revealed subsequent to the original apparitions. "The original revelations of Our Lady to the children were fine," he said, "those were the ones the Bishop approved. Much of the later accumulation is based on the memories of a holy nun who made her prophecies known after the events had happened. To the best of my knowledge there has been no official approval given to these—and most of the secrets and promises that cause all the furor are contained in them."

And why then did the Bishop now keep silent? "My guess is that he found the contents of his famous envelope unsuitable for publication," Monsignor Conway said. "As far as I know the Holy See has given no formal, positive endorsement to the apparitions of Fatima only permissive silence."

The nature of the unrevealed prophecy, which has had more publicity than any prophecy of the century, seems to vary with the nature of the observer. A Jesuit priest, rated an authority on Fatima, advised me casually: "It concerned something that was so trivial that it would have been absurd to make it known."

I did not question how he knew it was trivial.

"But the other prophecies were anything but trivial," I pointed out. "They concerned the chastisement of the West by the Russians."

"Most of this," he replied, "came from the recollection of the surviving nun, Lucy, and was not part of the original 1917 prophecy. And anyway, much more was made of the whole thing than ever should have been, since the source was three ignorant, superstitious children."

I pointed out that the children were also the source of the apparition story. "I suppose," I said, "the Church in Portugal considered it a heart-warming revelation at the time because of the depressed status of the Church in the country in 1917."

"Exactly," he said, "and it did serve some good purpose in revitalizing the traditional faith of the country."

"But at the same time," I said, "don't you think it odd that Russia should have been singled out as the chastiser, since Russia at that time was on its knees, recently knocked out of the war by Germany and on the verge of invasion by its former Allies?"

"Oh," he said, "there was undoubtedly something to the original vision; it's just that its importance in the realm of world affairs has been magnified beyond reality. And anyway, Russia wasn't mentioned till years later—by Sister Lucy."

Long before the preoccupation with the unrevealed prophecy, there had been a disposition within Church ranks to accept the Fatima story without too much question. A pamphlet published by the Catholic Information Society of the New York archdiocese, in December 1948, freely quoted from the original message along with the Lady's requests for penance and Rosary prayer: "If my requests are heard, Russia will be converted and there will be peace. Otherwise great errors will be spread through the world, giving rise to wars and persecutions against the Church; the good will suffer martyrdom, and the Holy Father will have to suffer much, different nations will be destroyed; but in the end my Immaculate Heart will triumph, and an era of peace will be conceded to humanity."

From its beginning, the pamphlet made clear, the message—and apparitions—seemed significantly interwoven with the fate of Russia. "Twenty-seven days after Lenin and Trotsky arrived at Petrograd [later known as Stalingrad]," this official Catholic report said, "to take command of the Socialistic Revolution in Russia, Our Blessed Lady, the Mother of God, appeared in a little cove outside the small town of Fatima, sixty miles north of Lisbon in Portugal. It was her sixth and last visit to warn the world of its folly and to offer a heavenly remedy."

In her revelations, Sister Lucy, who is still very much alive, had quoted not only from her own communications with the vision of Fatima, but from her little cousin Jacinta, who, with her brother Francisco, comprised the first audience at Fatima. It was Jacinta's vision, revealed before her death, according to Lucy, that graphically foretold some of the approaching horrors. Undoubtedly some of the fearful speculation about the unrevealed prophecy had stemmed from Jacinta's message, investigated by the Jesuit Father Fonseca. "Jacinta," Lucy had reported, "saw a 'very terrible' war, annihilated nations, many ruined houses, and streets filled with people crying with hunger and having nothing to eat. She saw the Holy Father before a table in a 'large house' with his face in his hands, crying. Outside the house there were many people, some of whom cast stones at him while others reviled and cursed him.

"Afterwards she saw also many of the persecuted faithful, among whom were slain priests . . . until the blood of martyrs had placated the wrath of God. Many people will die in this war, the great majority of whom will go to hell. God will send great punishments into the world and Spain will be the first country to suffer."

World War II has been thought by many to have begun in Spain, where the Communists and Axis Powers squared off in a prelude to the greater conflict.

Lucy herself had warned of World War II.

"Sister Lucy obviously saw the approaching war before it happened," one commentator pointed out, "because she referred it to the next pontificate, which would have been that of Pius XI, and though the war actually came in 1939, a few months after his death, many believe that Europe had been at war since 1936 when Hitler marched into the Rhineland. And of course, the Spanish Civil war broke out in that pontificate, too."

There is some confusion as to when Sister Lucy made her first significant reference to Russia. Though Russia's role in the prophecy was supposedly communicated by the vision in 1917, Lucy appears to have kept silent on this surprising reference to an avenging Russia—then a broken, defeated nation—for many years. This was in keeping, she said, with instructions from the Holy Mother.

But even in 1927, when Lucy was reliably reported to have

first divulged its role in the vision, the commentator pointed out that the Soviet was an insignificant force in world affairs, struggling with its five-year plan and in no position to menace anybody outside its borders.

Actually, there is no more reason to mistrust the story of the Fatima children and their prophecies now than there ever was. The content of the original 1917 message, together with the prophecies revealed then and subsequently, have not changed from the time they were first disclosed. And not the least Miracle of Fatima was the effect on the people of Portugal of this simple story of childish faith. It restored the vigor of the Church in a land where a dominant anticlerical intellectual clique was determined to eliminate the last remnants of Catholic worship. It touched off a counterrevolution, which returned Portugal to the Christian fold without shedding a single drop of blood—in itself a miracle. Its story had been treasured by Pius XII, the angelic pastor, and by the present Pope, John XXIII, who was conspicuously intrigued by its mysteries less than five years before the unrevealed message, recommendation, note, or what have you, was to have been opened in 1960.

In all of history there is probably a no more stirring call to faith, even to non-Catholics, than that contained in the Fatima story, a summons that has made the shrine at Fatima one of the most popular in the Catholic world.

As in all religious history, the visions at Fatima certainly came when they were most needed by the faithful.

When the Fatima children—Lucy dos Santos, ten, and her cousins, Francisco and Jacinta Marto, nine and seven respectively—saw their first vision on May 13, 1917, the Church in Portugal, known as the Land of Mary because of its traditional devotion to the Immaculate Heart of Mary, was in a state of acute distress. A revolutionary republican government, overthrowing the monarchy, had abolished the Catholic sacraments in this Catholic country. It boasted that it would stamp out Catholicism in two generations. But in the bleak hills of Fatima, the poorest parish in Portugal, the simple peasants clung zealously to their faith. The children of Fatima still said their daily Rosary. On this one day, having just done their Rosary, they were tending sheep in the pasture of Lucy's father, Antonio, on a high plateau known as the Cova da Iria. It was noon and the sun shone brightly from cloudless skies, but the three children were startled by two flashes of lightning. Then, as they looked up, they saw an iridescent radiance from a globe of light in the foliage of a small oak tree. In the center of the globe, enveloped in an aura, was a beautiful figure of a woman. She could not have been more than eighteen years old. As the children stood stock-still, the lady said softly: "Do not be afraid. I will not harm you." And then, not much later, she disappeared as dramatically as she had made herself known.

She did not identify herself at this time, but asked the children to return to the same spot on each thirteenth of the month until October, when she promised to tell them who she was. Meanwhile, she urged them to say their Rosary and do penance, and keep their secret.

Lucy urged the other children not to mention the incident, but they couldn't contain themselves. All three children were severely scolded by their parents for lying, and the parish priest also expressed his displeasure. Jacinta's mother was particularly outraged. She told little Jacinta that she was mad and beat her. But the girl wouldn't change her story.

The children were back at the Cova da Iria at noon on June 13, and with them were fifty or sixty curious villagers.

Lucy, the leader, recited her Rosary, and then turning toward the east, breathlessly exclaimed, "I've seen the lightning already. The Lady is coming."

The villagers listened entranced to Lucy's questions, watching her face grow ecstatic, but, of course, only the children heard what the Lady said—or saw her, for that matter. She did not stay long. She said that she would soon be calling Jacinta and Francisco, but that Lucy must remain to spread the message of the Immaculate Heart of Mary.

And the message was spreading, fanned by faith and hope. Although there were only a few hundred inhabitants in the village of Fatima, five thousand people turned up for the Lady's third appearance at noon on July 13. To the children she promised a miracle on October 13 to convince an unbelieving world of Her presence. It was at this time, Lucy revealed later, that she predicted that World War I, in which Portugal had become embroiled the year before, would soon end. "But if people do not cease to offend God, not much time will elapse, and in the next pontificate, another and more terrible war will begin." There would be a sign from the heavens. "When there is seen a night illuminated by an unknown light, know that this is the great sign which God is giving that He is about to punish the world for its crimes by means of war, famine, persecutions of the Church and of the Holy Father."

And then came a request to consecrate Russia to the Immaculate Heart—not to be revealed for years—so that "Russia will be converted and there will be peace." Otherwise, Russia, like Attila and his Huns, might become the Scourge of God. But in the end, Christianity would triumph anyway.

By now the story of Fatima was sweeping through Portugal. A hostile government, which had broken with Rome, was quick to move. On August 13, date of the next scheduled apparition, the children were arrested and flung into jail. Government officials, cajoling, wheedling, bullying, tried to get them to retract. They were led to a cauldron of boiling oil and told they would be thrown into it. But they kept insisting they had seen the vision, although they refused to divulge what they had been told; this was secret.

Not knowing what had happened to the children, fifteen thousand people had gathered at the Cova for some heavenly sign. They saw only a white cloud and a flash of lightning on a cloudless day. It had no more significance for them. But the arrest of the children had stirred up the country, and they were released. A few days later, the children again went to the Cova da Iria, and again Lucy reported the vision. Excitement was mounting in Portugal. The officials could do nothing to stop it. Some thirty thousand of the faithful assembled on September 13 before the small oak where the children had reported the first vision. Taking their cue from the children, the crowd eagerly scanned the sky.

Many reported a globe of light in the tree trailed by the now-familiar white cloud and rain in a clear sky, and they saw the luminous globe moving from east to west. "I shall never forget," one witness said, "the thousands of people, at the voice of a child, falling on their knees and, with tears streaming, praying with confidence for the maternal protection of the Queen of Heaven."

By now all of Portugal, despite the anticlerical posture of its government, was intrigued and excited by the reports from Fatima. The Catholic Church exhibited its customary reserve on miracles. One Catholic diocesan newspaper in Portugal suggested frankly: "Real Apparition or Supposed Illusion." Meanwhile, the free-thinkers and liberals were decrying the reported miracles as the Farce at Cova da Iria. The Reverend Doctor Manuel Nunes Formigao a respected dignitary, had been asked by the Church in Lisbon to investigate the strange stories coming out of Fatima. He was struck by the similarity of Lucy's story with that of two shepherd children who had reported Our Lady appearing in vision at La Salette, France, and giving them secret warning of great calamities if the people of France did not stop offending God.

Lucy's mother was familiar with the La Salette story. She recalled reading an account of the French miracle to her daughter, but had not thought it had impressed the child because she never mentioned it again.

Lucy unhesitatingly recalled having heard the story, but said she had not thought about it again, and she steadfastly refused to reveal the prophecy—the one of July 13, under the most skilled questioning. But the Reverend Doctor Formigao persisted in his efforts to pluck at the secret.

"If the crowd knew the secret," he asked, "would they be sad?"

Lucy nodded her head and added that only she and Jacinta had heard the secret, Francisco had seen only the vision. But she repeated that the Lady had promised a miracle on October 13, her sixth and last appearance, at the usual time, as a reassuring sign.

The investigator could not decide how much the children had seen and how much they had fabricated. The only thing he could do, with the others, was to wait for the day of the miracle. On this appointed day, October 13, all paths appeared to lead to Fatima.

The roads were clogged with farmers and factory workers, the rich and the poor, the sick and the strong. Many had traveled all night to get to the Cova da Iria by the hour of noon. Some carried crippled and ailing children in their arms, others hobbled with crutches and canes. It was a cavalcade that even disinterested reporters would not forget for a long time. "Nearly all, men and women," wrote the anticlerical editor, Avelino de Almeida of the newspaper *O Seculo*, "have bare feet, the women carrying their footgear in bags on their heads, the men leaning on great staves and carefully grasping umbrellas also. One would say they were all oblivious to what was going on about them, with a great lack of interest in the journey and in other travelers, as if lost in a dream, reciting their Rosary in a sad rhythmic chant."

Some seventy thousand made their way to the hollow, trampling the pastures of old Antonio dos Santos, Lucy's father, who was already morose about the whole affair. The Lisbon newspapers had sent their best editors and reporters, and *O Dia*, one of Lisbon's leading dailies, added its dramatic report on the march of the faithful:

"All night long and into the early morning a light persistent rain fell. It soaked the fields, soddened the air, and chilled to the bone the men, women, and children and the beasts plodding their way to the hill of the miracle. The rain kept falling, a soft unending drizzle. Drops trickled down the women's skirts of coarse wool or striped cotton, making them heavy as lead. Water dripped from the caps and broad-brimmed hats of the men. . . . The bare feet of the women and the hobnailed shoes of the men sloshed in the side pools of the muddy roads. They seemed not to notice the rain."

Long before noon the ground in the Cova was a quagmire. A sea of umbrellas covered the vast crowd. Yet when little Lucy suddenly cried, "Put down your umbrellas," the huge throng obeyed as one, and stood in the downpour, waiting.

As the appointed hour of noon arrived, the crowd was beginning to show the first signs of restlessness, and a priest there as an observer was getting ready to lead the children away, when Lucy looked into the leaden sky and cried exultantly: "She is coming. Kneel everybody."

A hush fell over the crowd.

Then Lucy's tremulous voice was heard again.

"What do you want of me?" she asked the Lady.

No matter how the crowd strained, only Lucy's voice could be heard in her colloquy with the apparition. But then came a sign, which all could see—the miracle that the Lady had promised.

The downpour suddenly stopped and the clouds parted revealing the great orange globe of the sun shimmering in an azure-blue sky. And then, as the thousands watched, spellbound, the shining orange disk seemed to spin, and as it spun it gave off fiery fingers of light reaching across the sky. The earth first cast a red shadow, and then, in bewildering succession, orange, yellow, green, blue, indigo, and violet.

Three times this phenomenon repeated itself. Then high in the sky the sun seemed to shudder and started to plunge to earth. Nearer and nearer it came in an electrifying power dive, shimmying violently as it approached the earth. The crowd began to cower in horror. "It's the end of the world," shrieked one woman, falling to her knees.

All around her people dropped down in terror. Some stretched flat on the ground, beseeching God for mercy. Others, speechless from fright, prayed silently.

For ten minutes the celestial display continued, until finally the sun started to climb again, resuming its normal position in the sky. And then came the realization of the miracle. The greatest of the skeptics, editor de Almeida, a freemason with a mistrust of miracles, was impressed along with the most hysterical. "Certainly beyond all cosmic laws," he reported, "were the sudden tremblings and movements of the sun, dancing as it were, in typical language of the peasants, before the astonished multitude who gazed in awe." Though unimpressed by a vision that he could neither see nor hear—except through the eyes and ears of a ten-year-old child— de Almeida did pay his respects to the Miracle of the Sun. "It remains for those competent to pronounce on the *danse macabre* of the sun, which today at Fatima has made hosannas burst from the breasts of the faithful and naturally has impressed—so witnesses worthy of belief assure me—even freethinkers and other persons not at all interested in religious matters." To this unbeliever, it was "a spectacle unique and incredible if one had not been a witness to it." But he had witnessed it and he drew a graphic picture: "One can see the immense crowd turn toward the sun, which reveals itself free of the clouds in full noon. But now bursts forth a colossal clamor, and we hear the nearest spectators crying, 'Miracle, miracle.'"

All of Portugal was now caught up in the Miracle of the Sun. The children of Fatima were marked personages. Everything they said or did was committed to memory or writing. They were constantly badgered and questioned. They had no peace. They began to draw to themselves. Jacinta, who had been a pious but happy-go-lucky child even while anticipating her own death, started having prophetic visions. She foresaw the fearful bombings almost a quarter of a century before they were enacted upon the roads of France and Holland and in the ruins of London and Frankfort.

She had visions of an oppressed Pope, and was troubled by them. "Poor little Holy Father," she said, "we must pray a lot for him."

Jacinta and Francisco had been told by the Lady they were going to die early, and they accepted their fate cheerfully, even eagerly.

In January 1919, Francisco contracted influenza. He succumbed that April. He was eleven years old. A few months later, his sister also came down with the flu. Specialists were summoned and they recommended a difficult chest operation. While Jacinta lay ill she reportedly had several visions applying to the mundane things of this earth. She told her nurse prophetically: "Our Lady told me that I am going to Lisbon to another hospital and that I will die alone."

Six weeks later the child was moved to St. Stephen Hospital in Lisbon so she could get needed care and surgery; her prophetic visions appeared to continue. Mother Gohindo, a Franciscan nun who saw her daily, remarked one day what a wonderful sermon a certain priest had delivered. Jacinta's comment startled her. "You will see," the child said closing her eyes, "that the padre is wicked." Within a few months, the nun was to recall, the priest had left the order under a cloud.

Jacinta was not a comforting visionary. When a doctor blandly suggested she pray for him before she went to heaven, she said without rancor, "You and your daughter will be there before me." Though she died but a short time later, they had already preceded her.

Even her death was prophetic. One afternoon the child wanly asked a nurse if she could see a priest. He administered First Communion, heard confession, and promised to bring her the Holy Eucharist in the morning. "That will be too late, Father," she said. "I'm going to die tonight."

The priest consulted with the doctors. They saw no immediate danger, and so he decided to return as he had planned, in the morning.

At ten-thirty that night, two hours later, the girl took a turn for the worse; her nurse rushed down a corridor to summon a doctor. When they returned, Jacinta was dead. She had died alone, far from relatives and friends, as she had predicted. The date was February 20, 1920. She would have been ten in three weeks.

The Cardinal Patriarch Manuel Arejeira, a conservative prince of the Church, had been impressed by the "astonishing phenomenon of the sun, which scholarly astonomers had not foreseen." And now he was impressed by the children's deaths: "The three little children confess that the Heavenly apparition had predicted that she would soon come for two of them to take them to heaven. During the illness that struck both, they insist that prayers and doctors will never cure them. One of them asserts that she will die alone, far from her family in a hospital, while the other runs from school to go to Church, since it is not worth his while to learn how to read, and it all took place as they had predicted."

With her two companions both dead, Lucy shortly thereafter entered a convent school and later took the name Sister Maria das Dores—Sister Mary of Sorrows. To Lucy, her mission was clear— the perpetuation of the message at Fatima, for had not the Lady said to her, when she told Jacinta and Francisco that they would be taken: "God wishes you to remain in the world for some time, because he wants to use you to establish in the world the devotion to my Immaculate Heart. I promise salvation to those who embrace it."

For several years, Sister Lucy clung stubbornly to the most secret of the predictions that had come through to the vision—the chastisement by Russia, with its eventual consecration to Christianity. And then in December of 1925, while studying in the convent of the Sisters of St. Dorothy in Tuy, Spain, across the border from Portugal, she had another vision, of both the Blessed Mother and the Christ Child. The Mother spoke: "My child, behold my heart surrounded with the thorns that ungrateful men place therein at every moment by their blasphemies and ingratitude. You at least try to console me."

Shortly thereafter, Sister Lucy began to ask for a special devotion. "She began to speak to her confessors about Our Lady's desire for the devotion to her Immaculate Heart in 1926, 1927, 1929, and in a letter to Pius XII in 1940," an official Catholic source told me. In November 1926, Lucy became a novice at the age of eighteen. In 1927, she had two visions in which Christ appeared, confirming the requests of His Mother concerning the devotions, and giving her permission to reveal certain things, but not the last secret, which apparently was to be saved until 1960. In 1927 came the revelation of the Russian threat, not as startling then as it would have been in 1917. World War II also engaged Sister Lucy. The children had been told to look for a warning light in the sky. On the night of January 25, 1938, those lights apparently appeared over most of Western Europe. They lit up the skies with a crimson glow that one startled observer described as a "reflection of the fires of hell." One newspaper headlined, "Aurora Borealis Startles Europe; People Flee in Fear," And it reported: "The lights were seen clearly in Italy, Spain and even Gibraltar . . . they spread fear in parts of Portugal, while thousands of Britons were brought running into the streets in wonderment."

But though she privately talked about the approaching war, Sister Lucy did not formally comment until three years after the lights had appeared, when she wrote her diocesan Bishop of

Leiria: "Your Excellency is not unaware that some years ago God manifested that sign which the astronomers choose to designate by the name Aurora Borealis. If they look well into it, they will see that it was not and could not be, in the form in which it appeared, such an aurora. But be that as it may, God was pleased in this way to make me understand that His justice was ready to let fall the blow on the guilty nations, and in this way to begin to ask with insistence for the reparatory communion of the first Saturdays and the consecration of Russia."

In a remarkable interview with the American Catholic scholar William Thomas Walsh, in 1946, before convent witnesses, Sister Lucy renewed her plea for devotions for the consecration of Russia: "What Our Lady wants is that the Pope and all the bishops in the world shall consecrate Russia to her Immaculate Heart on one special day. If it is not done, the errors of Russia will spread through every country in the world."

"Does this mean, in your opinion," Walsh asked, "that every country without exception will be overcome by communism?"

She answered with a simple "yes."

Walsh's observation, in his very readable *Our Lady of Fatima,* was a model of restraint. "It was plain," he commented, "that she felt that Our Lady's wishes had not yet been carried out. People must say the Rosary, perform sacrifices, make the five first Saturday communions, pray for the Holy Father."

At this time she also cleared up a point in Jacinta's vision of deplorable injury to a pope. "Some persons," Walsh said, "believe that Jacinta's vision of a persecuted pope referred to some particular pontiff. Some believe the present Holy Father [Pius XII] was the one she saw."

And Sister Lucy replied: "Jacinta said it was a pope. There was nothing to indicate any particular pope."

Oddly, it was Pius XII, consecrated a bishop in Rome on the very day and at the very hour of the first vision, May 13, 1917, who was to consecrate the Church to the Immaculate Heart of Mary, as requested through Sister Lucy on October 21, 1942, virtually the twenty-fifth anniversary of the sixth and final apparition at the Cova da Iria.

In December of 1957, Sister Lucy, now a nun of the Discalced Carmelites in the Convent of St. Theresa of Jesus, in Coimbra, Portugal, gave a revealing, if controversial, interview in which she delivered her latest warnings, if one excludes the unrevealed message of 1960, to an erring world. Her warning was communicated to the Reverend Augustin Fuentes, appointed Roman Postulator for the causes of the beatification of Francisco and Jacinta Marto. It was revealed with the approval of his superior, Manuel Pio Lopez, Archbishop of Veracruz, in whose archdiocese he was a priest.

Lucy, when the Reverend Fuentes saw her at the convent the day after Christmas, appeared pale and emaciated, and seemed downcast as she told him: "Father, the Blessed Virgin is very sad because not many respect her Fatima Message, neither the good nor the bad. The good do not because they go along their way of goodness, of apostolate, of virtue, but without paying attention to this message. The bad do not because the chastisement of God is not immediately hovering over them, because of their sins, and they proceed on their way of evil without paying attention to this message. But believe me, Father, God is going to chastise the world."

She briefly mentioned the message to be opened in 1960, less than three years from then. "I cannot go into greater detail," she said, "since it is still a secret, one that through the will of the Blessed Virgin may only be known to the Holy Father and the Bishop at Fatima."

And this is what the Reverend Fuentes said that the surviving child of Fatima told him: "Tell them, Father, that the Blessed Virgin said many times to my cousins, Francisco and Jacinta, as well as to me, that many nations would disappear from the face of the earth, and that Russia would be the instrument of the chastisement of Heaven for all the world, if before this we did not bring about the conversion of that unhappy nation."

As he left the convent, the good Father reflected long on what Sister Lucy had said. In Italy—in Rome itself, the seat of the Church, he had seen the spread of malignant communism with fifteen million active Communists in Italy. The Russians were hurling their threats, defiance, and insults at the world. Their following grew in Asia, Africa, and Latin America. He had seen Russian propaganda, including Khrushchev's latest threats, chalked on the walls of Rome, and he had come to the conclusion that Sister Lucy had clearly foreseen the hazard: "If Russia makes war against the world," he decided, "she will do everything possible to triumph, but if by chance she is conquered, who knows how many of the Western nations, before Russia falls, may first be destroyed, no matter how well armed they may be."

And the Lady, according to Lucy, had foreshadowed a decisive battle. There would be no mistake about the winner. "A decisive battle is a final battle, in which one is going to know who is the victor, and which side is beaten!"

Sister Lucy was not trying to frighten anyone, Father Fuentes said. Her motivation was spiritual. "Sister Lucy emphasized the fact that all this is not for the purpose of filling souls with terror but to make souls realize the reality of the circumstances in which we are living."

Despite the many critics of the Fatima prophecy within the Church, Pope John XXIII, when he was Cardinal Roncalli, indicated a belief that the story of Fatima had much more to it, mystically, than the Miracle of the Sun. "For my part," he said in 1956 before a throng of pilgrims at the world-famous shrine, "I am not far from believing that when the mystery of Fatima shall be completely revealed, there will appear in a clearer light the various small events—more striking than the sun—which, at length, culminated in the great act of historic significance: the solemn consecration of all the Portuguese nation on May 13, 1931 to the Madonna of Fatima."

Notwithstanding the controversy about the prophecies, the devotional message of Fatima appears to be spreading, serving, in the words of Pope John, as "an inexhaustible source of graces and prodigies, which turn themselves in torrents upon Portugal, and from there spread out over the entire Church and the world."

In a poor Bronx parish in New York City, the Monsignor Joseph Cacella, a Portuguese priest who knew the families of the three Fatima children, has shown what faith in the Fatima story can do. He has had notable success with his Fatima Club, which, with faith as a fulcrum, has added to the wonders of Fatima. Using a few drops of Fatima water drawn from a spring tapped at the shrine, many ailing have reported cures from disorders ranging from a slight pain in the neck to acute mental depression. "But the water," as the Monsignor pointed out, "has no magical properties. Its use presupposes purity of soul, a lively spirit of faith, and an abiding confidence."

And with this outlook, reinforced by faith, too, in the prophetic wonders of Fatima, the Miracle of the Water has at times outshone the Miracle of the Sun. It is remarkable what faith and a little water can do. "A patient was admitted to the hospital in Watertown, New York," reported Sister Mary Leonard of Fort Edward, New York, "suffering from severe convulsions. The specialists found that he had an irritation on the brain and on the lung. After the use of the Fatima water, the infection in the lung cleared completely, the convulsions were eliminated and the irritation of the brain greatly diminished so that the patient was able to be up and about and walk to his home and his job."

Not by its prophecies, nor its reputed cures—of which hundreds have been reported at the shrine—but by the Miracle of the Sun does the Catholic Church accept the the Miracle of Fatima. But since it is a "private" revelation, its prophecies need not be accepted by Catholics, though its devotional message is in keeping with Catholic dogma. Non-Catholics, unfamiliar with the Fatima story, have also questioned the Miracle of the Sun, despite the thousands of witnesses.

Wondering myself whether the sun's gyrations might not have been the consequence of a natural phenomenon, I telephoned an astronomer at the renowned Hayden Planetarium in New York, and asked if anything unusual, celestially, had occurred on the thirteenth of October 1917.

The astronomer was puzzled. "What was the occasion?"

"The Fatima Miracle of the Sun."

He groaned. "Don't quote me on that one; I've already got my head in a sling."

While appearing as a guest on a television show, the scientist had been asked if there was any logical way, astronomically, of accounting for thousands having seen the sun dive-bombing over a Portuguese village at this time. A Protestant, steeped in his scientific work, he had never heard the word Fatima before. With an unwitting laugh he had observed:

"It must have been a good vintage year in Portugal."

And the next thing he knew, the roof had fallen in on him. He was busy defending himself for weeks. "But seriously," he told me, "astronomically, such a phenomenon is unknown; it couldn't have happened."

"But what about the seventy thousand people who reported it happening?"

"It might have been mass hypnosis," he suggested.

I laughed. "Even so, that would be a miracle—for who could have hypnotized so many?"

The fact that the Miracle of the Sun had *not* been recorded by any observatory contributed to Church recognition of the miracle. "This phenomenon, which was not registered in any astronomical observatory," the Bishop of Leiria pointed out "—a fact which shows that it was not natural—was seen by persons of every class and grade of society, by believers and skeptics, by journalists representing the principal Portuguese newspapers and even by persons miles away. This destroys any explanation based on collective illusion."

Even to Church skeptics, decrying the importance given the unrevealed message of 1960, the Miracle of the Sun was a clear-cut, confirmed act of prevision which thousands had been told to expect. "The boldness of this prophecy is breath-taking," observed the Portuguese-born Monsignor Cacella. "It is rare in the history of miracles that a prediction was made with such exactness of detail. No nebulous augury in hoary verses! The exact date, the appointed hour, the definite place were fixed. It was a challenge to the modern world to come and see."

The Portuguese priest, now the head of St. Anthony Center in the Bronx, has made frequent pilgrimages to his native land to study the Fatima story and talk to witnesses who are still alive. Once with an Archbishop, who was a seminary classmate, he visited the most important witness of all, Sister Lucy. "A religious festival was in progress at the time," Monsignor Cacella recalled, "and the Archbishop asked if Sister Lucy would like to watch it."

Sister Lucy only smiled and shook her head. "Your Excellency," she said gently, "after what I have seen, what more is there for me to see?"

15 NOSTRADAMUS—THE OLD MASTER

"I wouldn't touch Nostradamus if I were you," the editor said. "Nobody could tell what he was predicting until after it happened."

But Oxford-bred Stewart Munro Robb only scoffed. "That shows how little people know about the Great Seer," observed this Nostradamus scholar extraordinary. "For more than four hundred years Nostradamus has been predicting the impossible, and on the basis of his predictions people who aren't the least psychic have been able to make their own predictions of the most unlikely events."

Nostradamus was no glib sorcerer but a prophet in depth. He not only predicted World Wars I and II, but foresaw the aerial warfare and submarine attacks on shipping that no other wars had experienced. In appraising a great event he didn't seem to miss a detail—Hitler's aggression, England's reluctance to arm, the French fiasco behind their vaunted Maginot Line, all were there for the skilled reader of Nostradamus. "Before World War II," elaborated scholar Robb, "even as the French generals put all their confidence in their great chain of underground fortresses, students of Nostradamus, without the slightest military background, knew the generals were completely wrong. They also knew that the impregnable line would collapse when war came —and they knew that war would come."

Robb himself was so confident of his Nostradamus that he predicted who would win the war and published his prediction at a time when England was standing alone against the might of the conquering Axis. "It was all there," he said, "as plain as day."

In the same way, Nostradamus scholars were forewarned of the atom bomb, flights through space, the rise—and fall—of the Soviets, and now—some thirty-five years away—they anticipate the first war between the planets, but hold out hope for a Golden Age following a period of woe and destruction.

Down through history, they point out, the wise old astrologer, making his predictions back in the sixteenth century, has seldom been wrong—describing the French Revolution, the coming of Napoleon, Cromwell's rise in England, English supremacy of the seas for three hundred years, the American Revolution. He saw plagues, fires, disasters, and, confounding those who claim a prophet can't predict for himself, foresaw his own death in time to help with the funeral arrangements.

Although some predictions disturbed him, he still felt compelled to make them, sadly predicting the downfall of his beloved Church, and then, happily, foreseeing its eventual restoration.

In his more than nine hundred prophetic stanzas, he foresaw events a few months or a few centuries off with equal clarity. Some were already in motion in his own time, and others, more wondrously, did not even begin to take shape until long after his death. He was an astrologer, but unlike the modern astrologer, he insisted that the destiny he foretold was fixed and certain, not allowing for the freedom of choice in the comforting litany:

"The stars impel, they do not compel."

So sure was he of the inevitability of his prophecies that he once told a crowd of hecklers: "You will not make me swallow any of these words, neither in my lifetime, nor after my death."

Endowed with psychic powers, he did not need the stars to see the future. He looked once at the eleven-year-old prince of the minor state of Navarre, and told the boy's governess: "If God permits you to live as long as the Prince, you will have as a master a King of France." And years after the prophet's death, Protestant-bred Henry IV, against all odds, ruled Catholic France.

To the uninitiated, though he could be terribly specific when he wanted to be, Nostradamus was difficult going. He was often deliberately vague and ambiguous, lest he give offense to the Great Ones of the court. "Had I given these prophecies clearly," he told his son Cesar, "these rulers, sects, and religions would find them so little to their liking that they would condemn them." But he still warned the ruling house of France, of which he was a loyal subject, that heads would one day roll, and he named the date—1792—and even identified the princely owners of the heads. But, of course, it did no good.

As an author-prophet, Nostradamus was also jealous of lightly handing out his pearls to the vulgar and ignorant. "My writings," he said confidently, "will be better understood by those who come after my death and by those who penetrate my meaning."

The erudite Robb agreed. Before he reached the point where he could predict from Nostradamus, the scholar discovered that he had all he could do to follow him. "You have to study him for years," Robb said with a smile, "before you suddenly discern a pattern in his poetry and prose, and with this insight all the vagueness and ambiguity, *double-entendre,* and obscurity that make Nostradamus an enigma swiftly crystallize into a thrilling preview of the future."

Robb soon learned that the Prophet was moved not only by caution in employing his abstruse figures of speech, but by a flair for imagery. He loved playing with words. England could be England, or Neptune, the Islands, or even, remarkably, Great Britain before there was a Great Britain; place names like Venice, Genoa, Angoumois, the Dnieper stood for the country of origin, just as the Potomac would have meant the United States. And, Robb said, Nostradamus would have been a wonder with cross-word puzzles and acrostics the way he dealt in anagrams. "He called Hitler 'Hister,'" Robb pointed out, "scrambled Napoleon into Pau Nay Loron—Napoleon Roy, introduced Cromwell by an anagram of his nickname Old Noll, called America the Occident, and the Church of Rome the Fishing Boat."

There were a thousand and one similar references but, as Robb discovered, simplicity was still the quickest road to the heart of the Prophet. And that is how scholar Robb, nearly four hundred years after the Prophet's death, was able not only to see the doom of Axis partners Hitler and Mussolini, but to call the turn on Franco's defection from his brother dictators when everybody else thought he was going to join forces with them.

But Robb knew better—for he had seen it all clearly in one simple stanza. Even before the fall of France, which he had already anticipated from the Seer, he was looking for the Axis powers to confer with Spain over a possible attack on the British stronghold of Gibraltar from the Spanish mainland. Nostradamus had said the meeting would take place on the Riviera, and that Franco—mentioning the Spaniard by name—would send his emissaries. But there would be an unexpected rebuff to the Axis, with access to the great gulf—the Mediterranean—denied. Nostradamus could not have been more specific:

> De Castel Franco sortira l'assemblee
> L'Ambassadeur non plaissant fera scisme;
> Ceux de Riviere seront en la meslee,
> Et au grand goulphre desnieront l'entree.

Which in English went:

> The assembly will go out from the Castle of Franco,
> The ambassador not satisfied will make a schism;
> Those of the Riviera will be involved,
> And they will deny the entry to the great gulf.

Robb was so sure of this prediction, before the fact, that he began combing through the newspapers for hint of such a meeting early in 1940, even before France collapsed and the Germans took over the southern part of that country. Not only that, he went on record with his prediction of an unexpected Axis diplomatic setback, in a pamphlet put out before the predicted event. He was not surprised, though perhaps pardonably elated, when months later his search through the newspapers was finally rewarded. A New York *Times* dispatch from Occupied France revealed that the Axis powers were to confer shortly with the Spaniards on the Riviera. By this time, there was no doubt in anybody's mind what the agenda was to be. But as Allied commentators glumly forecast a backdoor Axis assault on Gibraltar, Robb, who had written about the meeting long before it was scheduled, again knew better. "When Nostradamus was wrong," Robb observed confidently, "it was usually because he had been misinterpreted. But there was no chance of making a mistake here."

Since he "discovered" Nostradamus some twenty-five years ago, Robb has kept atop world events. In 1939, just before the outbreak of World War II, he read that the Frenchman de Fontbrune, basing his prognostication on a Nostradamus verse, had predicted the fall of the invincible Maginot Line and the taking of Paris. Robb was struck by the Prophet's detailed description of the underground network of the fortresses. It was the first adverse report on the Line behind which the French were complacently prepared to sit out the war.

As though he had made a tour of inspection, Nostradamus accurately referred to fifteen hydrographic sections, divided by water, placed them near a great river, clearly the Rhine, and then with astonishing clarity described the shocking impact on the people of Paris—always "the city"—in Nostradamus:

> Near the great river great retrenchment, earth withdrawn,
> It will be divided by water into fifteen sections;
> The city will be taken, fire, blood, cries, all turmoil,
> And the greater part of the people confused by the shock.

Although Robb thought Paris would fall, he never doubted that the Allies would be victorious. In no uncertain terms Nostradamus had described the Axis defeat. And Robb was so confident the Prophet was right that in May of 1941, with France crushed and England just hanging on, the scholar completed a book citing Nostradamus as his authority for the Hitler-Mussolini debacle:

> The two satisfied ones will be joined together,
> When most of the nations are conjoined to Mars,
> But the big man of Africa will be in fear and trembling,
> When the two joined dictators [Duumvirat] are disjoined by the fleet.

Nostradamus never employed an expression idly. Reaching for the Latin term *Duumvirat* to describe this precious pair, Nostradamus had given the partnership a more appropriate tag then the partners themselves had given it. "Nostradamus," Robb explained, "strayed from the French only in making a special point, and *Duumvirat* was the only expression in any language that implied a two-man dictatorship with fascist tendencies." It was remarkable at times to see how Nostradamus' mind worked. "Mussolini, by virtue of his tarnished Ethiopian conquests, was certainly the big man of Africa," said Robb, "and the complacent twosome, imagining victory already in their grasp, were given an unexpected setback when their lifeline to Africa was severed by the British Mediterranean fleet."

Elsewhere in Nostradamus, Robb rounded out his picture of an Axis defeat. One prophecy practically named Hitler, referring to him as Hister, the alteration of one letter being a common anagram form at that time. Another described him as a dark, baseborn, iniquitous man, and foretold a bitter war of attrition, Germany finally compelled to fall back on striplings in uniform:

> Greater part of the camp will be against Hister,
> It will have the great man carried in an iron cage
> When the German child watches the Rhine.

To Robb it was all quite clear. The French for "iron cage" was contemporary usage for prison, and some suggest that Hitler made a prison of the Berlin bunker that was to become his mausoleum.

As a World War II pattern became apparent, it was then a simple matter to forecast Italy's defeat and Il Duce's ignominious end from this reference to aerial warfare, though Italy itself was not mentioned:

> The Armies will fight in the air a great while . . .
> When the monarch of Adria (Adriatic Italy) shall fall.

And the manner of his fall, trussed up by his bootstraps in a city square, reviled by the very mob that once adored him, was equally clear:

> The tree shall fall in the middle of the city,
> Vermin, scabs, sword, firebrand in face.

From the Prophet's curious figures of speech, Robb has predicted that many living today will one day be witnesses, or victims, of the interplanetary war usually associated with science fiction until Colonel John Glenn and the Russians showed the world how to maneuver a ship in space. The date for the struggle is in cold type—July 1999—and when Nostradamus gives dates, the events are truly momentous, Robb pointed out, and he is seldom wrong:

> In the year 1999 in the seventh month,
> A great king of frightfulness will come from the skies
> To resuscitate the great king of Angoumois,
> Around this time Mars will reign for the good cause.

And what does it all mean?

In keeping with the Prophet's code, interpreters recognized that Angoumois stood for France. And France, reasoned Robb, would not be engaged in a great war without its traditional allies. For well over three hundred years, the quatrain had baffled the most enterprising interpreters. Then with the airplane, some thought they had the answer—aerial bombing. "But now with interplanetary travel a possibility," Robb observed, "the literal meaning can be applied, an actual descent from the skies, with favorable consequences for the Allied cause."

That very day, in February of 1962, when Robb and I sat talking, I had leafed through the New York *Times,* my eye catching the headline: "Contact With Worlds In Space Explored by Leading Scientists." I read on: "So real is the possibility of communication with other worlds," the article began, "that the National Academy of Sciences has sponsored a conference held quietly at Green Bank, West Virginia, to review the situation." Further along, the story announced that astronomers felt that establishing contact with other worlds might save this one from self-destruction. "They [the scientists] point out," it went on, "that we still do not know whether or not self-destruction is an inherent characteristic of civilizations that occurs throughout the universe, whenever a culture achieves the ability to destroy itself."

"Is this it?" I asked Robb with a tolerant smile.

With a smile he replied: "I was very amused to read in one of the tabloids the other day that Nostradamus had predicted the end of the world in 1999. Of course, he did nothing of the sort; he has predictions for almost another two thousand years, and he sees life continuing with all its turmoil and strife long after that."

Many, like my editor friend, scanning Nostradamus idly, have been confused, bewildered, and often bored by the apparent double-talk of the incomparable soothsayer. But when the thin veil of rhetoric was pierced, Robb often found Nostradamus brutally frank and precise.

In his own time, Nostradamus won fame for prophesying the remarkable death of his benefactor, Henry II of France. Tactfully, he refrained from telling the king that he would die from a chance stroke in single combat, but warned him against engaging in duels. The king chose not to listen, just as sensible people today would scoff at any psychic. Henry felt himself master of his fate, and Nostradamus did not argue the point. And with the king's hearty laugh ringing in his ears, the Prophet returned from court to provincial Salon to pen a prophecy published only a year before the king's death in 1559:

> The young lion shall overcome the old,
> On the field of battle in a duel [duelle],
> He will pierce his eye in a cage of gold,
> This is the first of two blows, then he dies a cruel death.

This was not the only warning the French monarch had received; Nostradamus' predecessor, Luc Gauric, a favorite of the Italian-born Queen, Catherine de Medici, had also warned him to beware of duels. But defying tradition—and fate—the king ordered the youthful Earl of Montgomery to joust with him at games marking the betrothal of his Princess daughter. As they went to their horses, the king eager and flushed, the Earl pale and hesitant, many noted in alarm that both Henry and his young opponent wore the device of the lion on their armor.

There was a brief flurry as the two men and their mounts collided. The Earl weakly poked out his lance, barely grazing the king's throat. But deflected by Henry's own lance, it shot up, knocking open the protective vizor of his gold helmet, and splintered off into his eye. Cruelly wounded, the king lingered painfully for days before fulfilling the prophecy he had ignored.

When Nostradamus saw an event, he saw an endless chain of consequences, all tumbling together toward a grand climax. And so, just as he saw Henry's death, he foresaw the impact on young Montgomery. Forgiven by Henry on his deathbed, the Protestant Montgomery discreetly took himself to England, but after a decent interval returned to claim his estates. Although Nostradamus' quatrains were even then the vogue, it is doubtful that Montgomery had read the one so aptly applying to himself:

To him who in strife and arms in the warlike field
Shall have carried away the prize from one greater than himself,
By night in bed six men shall attack him;
Unprotected, he will be surprised, naked and unarmed.

Even in exile, the Earl had not been far from the mind of a vengeful widow. While asleep in his Domfret castle, he was seized by a half dozen armed guards ordered out by Catherine and carted off to dungeon. Another prophecy had fulfilled itself.

While Nostradamus considered personal readings beneath his dignity, he could not refuse his benefactors at court. He was beholden to the King and Queen, who had not only appointed him court physician, but had made him financially independent.

Before Henry's violent death, the Queen had asked Nostradamus to examine the future of her three sons. The Prophet tactfully explained that he saw each occupying a throne. Since the princes were in the same age bracket, the Queen happily assumed they would rule over three different countries, and the Prophet diplomatically said nothing to discourage her. "If he had told the Queen what he actually saw," Robb observed, "he may well have lost his own crown."

Like a modern astrologer reluctant to impart bad news, Nostradamus had glossed over his vision with an innocuous remark that was still true. "He had seen the princes on a throne," Robb said, "but it was the same throne, and he could hardly have voiced this prediction without implying brief and uneasy reigns for at least two of them."

Only after the event—and the Prophet's own death—were the predictions for all three sons amazingly revealed. All died young, and as Nostradamus foresaw:

> The eldest son leaves, with his wretched marriage
> Widow, no children, and two isles in strife,
> And dies before eighteen, incompetent of age.
> The younger son will reach an accord earlier still.

"After being briefly married to Mary Stuart," Robb said, "the eldest son, Francis II, died six weeks before his eighteenth birthday, and his childless widow returned to Scotland to quarrel with England's Elizabeth over their island kingdoms."

Francis' successor, Charles IX, was engaged to marry when he was but eleven, and as the instigator of the St. Bartholomew's Massacre in which Protestants by the thousands were slain and hung by their heels, he emerged as a bloodthirsty monarch who stood at a palace window taking potshots at his luckless victims:

> The savage king, when he shall have tried
> His bloodstained hand with fire, sword and bows,
> All the people shall be terrified
> To see the great hung by the neck and feet.

Charles was followed by the third brother, Henry III, whose assassination was already clearly drawn in Nostradamus' book of verse:

> A great king taken by a young man's hand . . .
> Three brothers perish; this death takes the last.

Before becoming King of France, Henry had briefly held the Polish throne; the prophet pinpointed his assassination with remarkable directness:

> The twice king [le roy-roy] dies, by Clement hand is slain.

Even for Nostradamus, this is a singular line. Thirty-five years after its publication, in August 1589, Henry was fatally stabbed by a gentle young monk. His name was Jacques Clement.

When he first began his study, Robb found it difficult to believe that such complex events could have been predicted so far ahead with so much accuracy. Like other skeptics, he suspected the authenticity of quatrains so rich in detail they stood out from the carefully contrived ambiguity of most stanzas.

One in particular he could not accept. It detailed events, places, and names of the French Revolution, which materialized three hundred years after Nostradamus' death. As he examined it incredulously, Robb decided that an unscrupulous publisher had slipped the quatrain into some edition after the Revolution, imitating the terse compact style Robb has come to know so well:

> The husband alone, afflicted, will be mitred.
> Return, conflict, will take place at the Tuileries.
> By Five Hundred, one betrayer will be titled,
> Narbon and Saulce, we have oil with knives.

It was little wonder Robb was suspicious. When this prediction was ostensibly made, back in 1558, the Tuileries palace had not yet been built and was the site of an old tile kiln. The red cap of liberty, the Phrygian bonnet or mitre, had not been forced on the "husband," as Louis was derisively known by the Revolutionary mob invading his palace. The glorious Five Hundred had not staged their dramatic march from Marseilles, singing their grand anthem, to storm that symbol of tyranny, the Bastille. Narbonne, of course, was Louis' plotting Secretary of War who was summarily dismissed; and Saulce or Sauce was the Mayor of Varennes who turned the fugitive royal family over to a Revolutionary tribunal. Operating a general store, oil and cutlery were his coat of arms.

Diligently, Robb set out to find the oldest available version of the prophecies. In the Rare Book Room of the New York Public Library, he came upon an original English translation by Theophilus Garencieres, a doctor in the College of Physick, London. It was published in London by Ratcliff and Thompson in 1672, antedating the French Revolution by more than a hundred years. There was no chance of forgery. Thumbing through the nearly three-hundred-year-old volume, Robb found his quatrain. It was virtually the same as the one he had read before.

Like Robb, I visited the library, consulting *The True Prophecies*. The Tuileries, the Five Hundred, Narbon and Saulce, they were all there. As I kept leafing through Garencieres' musty pages, my eye was caught by another stanza, a date—the year 1700. I read carefully:

> A great while before these things [the previous quatrain],
> Those of the East by virtue of the Moon,
> In the year 1700 shall carry great droves
> And shall subdue the whole Northern Corner.

A true researcher, Garencieres urged later scholars to check the prediction—and his interpretation—at the appointed time, twenty-eight years hence. He himself died in 1680.

"I [Garencieres] desire posterity to take special notice of this stanza that in case it should come to pass, our Author [Nostradamus] may be admired for the specification of the time, which is so punctually set down here that it admitteth no ambiguity." Criticizing other interpreters, for "expounding the stanzas according to their fancy," Garencieres then allowed his own fancy to roam:

> The plain meaning is, that the Turks, which he
> calleth those of the East, by virtue of the moon,
> which is their ensign and badge, shall in the year
> 1700 carry away abundance of people—and shall
> subdue almost the whole Northern Country, which to
> them is Russia, Poland, Hungary, Sweden, Denmark.

Consulting a convenient encyclopedia, I discovered that in the year 1700, Charles the Twelfth of Sweden, a military genius of eighteen, had tackled a coalition of Russia, Denmark, Poland and Saxony, subduing one after another and taking many prisoners. Later defeated, he fled to Turkey, where he was first befriended and then driven out as the Turks made peace with Russia. The conflict of 1700 in which Charles subdued the whole Northern Corner was known as the Northern War.

Nostradamus had correctly predicted the time, place, and circumstances, though the military lineup was vague. Garencieres, mindless of his own admonitions, had reasoned Turkey into the stanza but given it Sweden's role; however, he had his excuses: "He [Nostradamus] doth sometimes deliver the thing in so obscure terms that without a peculiar genius, it is almost impossible to understand it."

The Great Seer came by his powers naturally. Both his grandfathers were court physicians, astrologists, and Kabalists, and though converting from Judaism to Catholicism, in accordance with a royal decree, they never ceased delving into their ancient mystical lore. Though a devout Catholic, Nostradamus was proud of his descent from the Biblical tribe of Issachar, "to whom it is given to know and discern the times . . ." Schooled in medicine and philosophy at two universities, he eventually became court physician to three kings—Henry II, Francis II, and Charles IX. But considering astrology a higher art, he made medicine a secondary career; still he is credited with ending two plagues with his uncanny healing powers.

As a young man his gift of prophecy first became apparent when he was traveling in Italy and came upon a group of Franciscan friars. After greeting all, he suddenly fell to his knees before the youngest, a dark-eyed village lad from Ancona, named Felice Peretti.

"Why this unseemly homage?" the older monks demanded crossly.

Nostradamus replied piously, "It is necessary that I kneel before His Holiness."

The monks turned away scornfully, but years later young Peretti became, first, Cardinal of Montalto, and in 1585, some twenty years after the Prophet's death, His Holiness, Pope Sixtus the Fifth.

Like the prophets of old, Nostradamus felt close to the all-seeing Creator, for as Garencieres explained: "Knowledge of future things belongeth to God alone, but sometimes he revealeth them to his servants or to some particular man as he pleaseth." Nostradamus himself once explained, discussing his power:

"Aside from astrological calculation, one must be inspired by the prophetic spirit which is the gift of Providence."

Truly humble, he suffered misfortune without complaint. His wife and two children perished in the plague while he was away ministering to others; he bowed in sorrow, murmured a prayer, and went on saving lives. Later, he married again, and had four children, one growing up to become a priest.

No recluse, he enjoyed discussions with friends and was modest in his claims. There were many prophets, he said, among the obscure and the childlike, and saluting them, he quoted from the greatest Prophet of all: "Thou hast hidden these things from the wise and prudent and hast revealed them to the small and weak."

He was careful of his appearance, but not vain. His features were regular, his eyes deep-set, his mien aristocratic. His trim, pointed beard and serene gaze gave him a striking resemblance to the poet Shakespeare, who arrived on the scene almost as Nostradamus was leaving it in 1566, at sixty-three. With all his eccentricity, he was a kind husband and father, and his family was devoted to him. His wife composed his eulogy, commending Michel de Notredame—Nostradamus—to His Maker, and arranged that his remains lie in a church vault.

No prophet had greater honor in his lifetime. Because of his predictions on affairs of state, courtiers and diplomats eagerly perused the successive editions of his quatrians for clues to French policy and hints of royal alliance. But when personally consulted by visiting ambassadors, he would only smile enigmatically, and refer them to his enigmatic verse. He provoked consternation at court once, predicting a thinly disguised plot by a Robin. And, perforce, had to explain that the traitor Marshal de Biron, for whom "Robin" was a perfect anagram, would not be plotting with the Spaniards for another generation or so. And would be put down, anyway.

He was forever being tested by friends and strangers, who doubted that mortal man could work his reputed wonders. He was visiting the nobleman Lord Florinville at his estates in Lorraine, for instance, when his host thought he would have this joke at the Seer's expense. Having a black and a white pig, he asked the seer which, if he knew so much, would be served at dinner that evening.

"The wolf will eat the white pig, and we shall have the black," Nostradamus told his host.

Laughing to himself, the nobleman went into his kitchen and ordered the cook to prepare the white pig, staying there as it was butchered. Later, as the servants brought in the barbecued delicacy, Florinville, with a pleased chuckle said to his guest, "And now enjoy the white pig."

Nostradamus smiled. "It is the black pig, my Lord, but white or black, it does you honor."

Lord Florinville smiled tolerantly. "It is the white pig," he said. "I saw it killed myself."

Nostradamus shrugged. "It is the black all the same."

Florinville's smile broadened. "I will call the cook," he said, "and prove the Great Seer wrong."

As the cook appeared, his master said, "My guest insists this is the black pig."

The cook paled and trembled. "Master, forgive me," he pleaded, "but a wolf came in through the window and took the white pig, so I had to kill the black pig."

Even in his lifetime he was misquoted and misinterpreted, and contemporary mystics, some real, others fraudulent, tried to capitalize on the vogue inspired by his success. Many, from selfish motives, sought to read meanings into his verse that he never intended; others were impelled by wishful thinking, causing Garencieres to lament: "Many pretending to understand the author have made a quantity of false prophecies as if God had given them the same understanding that he gave the author."

The misconstruction of Nostradamus continues. At a public meeting recently, a self-proclaimed authority announced that the Seer had predicted the trial and conviction of Adolf Eichmann for the mass murder of six million Jews.

And the basis for this claim? "A quatrain," said Robb, "in which Nostradamus predicted an arsonist would be brought to bay for his crimes." He smiled. "Nostradamus never threw off the initiated. His allusions were invariably true, and he was always fair with those who would be trying to solve his riddles. When he meant fire, he said fire, and in the great fire of London even suggested the date—1666."

Through his very indirection, the Prophet made himself doubly clear to the scholars. Many have wondered why Nostradamus should call Franco by name, and then obliquely refer to Hitler as Hister. "That's easy," Robb observed. "Hister conveyed much more than Hitler to the generations who preceded him. Hister was an ancient name for the Danube; it suggested the future dictator was Austrian; likewise, stemming from the Greek root for hysteria, it provided a clue to the future tyrant's personality."

Despite a flair for the mystifying, Nostradamus often penned the headlines of history more precisely before the event than many historians have done thereafter.

Some likened the prophet's precision to that of a master journalist writing concise, pithy headlines. The Great Fire of London, for instance—"London, burnt by fireballs in thrice twenty and six"; and London's Great Plague—"the great plague of the maritime city shall not diminish till death be sated for the just blood [Charles the First's]." In three lines, he foresaw the bloody revolution in England and the rise of the commoner Cromwell:

> More butcher than King in England
> Of obscure birth, he will seize the Empire by force,
> His time approaching so near that I sigh.

And in still another verse he virtually named the usurper, referring to him as Lonole, a perfect anagram for Cromwell's popular nickname of Ole Nole or Old Noll.

> The young prince of the Kingdom of Britain
> Whose dying father will have recommended him,
> This one being dead, Lonole will perorate
> And snatch the Kingdom from his very son.

Together the two quatrains covered a library full of history. "James I of England, who was also James VI of Scotland, was born in June 1566, only two weeks before Nostradamus passed away," Robb pointed out. "He attained the English throne in 1603, commended his son's claims to the Scottish lords, and in 1625 was succeeded by that son, Charles I, from whom Ole Nole ruthlessly snatched the throne."

Long before England turned back the Spanish Armada in 1588, Nostradamus predicted that the tiny island empire would become the world's dominant power, holding sway for a period only recently concluded:

> The Great Empire will be by England,
> The all-powerful for more than three hundred years.

And then, amazingly, he foresaw the breakdown of the League of Nations; a slow-to-arm England remarkably allied with the French and a Semitic people—"Punic" for Carthage—engaged in a death fight with the Nazis, the struggle hinging on control of the skies:

> Great Neptune from the depth of the sea,
> Mixed with the Punic and the Gallic Peoples,
> The Isles bloodstained for having neglected to arm

> Because of the Germans, they and their neighbors around them
> Will be in wars for the control of the clouds . . .
> The shortcomings of Geneva will then be laid bare.

Predictions didn't spill out of the Great Seer in any chronological order. He recorded things as they came to him; a quatrain prophesying the end of the world might stand next to the War of the Spanish Succession. He made scanty references to America, but these were momentous. The first dealt with the birth of the infant nation itself. Nearly a hundred years before the first landing at Plymouth Rock, he foresaw the American Revolution:

> The Occident, free from British Isles,
> Not satisfied, sad rebellion.

And eventually, fulfilling the cycle of England's rise and fall, he foresaw a reunion, still to come, between the States and the Mother Country, with America taking over—and this at a time when the continent was only a wilderness peopled by savages:

> There will be a head of London from the government of America.

For his own France, which he saw torn by history's bloodiest revolution (until then), Nostradamus wrote headlines edged in crepe. It was almost more than the old royalist could bear. "For this reason perhaps," Robb considered, "he may have been more specific than usual, feeling the need to warn of the future." He virtually sketched the whole course of the Revolution, giving dates and details with startling accuracy. And suffering with each sweep of the guillotine, some two hundred and fifty years away, he reluctantly pictured his beloved Paris as the "city of the blade," and deplored the Revolution's attack on the Church. Scornfully, he denounced the so-called Age of Reason—decrying the "greatest persecution of the Christian Church, worse than that which took place in Africa," and he warned, "This will culminate in the year 1792, which people will think to be a renovation of the age." As it turned out, the Christian calendar was officially abolished by the Revolution on September 21, 1792, and year one, Age of Reason time, was formally proclaimed, as Nostradamus had vainly warned.

The deaths of Louis XVI and Marie Antoinette haunted his dreaming and waking hours. For all his bumbling indecision, which appeared to seal his fate, Louis' downfall had been long ordained in Nostradamus:

> Led to the head, made second, betrayed,
> The city of the blade burns the face with powder.

Before losing his head, Louis signed a document subordinating his authority to the Revolutionary tribunal. Afterward, his corpse was sprinkled with powder—quicklime—and buried in an unmarked grave. Exhumed years later, only bits of calcined bone remained. The powder had done its job well.

The Revolution spread itself clearly before the Prophet, as though it were only yesterday instead of tomorrow. Through the timeless windows of his mind, he saw the execution of a queen, at a time when a slight to a queen would have been blasphemy. There was no rumbling of Revolution, no prophetic murmurings among the people in his time. Still, Nostradamus saw a queen of ill repute sharing the fate of husband and son, condemned by a jury chosen by lot—the only queen in history condemned by such a jury:

> The Government taken over will convict the King,
> The Queen sent to death by jurors chosen by lot,
> They will deny life to the Queen's son.
> And the prostitute shares the fate of the consort.

Nostradamus was obviously alert to the Queen's niche in history, and of the rumors that scandalized Paris and helped to foster public discontent. The "prostitute" was the courtesan DuBarry, and the two women went to the guillotine in the same year.

Appraising the Revolution, Nostradamus had seen what was essentially a social upheaval. "Then will come the beginning, including in itself what will endure." But of the Revolution came Napoleon, a transient, political fluke, and the more enduring framework of the French Republic. Napoleon himself was discounted as an upstart and "butcher." Everything about this "crophead" irked the Prophet—personality, birth, career:

> An emperor will be born near Italy
> Who will be sold the Empire at very dear price.
> One will say from the men he rallies around him,
> That he is less a prince than a butcher.

A million different events had to conspire before a Napoleon could rise in France, and a dynasty end that had ruled France for a thousand years. Even the Empire itself did not exist until a simple soldier carved it from the debris of the Revolution. And what ruler of Catholic France, traditionally His Most Christian Majesty, could predictably be anti-Catholic?

> From a simple soldier he will attain to Empire,
> From the short [military] robe, he will attain the long.
> Valiant in arms, in the Church, where he is worse,
> He will vex the priests as water does the sponge.

Nostradamus was particularly explicit with Napoleon, who ruled France from November 1799 until April 1814, after winning his spurs in the siege of Toulon:

The crophead will take the satrapy,
From the marine and tributary city,
He will drive out as sordid all who oppose him;
For fourteen years he will hold the tyranny.

As though he were there, Nostradamus pictured the widespread disillusionment following the first proud surge of nationalism as France mourned its dead on the battlefields of Europe:

It will have made a very bad choice in the crophead,
It will suffer more than its strength can bear;
Such great fury and rage will make it said
That he is destroying the entire sex by fire and sword.

Nostradamus was not displeased to note Napoleon's defeat:

The captive prince, conquered to Elba
He will pass Genoa by sea to Marseilles.
He is completely conquered by a great effort of the foreign forces,
Though he escapes the flames, the bees yield liquor by the barrel.

After escaping Elba, Robb pointed out, the Emperor took the sea route described, to meet his Waterloo at the hands of Allied troops commanded by Blucher and Wellington. "Napoleon was the only French ruler to use the bee as an emblem of power," Robb said. "He escaped with his life, but his strength was sapped."

Because of Nostradamus' success with the French Revolution, the curious have leafed through his pages searching for news of its Russian counterpart. They have not had to look far. But while the Prophet was horrified by the French Revolutionists, for the Russians he felt only contempt, both for the Revolutionary leaders themselves, and a people so easily duped:

Songs, chants and slogans of the Slavic people
While princes and Lords are captive in the Prisons
In the future, by idiots without heads,
Will be received as divine oracles.

In still another stanza, Robb saw a definite allusion to the Romanoff overthrow and the rise of Lenin, a bourgeois from a small town:

The Slavic people in a martial hour
Will become in a high degree very lifted up
They will change their prince; the successor to be born a provincial . . .

But the Reds are to go the way of Hitler and Mussolini. On the basis of his Nostradamus, Robb has been predicting the imminent downfall of communism, the first break coming in the country of its origin, Russia. Robb's confidence stems from the so-called "More verse," a remarkable reference to Sir Thomas More's "Utopia," a fictional conception of the ideal communal community and a best seller in Nostradamus' day:

> The law of More will be seen to fail
> Before another much more seductive,
> The Dnieper will be the first to fail,
> Through gifts and tongues of one more attractive.

In his inimitable manner, Nostradamus indicates democracy may be this charmer:

In a place and time when flesh gives way to fish,
The common law will be constrained,
The Old Man will make a strong stand, then taken from the midst
All things in common among comrades badly set back.

The clue is in the last line, which Nostradamus takes pains to set down in the Greek: *Le panta choina Philon.*

And since Greece is the traditional home of democracy, Robb pointed out, this could well be a hint to the wise. Flesh giving way to fish could signify Eastertide, or the triumph of Christianity, or wishful thinking.

But there was also bad news for his beloved Church. He saw not only the afflictions of the French Revolution, but even greater adversity perhaps at a later date:

> Oh great Rome, thy ruin approach,
> Not of thy walls, but of thy blood and substance,
> The printed word will work terrible havoc
> The pointed sword driven home to hilt.

With more imagery and equal foreboding, he devoted himself to the same theme:

From the top of Mount Aventine, a voice was heard
Get you gone, get you gone on all sides,
The choler shall be fed with blood of the red ones
From Arimin and Parator, the Colonnas shall be driven away.

Mount Aventine was one of the seven hills of Rome; the red ones were defined as Cardinals, the Colonnas, as traditional defenders of the Pope, symbolized Papal might. But the Church was to come back strongly. Nostradamus, in a notable quatrain hinting at the identity of an anti-Christ, penned hopeful news of the Church's restoration:

Of Trojan blood shall a Germanic heart be born,
Who shall attain to a very high power;
He shall drive out a foreign Arabic people,
Returning the Church to her pristine pre-eminence

While this champion of the Church is unrevealed, some interpreters feel the chronology itself is clear, correlated to the predicted events of 1999, when the entire Western culture, according to Nostradamus scholars, may be under attack from the East:

The Oriental shall come forth from his seat,
To pass the Appenine mountains to see France,
He shall pass through the sky, the waters and snow,
And shall strike everyone with his rod.

Nostradamus doesn't pinpoint the enemy's nationality, but some insist it is Arabic; others with an eye to current history say China. However, it may again be the Japanese, or India, or even the Indonesians—Asiatics all.

With all this turmoil, the Great Seer somehow saw the world limping along to the year 3797 A.D., for which he made his last dated prediction. But long before, he foresaw a peaceful millennium, presumably after the turn of this century. And he predicted, happily, a revival of Christianity:

The body without soul will no longer be as sacrifice
Day of death will change to day of birth.
The divine spirit will make the soul happy,
Seeing the world in its eternity.

It was not Nostradamus' practice to dismiss events of such magnitude in a single quatrain. As though trying to satisfy his own curiosity he kept harking back to the same subject:

> At the revolution of the great number seven,
> It will happen, in the time of the games of the hecatomb,
> Not far from the great age thousand
> That the dead will rise from the tombs.

All this is by way of again emphasizing the year 2000 A.D., according to Robb's calculation. "Nostradamus picked out the year 7000, equivalent in his tradition to 2000 A.D. since Christ's birth was placed in the five thousandth year." The interpretation is less complex: the symbolic triumph of Christianity, the Resurrection after the great slaughter—the games of the hecatomb.

While by no means a pessimist, Nostradamus, as an honest historian, felt compelled to report an end to this human habitat. Characteristically, he offered a number of clues as to how and when this end would occur:

> Twenty years after the reign of the moon passes,
> Seven thousand years another will hold his monarchy,
> Then the sun takes his weary days,
> Then is my prophecy accomplished and ended.

But fearful that not even the keenest scholar would penetrate his meaning, the Prophet passed out a few additional hints in prose, picturing a towering mass of water overshadowing even the Biblical flood in its destructive sweep: "So many great inundations that there shall scarce be any land that shall not be covered with water, and this shall last so long that except for ethnographies and topographies all shall perish."

And how will this flood originate? Students of Nostradamus believe the Prophet has the answer: "Before and after these inundations in many countries, there shall be such a scarcity of rain and such a great deal of fire and burning stones shall fall from heaven that nothing unconsumed shall be left."

Or as one interpreter said:

"If this isn't the daddy of all H-bombs, Nostradamus has made his first mistake."

16 DESPISE NOT PROPHESYINGS

I was sitting in a corner of the room ruminating about Biblical prophecy, of all things, when a large woman with a determined eye descended on me. At this stage I had very mixed feelings about Bible interpretation in general and Biblical prophecy in particular. It seemed to mean all things to all people, though my feeling was it had not been intended that way. I could not agree with Thomas Paine, the patriotic pamphleteer of *The Age of Reason,* that the early prophets were nothing more than official balladeers, much like Homer was to the Greeks, nor could I agree that every Biblical warning or exhortation was applicable to every age, though well it might be, for certainly this was true of the rest of the message.

This was about what I was thinking when this overpowering figure of emancipated womanhood swooped down on my little corner of the world some thousands of years away from the subdued chatter of the politely murmuring guests. I knew who she was, of course. She had composed a best seller concerning one of the most beloved of the disciples, and she was full of the Bible and its prophecies, and, like so many others, of forebodings of the end, the promised Armageddon, the last grueling struggle on the plains of Palestine between good and evil. "It shall come to pass in that day," the prophet Zechariah had said, "that a great tumult from the Lord shall be among them. And Judah shall also fight at Jerusalem."

I smiled politely. "The world," I said dryly, "ends with every millennium."

But the writer had specific clues, and the *modus operandi* besides—not by the atom bomb, which I had been hearing about for

some time, but through radiation. "The neutron," she said in a
whisper.

I gathered it was some sort of ray, which left buildings intact
but destroyed all life therein.

"Matthew and Joel," she said, "it's all there. Look at Matthew 24:15 under prophecies and warnings. If that isn't a warning
of radiation and its contamination, I don't know what is."

Referring to a prophecy made six hundred years before his time,
Matthew had warned: "So when you see 'the abomination of
desolation,' of which the prophet Daniel spoke, standing in the
holy place (let the reader understand), then those who are in
Judea must take to the hills. If a man is on the roof, he must not
come down to fetch his goods from the house; if in the field, he
must not turn back for his coat. Alas for women with child in
those days, and for those who have children at the breast! Pray
that it may not be winter when you have to make your escape, or
Sabbath. It will be a time of great distress, such as has never been
from the beginning of the world until now, and will never be
again. If that time for troubles were not cut short, no living thing
could survive; but for the sake of God's chosen, it will be cut
short."

If this weren't enough, there was Joel. Not even the animals
were spared here. "Alas for the day! for the day of the Lord is at
hand, and as a destruction from the Almighty shall it come. . . .
How do the beasts groan! the herds of cattle are perplexed, because
they have no pasture; yea, the flocks of sheep are made desolate."

Joel told of the "valley of decision" and of celestial fireworks.
"And I will show wonders in the heavens, and in the earth, blood,
and fire, and pillars of smoke. The sun shall be turned into darkness, and the moon into blood, before the great and terrible day
of the Lord come."

The "pillars of smoke," of course, meant but one thing to my
interpreter. "Can't you just see the mushroom over Hiroshima,
magnified a thousand times?"

She was strangely unworried. All this, she felt, was the inevitable forerunner of the second coming, and, as had others, wondered
whether the Messiah returning might not also be happily recog-

nized by the Jews by whom He had gone unrecognized two thousand years ago. And then perhaps just as a star marked the birth
of the child of Bethlehem, ushering in the Piscean Age, there
would be another sign in the skies, perhaps another unusual con-
stellation, portending His rebirth on earth. Perhaps it was this
sign, ushering in a new Aquarean Age, some say, that was seen
in the unique planetary lineup on February 5, 1962. "Then will
appear in the heaven the sign that heralds the Son of Man." Perhaps a new Child was born—or so some felt.

With these signs, Christ had said, "You may know that the end
is near." It was all very clear to the best-selling writer.

In apparent contradiction of those who see the final judgment
only now approaching, He also said, "The present generation will
live to see it all." But a standard dictionary serves to reconcile the
discrepancy for some. Generation once meant "race, kind, breed
or stock," in other words, humanity. However, none can pinpoint
the time. "But about that day and hour, no one knows . . . only
the Father."

I had heard many times of the heralded end of the world. It
had beeen ending almost since it had begun. In 1843, the
Millerites, predecessors of the Adventists, had given away their
earthly possessions, donned their ascension robes, and waited ec-
statically for the world to stop. It hadn't, and founder William
Miller, owning up to an error in his Biblical calculation, braced
his followers for a second assault on Heaven the following year.
In 1849, the Massachusetts-born prophet died, a disillusioned
and broken man. The world had ended for him.

Every crisis, every great war appeared to flush forth a new flood of
Biblical interpretations foretelling the end. With an approaching
millennium, a new age had dawned, astrologically, if in no other
way, and with it the conviction of impending disaster and redemption. And the restoration of Israel as a nation, a promised forerunner of the last good fight, served to quicken this feeling.

In 1878 Dr. Grattan Guinness, English student of the Bible,
had seen prophetic indications that "the cleansing of the sanctuary
and the restoration of Israel are not too distant." With this return
of the Jews to the Holy Land, the scholar had foreseen the

prophesied war to end all wars: "Then the last warning bell will have rung; the last of the unfulfilled predictions of scripture as to events prior to the great crisis will have received its accomplishment. Then the second advent of Israel's rejected Messiah to reign in conjunction with His glorified saints as King over all the earth will be close at hand."

It certainly seemed as though the stage was ready. For had not the prophet Isaiah said, some hundreds of years before Christ: "And it shall come to pass in that day, that the Lord shall set his hand again the second time to recover the remnant of his people, which shall be left. . . . And he shall set up the ensign for the nations, and shall assemble the outcast of Israel and gather together the dispersed of Judah from the four corners of the earth."

Though I had long pored over the Bible, losing myself in the blood and thunder of the Old Testament and the gentle parables of the New, I was no Bible scholar. I sought out qualified authorities in the churches and seminaries, in the hope that they could see more than I. And though their interpretations often did not admit of as much prophecy as the Apostles themselves recognized in their day and age, I could sympathize with the need for conservatism in this day and age. But the liberal interpreters of the Bible were certainly more provocative.

There was, it appeared, a rhythmical pattern in the words of the prophets. By synchronizing the major prophecies from Isaiah and Daniel through Ezekiel to St. John the Divine, the liberal interpreters have convinced themselves that all take the same high road to the millennium. From John's prophetic book of Revelation, which the conservatives see only as a message for the early Christians suffering martyrdom under the Emperors, the liberals more romantically foresee the final tussle with the anti-Christ, with victory for the good cause: "When the thousand years are over, Satan will let loose from his dungeon; and he will come out to seduce the nations in the four quarters of the earth and to muster them for battle, yes, the hosts of Gog and Magog, countless as the sands of the sea. So they marched over the breadth of the land, and laid siege to the camp of God's people and the city that he loves. But fire came down on them from heaven and consumed them."

Despite liberal interpretations, revelation is often inscrutable in its symbolism. The Four Horsemen of the Apocalypse sweep through the sky, as they have before virtually every crisis in nearly two thousand years, with a chilling message of war, famine, pestilence, and death. John saw the destruction, in a single hour, of the greatest city in the world. Symbolically, he called it Babylon, though long-fallen Babylon was clearly not intended. No destruction of a city fitting this description has yet occurred, leading some to suggest that its destruction is yet to come as part of the promised day of reckoning. Its identity—and fate—is colored with symbolism: "Fallen, fallen is Babylon the great! She has become a dwelling for demons, a haunt for every unclean spirit, for every foul and loathsome bird. For all nations have drunk deep of the fierce wine of her fornication. . . . Mete out grief and torment to match her voluptuous pomp. She says in her heart, 'I am queen on my throne! No mourning for me, no widow's weeds!' Because of this her plagues shall strike her in a single day—pestilence, bereavement, famine and burning—for mighty is the Lord God who has pronounced her doom." And the traders who profited through her will mourn and say, "Alas, alas for the great city, that was clothed in fine linen and purple and scarlet, bedizened with gold and jewels and pearls. Alas, that in one hour so much wealth should be laid waste."

This certainly seemed a provocative prophecy, but the conservatives were unimpressed. Not even the image conjured by the prospect of a great city's destruction in an hour could ruffle their calm.

"That was purely allegorical, all that fire and thunder and brimstone," one conservative told me, "and it is only a manner of speaking." He was a distinguished man of the cloth, and he chewed on his pipe as he interpreted for me. "I can't emphasize too much that the prophets and disciples were fundamentally rooted in their own age, commenting on the problems of their own times."

"How about the coming of Christ?" I said. "Isaiah seemed to have foretold that centuries ahead: 'Behold a virgin shall conceive and bear a son.' or, 'For unto us a child is born, unto us a son is given; and the government shall be upon his shoulder, and his name shall be called Wonderful, Counsellor, the mighty God, the everlasting Father, the Prince of Peace.'"

He nodded sagely. "First off," he said coolly, "which Isaiah do you mean? There were three of them, scholars realize today, and the first Great Isaiah, living about 750 B.C., foresaw the Babylonian captivity. Then there was the Isaiah of the captivity, and another between 400 and 300 B.C."

I was puzzled. "Whichever Isaiah it was," I pointed out, "still predicted well ahead of the future."

He smiled. "I don't question that. We only question the fanatical prominence given the prophecy rather than the teacher." He laughed. "At the rate the world is going, I wouldn't be surprised if it stopped today, or tomorrow, or the day after tomorrow, but I see no specific warning of it in the Bible for us. Every day is Judgment Day in a sense."

I wondered what would have happened in Christ's time if His people had been as skeptical of the ancient prophecies. "Wasn't this rather specific?" I asked, quoting from the prophet Zechariah, living five hundred years before Christ: "Behold, thy King cometh unto thee: he is just and having salvation; lowly and riding upon an ass, and upon a colt the foal of an ass . . . and he shall speak peace unto the heathen; and his dominion shall be from sea even to sea, and from the river even to the ends of the earth."

The authority nodded conservatively. "Yes, that is recognized as prophetic, for Christ would certainly have been the only king, of his own choosing, to meekly ride into a city on a donkey." He laughed. "To any other king it would have been impossibly demeaning."

And how about Christ's betrayal? Many have thrilled with Zechariah's: "And I said unto them, If ye think good, give me my price, and if not forebear. So they weighed for my price thirty pieces of silver." It was rather distracting to see my authority shake his head with a tolerant smile and rule out the reference as no more than coincidental, when the King James version of the Bible itself noted: "Next to Isaiah, Zechariah has the most frequent references to the character and the coming of the Messiah, and predicts his riding into Jerusalem upon an ass's colt, and foretells the betrayal, and the exact sum of money which was paid to Judas."

To many, Psalm Twenty-two has seemed a moving picture of Christ on the Cross: "My strength is dried up like a potsherd, and my tongue cleaveth to my jaws, and thou hast brought me into the dust of death. For days have compassed me: the assembly of evil doers have enclosed me, they pierced my hands and feet . . . All they that see me laugh me to scorn. They shoot out the lip, they shake the head, saying, 'He trusteth on the Lord that he would deliver him—let him deliver him seeing he delighteth in him.'" And then even more strikingly: "They part my garments among them, and upon my vesture do they cast lots."

Differing from two apostles, the seminarians insisted this was no clear-cut prophecy. "Behold, we got up to Jerusalem," Luke had pointed out, "and all the things that are written by the prophets concerning the Son of Man shall be accomplished. For he shall be delivered unto the Gentiles and shall be mocked and spitefully entreated, and spitted on."

And Matthew, too, who had trod with Christ, appeared to feel the old Hebrew prophecy had been singularly fulfilled: "They gave him vinegar to drink mingled with gall; and when he had tasted thereof, he would not drink. And they crucified him, and parted his garments, casting lots; that it might be fulfilled by the prophet, *They parted my garments among them, and upon my vesture did they cast lots.*"

All through the Bible, there appeared little doubt in the minds of Jesus and the disciples of the prophetic record of the Old Testament. Christ often seemed to take it as His timetable, once announcing, for instance, that it was not His "appointed" time to enter Jerusalem. He knew what the end would be.

But again the conservatives were unimpressed by prophetic fulfillment. "He didn't have to be psychic to know what was coming," one Biblical authority told me with a sardonic smile. "He was inviting this action by attacking the ruling church and political faction of the country. And He was prepared for the consequences."

"But didn't He say that all this was to fulfill the old prophecy in its own way? 'Day after day, I was within your reach as I taught in the temple, and you did not lay hands on me. But let the scriptures be fulfilled.'"

The minister eyed me speculatively. He was a learned man, sophisticated, assuredly better acquainted with the subtleties of the prophets than a reporter who could only wonder how subtle these men of simple faith could be. "Certainly," he said, "the people around Christ believed in prophecies, but you must understand"— he smiled rather patronizingly—"that they were essentially ignorant men with a superstitious belief in the supernatural."

I was slightly taken aback. "If they were so ignorant and superstitious," I responded mildly, "why do we listen to them two thousand years later?"

It had seemed so clear to me. At the Last Supper, Christ had been most specific in foreshadowing his fate. "Never again," he said, "shall I drink from the fruit of the vine until that day when I drink it new with you in the Kingdom of my Father." He singled out his betrayer from the group around the table, calling especial attention to the fact that an old prophecy was to be fulfilled: "He who eats bread with me has turned against me. I tell you this now, before the event, that when it happens you may believe that I am what I am."

Then Jesus exclaimed: "In truth, in very truth, I tell you, one of you is going to betray me." When the disciples looked up in bewilderment and asked who it was, Jesus replied: "It is the man to whom I give this piece of bread, when I have dipped it in the dish." He dipped it and gave it to Judas Iscariot, and said, "Do quickly what you have to do."

And He predicted to Peter, who protested he would lay down his life for Him: "I tell you in very truth, before the cock crows, you will have denied me three times."

Many scholars have thought Christ and the apostles uncommonly psychic. Others have remarked on their complete attunement with God. How else, some ask, did Saul, who was to become Paul, have his blinding vision on the road to Damascus, when he heard a voice saying, "Saul, Saul, why do you persecute me?"

"'Tell me, Lord,' he said, 'who are you?' The voice answered

'I am Jesus, whom you are persecuting. But get up and go into the city, and you will be told what you have to do.'"

Meanwhile, in Damascus, a disciple of Christ, named Ananias, had a vision in which he was directed to a certain house and told to "ask for a man from Tarsus named Saul."

"You will find him at prayer," Ananias was told, "he has had a vision of a man named Ananias coming in and laying his hands on him to restore his sight."

Knowing Saul as a relentless persecutor, on his way to Damascus to arrest those who followed the new way, Ananias demurred. "But the Lord said to him, 'You must go, for this man is my chosen instrument to bring my name before the nations and their kings, and before the people of Israel.'"

And so Saul, through a combination of two visions, was to become the greatest apostle of the new faith.

To some modern Biblical scholars, it was a noteworthy but by no means incredible development.

To somebody like Arthur Ford, the spiritualist minister, there was nothing remarkable about the psychic message of the Bible. "The trouble with many ministers," Ford said, "is that they don't believe what they read in the Gospel." Healing, predicting, clairvoyance, telepathy, even teleportation, were all an integral part of Christ's ministry, Ford pointed out, and, with faith, he feels this work can be continued. "If it weren't for its psychic message," he noted, "the Christian religion would be little different from many others." Christ's clairvoyance, Ford observed, was an instrument to point up His message. "To a simple yet skeptical people," Ford pointed out, "they were his symbols of authority." At the well Christ told the Samaritan woman, who acknowledged no husband, "You are right in saying that you have no husband, for although you have had five husbands, the man with whom you are now living is not your husband." At this, Ford pointed out, the woman was sufficiently impressed to spread the word that the stranger at the well might be the expected Messiah.

Similarly, Christ had healed the blind, in one case a man blind from birth. "This was no empty fairy tale," Ford stressed. "The people were skeptical, and Christ's enemies conducted an inquiry, questioning not only the parents to whom the son had been born blind, but the man himself and his friends. When he testified that Christ had indeed redeemed his sight, they threw him out of the synagogue to discredit the miracle."

Ford's Spiritual Frontiers movement, dedicated to reviving Scriptural psychic powers, is gathering many converts among the Protestant clergy. One night in New York, Ford, ordained himself in the Church of the Disciples of Christ, discussed the psychic revival in a Presbyterian Church, while flanked by ministers of the Congregationalist and Baptist persuasions. "If we do not accept the prophetic messages of the Bible," Ford asked, "what then do we accept?" He quoted from Corinthians: "'When a man prophesies, he is talking to men and his words have power to build; they stimulate and they encourage. The language of ecstacy is good for the speaker himself, but it is prophecy that builds up a Christian community.'"

"Do you really believe," I asked later, "that the prophets could make their predictions hundreds and thousands of years ahead?"

The spiritualist smiled. "To God, a day or a thousand years is all the same."

I thought of Gog and Magog, Armageddon, and all the rest. "Do you think the world is going to end?" I asked.

He laughed and then said seriously, "The sense of impending great events is in the air. I feel it wherever I go. It is almost a physical force. The time seems to be ready for great and auspicious events, as the Bible has foretold. The Jewish people are back in their national home; we have an assembly of nations gathered in covenant, the United Nations; and we are leaving the Piscean Age, the Age of dawning Christianity." He mused impassively. "Before Christ was born, the wise men looked to the stars. We might do well to look to the Heavens again for another sign."

Like my writer friend, had he been impressed by Matthew and Joel?

He replied simply, "I am a minister who believes in the Bible."

Already Spiritual Frontiers is making converts in lay ranks. "All our ministers have to do," Ford said, "is to bring the original message back to the Bible, and then bring the Bible back to the people."

Still, I couldn't understand how the average preacher not noticeably psychic could emulate the miracles of the apostles. But Ford felt there was a way of developing dormant psychic powers, if the wish was there. And in instances where a clergyman was outstandingly psychic, he might even become a great visionary. The popular evangelist, Billy Graham, Ford thought, was a case in point. "I heard him once in Miami, and the whole room vibrated with his message. He virtually hypnotized you."

A man of God who would practice the gospel of Corinthians had to deny himself alcohol, tobacco, and excesses of food; all these clouded the psychic potential. He could not give way to emotion, anger, fear, anxiety; it would not only subordinate the subconscious, but would upset the rhythmical breathing essential to relaxation. "Generally," Ford explained, "tense people aren't good psychics." Deep breathing helped, since oxygen increased the perceptive powers. And the student was to keep his spine straight, sitting, standing, or lying, permitting the energy force to rise easily to the head.

It did not seem to me that anybody could become psychic through merely practicing these simple exercises, but Ford insisted that such concentration, plus faith in the psychic message of the Bible, had already worked its wonders.

"In Trenton, New Jersey, recently," Ford said, "we had one of our ministers getting a sermon in automatic writing, his dead father supplying the content; in Mamaroneck, New York, the Reverend Edgar Jackson has been accomplishing healings for years; telepathy and precognition are becoming common."

The reference to the Reverend Jackson reminded me of Cayce. "Tell me," I said, "does it make any difference where the ailing subject is?"

He smiled. "If it's going to work, it will work in the same room or a thousand miles away. After all, it is love, wisdom, and concentration on one side that does it, with faith on the other."

In accomplishing his reported healings, Ford pointed out, Jackson strove first to build up a favorable emotional atmosphere, eloquently discussing the Bible and its cures and the powers of faith. "I am convinced," Ford said, "whether it is at Lourdes, Fatima, in a

Chicago church, or a minister's study, there is no healing without some hypnotic suggestion."

And there is nothing strange about it, he insisted. It has been done many times in the Bible, if Bible readers would only believe what they read.

He has had his difficulties with unbelieving ministers, too. "Do you believe in prayer?" he asked one clergyman.

Puzzled, the cleric nodded.

"Do you believe that God hears your prayers?"

Again the clergyman nodded.

"Even if you say them silently?"

The minister, becoming impatient, said, "Why, of course."

"Then," Ford said, "you must believe in telepathy."

Down through antiquity, corresponding with the Biblical period, the ignorant—and the informed—have accepted prophecy almost as a law of nature. The Greeks had their oracles, the Romans their soothsayers, the Indians their swamis. Prophecy flourished in the pages of Plutarch. Before the fateful Ides of March, that unparalleled biographer points out, Calpurnia was so convinced that her dream of her husband's death was prophetic that she would have prevailed on Caesar to dismiss the Senate had not one of the plotters, Decimus Brutus, taunted: What would your enemies say if anyone should tell them they should break up for the present, and meet again when Calpurnia should have better dreams?

Spurinna Vestritius, a soothsayer, had warned Caesar to beware the Ides of March. Encountering the seer on his way to the Senate meeting, the dictator leaned out of his litter and said with a laugh, "The Ides of March are here."

"Yes," said Spurinna, "but they are not yet past."

On the day Caesar Augustus was born, another chronicler tells us, his father Octavius arrived late at the Senate house. And a fellow senator, Publius Nigidius, who dabbled in astrology, solemnly forecast: "Some day that infant shall be the ruler of the world." Octavius was so startled by this threat to his beloved Republic that he was minded to go home and dispose of the infant, but then philosophized that the stargazers were more often wrong than right.

Augustus seemed to attract prophecies. The teen-aged heir of the divine Julius was sojourning in Apollonia with his friend Agrippa, later to be his prime minister, when the two, incognito, visited the astrologer Theogenes, a renowned soothsayer. As he noted Agrippa's hour of birth, the old soothsayer's eyes widened, and he predicted that few men would achieve his power in later life. Not wanting then to be cast in a bad light by his friend's glowing prospects, Augustus demurred at being read, but finally yielded to Agrippa's good-natured jibes and gave Theogenes his birth hour. Consulting his charts, Theogenes leaped from his chair and threw himself at the feet of the unknown youth. "And you," he said, "shall one day be master of the world." It was at Apollonia, ironically, that Augustus was to hear of his uncle's assassination.

Visions run a familiar course in history. The voices of the saints— Catherine, Michael, and Margaret—told a simple French peasant girl that she was to put the helpless Dauphin on the ancestral throne denied him by the British. At sixteen, illiterate and un-schooled, she took over the armies of France—in accordance with her vision—raised the siege of Orleans, and saw her prince crowned Charles VII at Rheims, as the voices had said. After her visions had been fulfilled, Joan's confidence seemed to desert her. She no longer gave commands with the same decisive force. Without a miracle to perform, she was once more a simple farm maid. "I have accomplished that which my Lord commanded me, to raise the siege of Orleans and have the gentle king crowned." She asked to be sent back home, where she could tend the sheep and cattle and browse carelessly through the meadows. But she was captured in battle by the enemy and cruelly imprisoned and tried. English soldiers tauntingly asked the Liberator of France when she would be "liberated." She smiled wanly and said, "Ask me in three months, and I will tell you." Three months later, May 30, 1429, she was burned alive at the stake, and in her own serene words, liberated. To the end, she had refused to divulge the nature of her sainted revelations. "You asked me," the gentle Maid of Orleans told a prosecuting bishop, "to tell something I have sworn not to tell."

Just as the ancient Hebrews invoked the prophecy of Jeremiah,

limiting their captivity to seventy years, to encourage and sustain
their people in Babylon, so too have other nations turned to prophecy for the mustering of morale in adversity. During the terrible
grueling months of trench warfare before Verdun in World War I,
as casualties mounted and troops mutinied, the French dug out the
hoary prophecy of Odile, patron saint of Alsace. Actually, the
prophecy, though current for centuries, was apocryphal, and appeared to have little bearing on that particular war. However, its
impassioned phrases were heartening in their Biblical fervor:
"Hearken, hearken, oh my brother, for I have seen the terror of
the forests and the mountains. Horror has frozen the peoples. The
time is come when Germany shall be called the most bellicose nation
upon earth. The epoch is arrived when from her bosom shall
arrive the terrible warrior who shall undertake the world war, and
whom the people in arms shall call anti-Christ, he who shall be
cursed by the mothers, as, like Rachel, they weep over their
children and refuse to be comforted."

It seemed to pick out a World War, all right, and it described
the Germans pretty well. "Twenty nations shall fight in this war.
The conqueror will start from the banks of the Danube. The war
he will undertake will be the most frightful mankind has ever
suffered. His arms shall be flaming and the helmets of the soldiers
covered with spikes, which will throw off sparks while their hands
brandish flaming torches.

"He will win victories on land, by sea, and even the air. For
his warriors will be seen winged in unimaginable career, riding
up into the firmament to catch the stars in order to hurl them
down on towns and ignite great fires. The nations will be astonished
and will exclaim: 'Whence comes this strength? How has he been
able to undertake such a war?'"

But then came a comforting prediction, which did not apply too
well since Verdun came in the third year of the war, in 1916,
lasting nearly a year, as French generals desperately sent up the
rallying cry: "They shall not pass."

And what had Odile promised? "The war will be very long,
and the conqueror will have reached the height of his triumph

about the middle of the sixth month of the second year of hostilities [1915].

"This will be the end of the period of bloody victories. In the flush of his triumphs, he will say: 'Accept the yoke of my dominion.' But his enemies will not submit and the war will continue. And he will exclaim: 'Misfortune will come upon them because I am their conqueror.'"

Again when Hitler's twisted cross flamed across Flanders and France the prophecy was resurrected, and this time the fit seemed better. An Austrian, the conqueror had come out of the Danubian area; he had persecuted the churches, and he had reached the apex of his career in June 1940, with most of Europe broken before his feet, and of all his adversaries only an unarmed England grimly holding on.

In this country we have had our prophets too. One, indeed, likened himself to the ancient Hebrews, and called himself Prophet. He founded a new faith on the strength of his visions, which he called prophetic, and which critics called fake. But he was believed unquestioningly by thousands of followers, earnest, upright men and women who walked in the ways of the Lord. His name was Joseph Smith, and, like Moses, he predicted that his people would find the Promised Land, but that he himself would never set foot there. "You will go to the Rocky Mountains," the Vermont-born visionary told his disciples in the Church of Jesus Christ of the Latter-Day Saints, "and you will be a great and mighty people established, which I will call [from Revelation] the White Horse of Peace. But I will never go there."

His people, the Mormons, recalling an earlier quest for a Promised Land, were driven and persecuted across the Western plains, from upstate New York to Ohio, Missouri, Illinois, and eventually Utah, which Joseph Smith, as he foretold, never lived to see. In June 1844, with his brother Hyrum, he was murdered by a mob that broke into a Carthage, Illinois, jail cell where he was being held on a trumped-up charge of sedition. Many years later, his successor, Brigham Young, was to report: "I heard Joseph say many a time, 'I shall not live until I am forty years of age.'" He was thirty-nine when he died.

He was a man of many prophecies. In 1833 he foresaw the Civil War, a generation later, proclaiming: "A terrible revolution will take place in the land of America, father against son and son against father."

He foresaw the discovery of gold, predicting accurately, many years before the find in Sutter's Creek, that it would be "shoveled like sand." And he predicted that the Constitution of the United States would someday hang like a thread.

His most notable prediction was reserved for the end of times, when he revived the promised Biblical struggle against Gog and Magog, but with two startling departures. He identified the enemy—Russia—hardly a factor in world affairs then, and he fixed the time, the century after the American Civil War. "England and France are now bitter enemies," he pointed out more than one hundred years ago, "but they will be allied together one day and united to keep Russia from conquering the world." He believed that the Lost Tribes of Israel had turned up in England, perhaps with the venturesome Phoenicians, a Semitic tribe that had founded Carthage. "The wisdom and statesmanship of England comes from having so much of the blood of Israel in the nation," he observed.

Although communism would wax great, he forecast its overthrow: "These kingdoms that will not let the Gospel preach will be humbled."

And with the Russian threat, he saw another menace from the Orient, with a threat to our West Coast by a slant-eyed people of the yellow race. But in the great showdown, America would lead the banners of Christ to victory: "The last great struggle that Zion will have to contend with will be when the whole of America will be made the Zion of Our Lord. Those opposing will be called Gog and Magog and their power will be great. But all opposition will be overcome, and then this land will be the Zion of Our God."

Only time, of course, would tell whether Joseph Smith, the marrying Mormon, was a good or false prophet. But the greatest Prophet of all had told His people what to look for on that eternal judgment day:

"Portents will appear in sun, moon, and stars. On earth nations will stand helpless, not knowing which way to turn from the roar and surge of the sea; men will faint with terror at the thought of all that is coming upon the world; for the celestial powers will be shaken. And then they will see the Son of Man coming on a cloud with great power and glory. When this begins to happen, stand upright and hold your heads high, because your liberation is near."

17 SUMMING UP

Somebody had shown me the French philosopher Tarde's discourse on the future shaping the present, not the present shaping the future, as I had always considered. It was very appropriately called *The Effect of Future Events*.

"Purposiveness," Gabriel Tarde wrote, "plays a role in the phenomena of life perhaps more important than that of heredity. The embryo is explained by the adult creature. . . . Evolution shows changes occurring not at random but apparently in accordance with a directing idea; when several events converge toward one important event, this future event has exerted an influence on the present."

Was Tarde trying to say that the future is already there, already ordained, determining the activities that would inevitably make that future materialize, though we generally did not know ourselves what that future was?

Had not Christ intimated pretty much the same thing on His way to the Cross, when He scolded a disciple for resisting those who had come to take Him: "Do you suppose that I cannot appeal to my Father, who would at once send to my aid more than twelve legions of angels: But how then could the scriptures be fulfilled, which say this must be?"

We often had striking notice of a greater authority then man's in the management of his own affairs.

Henry IV of England, because of a prediction that he would die in Jerusalem, called off a projected trek to the Holy Land, and later died unexpectedly in Westminster Abbey, in the Jerusalem Chamber.

As a child on the dreary island of Martinique, Marie Josèphe Rose Tascher de la Pagerie was told by a Negro seeress that she would one day be a queen. She laughed, and married, at sixteen, a minor French officer, Beauharnais. He was guillotined in the French Reign of Terror, which she luckily survived, and she married another French officer, Bonaparte. And when he became Emperor, she became Empress of the French.

In September 1939, as Hitler's forces mopped up in Poland, most Germans were confident of swift victory. But a thirteen-year-old German girl dreamed otherwise. In her vision she saw military operations coming to a halt near her home outside Munich, deep in Germany, and next morning told her parents the war would end in their village, with their house unscathed. Six years later, American troops occupied Marie-Luise Debus' village, and as as the last futile shot whistled over her house, the German batteries ceased fire. The war was over.

Theosophist Madam Bathsheba had warned Chicago's mayor, Anton J. Cermak, in January 1933, in the home of industrialist Vincent J. Bendix, to beware of shooting. "I know, I know," Cermak had said. But a few weeks later, his life was snuffed out by a bullet intended for President-elect Franklin Roosevelt, sitting next to him in a motorcar. At the last moment, the aim of the assassin, Zangara, had been deflected by a woman's upthrust arm.

In so many cases, as research had shown, warnings of the future didn't seem to alter the course of that future.

As my own notes revealed, I had been warned four times by psychics—and once by a nonpsychic—to get out of the stock market after January 1962, but I had not given it a second thought.

Madam Bathsheba had advised many of "her people" to dispose of their market holdings by March of 1962, two months before the crash. But a typical client, acknowledging this advice, told me lamely: "I disposed of what I could, but I had to hold some."

She lost heavily on what she "had to hold."

Knowing the predicted future, many still seem unable to avoid it, even when it is not what they think they want at the time. Not long after sensitive Maya Perez first read for me, I recall her reading for a young Greenwich, Connecticut, socialite named Barbara Williams. "You are interested in a young man in Japan," the sensitive told the pretty girl.

"I am not," the girl responded.

Miss Perez frowned. "That's funny," she said. "I see him very clearly, he's blond and fair, and well set up." She raised her eyebrows. "He's in the service, but he's a professional man." She looked up at the girl. "Do you know anybody like that?"

The girl nodded. "Yes, but I'm not interested. I just broke off the engagement."

Madam Perez laughed. "Well, whether you like it or not, you're going to marry that man—and you're going to have four children." The young lady laughed scornfully. But a year later she married flight surgeon Cadvan Griffith, a persistent suitor, on his return from Japan, and the last time I saw the blond doctor and his pretty wife, they were married more than seven years and were happily expecting their fourth child.

Many psychics, while fatalistic, still feel that some aspects of destiny are fluid; others insist that visions or warnings only serve to shape the individual's unchangeable destiny. Thus premonitions which appear helpful are part of that destiny, not a changing force. Suffragist Susan Anthony, vacationing in an Atlantic City hotel, dreamed one night of a terrible fire, and checked out in the morning with her niece not long before flames consumed her hotel and much of the resort's famous boardwalk. Was her premonition part of her destiny.

This problem of determinism is one that has intrigued everyone, even the most confirmed fatalist, who is aware of the conscious thought processes that apparently formulate his own decisions. It is one that the medium Eileen Garrett has treated engagingly. Reading for a friend of the late architect Frederick Bligh Bond, the sensitive reported her disappointment at not being able to establish clairvoyant contact, when suddenly a commanding voice told her to take a gun from the man's pockets. "As he was about to close the door," she said, "I obeyed the voice, rushed after him, and told him, 'Your mother says you have a gun in your pocket. She is terribly distressed because you plan to use it.'"

The man collapsed. "It was only a good deal later," Miss Garrett related, "that I heard from Bond that his friend, a Detroit business-man, had suffered a great financial loss. He had written a farewell letter to his wife, and taken a room at the Piccadilly Hotel in New York, where he intended to shoot himself. It was then that he came to me, and that I heard what appeared to be the voice of his dead mother commanding me to intercede."

Later she learned from Bond that the man, apparently impressed by the message, had returned to his wife, reinstated himself in the business, and lived another ten years before dying of a heart attack.

Miss Garrett, an energetic researcher herself, stated the immediate problem well:

"Did I actually hear the voice of a dead person while seeing her clairvoyantly? Did I tap the mind of the desperate man by telepathic perception? Did I precognize, but by my action prevent the occurrence of a future event?"

They were all interesting possibilities. But the fact that the normally unknowable future is predictable, implying that the future is fixed, does not necessarily mean that man has to wait for the future to catch up with him. In his hands still lie the seeds of his own happiness. "Man's freedom does not consist in his decisions being uncaused," Professor Ducasse had observed, "for they too are the effect of causes, but the fact that some of them [his decisions] do cause what he intended. Insofar as they do, man is free, but his freedom is limited since there are many things which his decisions are impotent to cause to occur."

In other words, the downpour is inevitable, but man decides for himself whether he should carry an umbrella. And in making that decision, he has exercised a degree of free will—and kept the rain off his back.

It is not the things that happen to us, an elderly philosopher had once observed, but the way we react to them that determines our eventual success. "Fate, karma, destiny, call it what you like," the Swami Paramhansa Yagonanda had told spiritualist Arthur Ford, "there is a law of justice that somehow, but not by chance, determines our race, our physical structure, and some of our mental and emotional traits. These are mediated to us through our genes, but the important thing to realize is that while we may not escape our own basic pattern, we can work in conformity with it. That is where free will comes in. We are free to choose and discriminate to the limits of our understanding, and as we rightly exercise our power of choice, our understanding grows."

In more direct Western fashion Dr. F. Regis Reisenman had come to virtually the same conclusion. "People who predict the future," he had told me, "virtually establish the fact that there is a future. And because it is predictable, it is obviously already laid out and established, but within the framework of that broad future—life, death, etc.—there is plenty of roaming space for the free will. For, quite manifestly, it is the way we respond to the expected and the unexpected, the disappointments and tragedies of life that determines our state of mind, not the actual event itself."

In connection with this "roaming space," I was reminded of a light incident that had occurred when I was making the rounds of the fortune-tellers with an experimental subject, June Baier, a young actress in her twenties. After the last visit, our careening taxicab almost collided with a truck, stopping with breath-taking suddenness to avoid an accident. "Please watch where you're going," the girl cried to the driver.

"You have nothing to fear," I said dryly. "The fortune-tellers all said you'd live to be eighty-five."

"I know," she rejoined, "but I don't want to spend the last sixty years of it in a cast."

In recognizing that the future is predictable, Dr. Reisenman had pointed out, man must inevitably accept that there is an order in the universe, a physical fact acknowledged by the scientist Einstein before his death. And by being in harmony with this order man may make the most of the future ordained for him. Even the trivial often points up the importance of accepting the future. In October 1961, for instance, a French gymnastics instructor predicted three times that an airliner due to take him from Paris to the African Ivory Coast would never reach Marseilles, and three times he was right. But even so, the gymnast, Jean Claude Cuisseau, to whom visions were not unfamiliar, did not take full advantage of his own premonitions. Before the first flight from Orly Airport, he casually told a stewardess that the plane would go no further than Lyons, and turn back. Over Lyons, the pilot announced he was returning to Paris because of a mechanical defect. The flight was rescheduled the next day, but as the passengers boarded the plane, Cuisseau announced it would go no further than the runway. Again, because of a technical difficulty, Cuisseau was proven right.

The flight was rescheduled for the next day at noon—October 4—but this time Cuisseau didn't even bother to leave his hotel room. "Tell the passengers they are wasting their time," he told a service employee, who had come to fetch him, "the plane will not take off." Minutes later, the flight was again postponed. As airline officials shrugged, Cuisseau explained: "I spent some time in India a number of years ago, and learned the methods of the wise men of that country. I get these powers when I am very tired."

By his foreknowledge he had saved himself a trip to the plane. He could have saved himself three.

But the readiness to accept the predictable future, and adjust to it, can be as imperative as life itself. Seeress Jeane Dixon has predicted that China, not Russia, will be the great menace to the United States one day; if her glimpse of the future is correct, could it not be that preparation for that day would spare the country much travail, even though an American triumph in any such conflict is still destined in her crystal ball? In the international sphere, Mrs. Dixon had also predicted—to the unbelieving brother of the King of Nepal—that Nepal would go behind the Communist Iron Curtain. She foresaw the failures of the Summit Conference in Paris before the U-2 incident ruffled Khrushchev, and British Prime Minister Anthony Eden's resignation over the Suez Canal.

How well it might have been for all concerned to have been

braced for these reverses. As it was, her warnings obviously accomplished little, and the politicians wouldn't have listened had she told them.

It is interesting to note that both Jeane Dixon and the late Edgar Cayce have predicted a threat to America through the Davis Strait, that little-traveled passage between Greenland and the mainland of North America, from which an over-the-pole attack could conceivably be launched. "I don't know why it should be," Mrs. Dixon remarked, "but that is a vulnerable area." Perhaps, this is warning to the wise.

Having enough problems on earth, we may be picking up more than we bargain for in space. Many psychics, including Mrs. Dixon, see life on other planets—and not all of it friendly. And even the scientists have speculated that even now we may be under observation by life on another planet.

Nostradamus, of course, saw an apparent space conflict not very far off, but despite his record in the past for accuracy, few will believe him. I find this difficult to accept myself, any more than as a very young man I could accept the fact that I would some day die. It was outside the dimension of my everyday thinking. In the same way, with others, I cannot take Edgar Cayce seriously when he tells of the imminent destruction of New York City and the two great cities of the West Coast. It matters not how right, again, Cayce has been in the past. Such destruction is outside the scope of my credibility, just as, I imagine, the Japanese could not visualize the annihilation of Hiroshima and Nagasaki before the bomb dropped.

It was more pleasant, and simpler by far, to dwell on the meaning of individual forecasts.

In the personal realm, the faculty of keeping in tune with an established order is intriguing because its potential benefits are more readily recognized through an easy process of self-identification.

An advertising man I know quite well, uneasy about his approaching marriage to a younger and immature girl, was roused from a restless slumber one morning by the insistent throb of the phone. As he sleepily picked up the receiver, a familiar voice said, without a preamble, "Don't do it, don't do it."

"Don't do what?" he asked, annoyed, without quite recognizing the voice.

"Don't marry that girl," the answer came.

And then he recognized the voice; it was that of psychic Maya Perez, whom he had not seen since her departure for California a year before.

Not bothering to ask how she knew he was dourly contemplating marriage, he asked rather gruffly:

"Why not?"

"She's bad for you. You'll be terribly unhappy."

"How do you know," he asked, "you've never seen her, and don't even know her name?"

Maya stuck to her guns. "She's not right for you," she said.

Aware that she had been predicting events for years as though they were inexorable, the advertising man said roguishly: "If you see something in the future, isn't it your belief that this something is bound to happen?"

"Why, yes."

"In other words you can't change your fate?"

"No," Maya intoned doubtfully, "you can't."

"Then," the man said, "if I am fated to marry this girl, or some other girl, nothing can change it. The whole force of my personality, the influence of the planet I was born under, everything that I am or hope to be is driving me toward that decision."

She appeared more doubtful than before, but still agreed.

"Then," the prospective bridegroom said, "I might as well relax, for even knowing the future, forewarned, the best that I can hope to do is prepare myself for a marriage I am fated to make—and make the best of it."

She drew in her breath. "Robert," she said, "you're really learning."

Robert assumed that the clairvoyant had got a telepathic message communicating his misgivings about the marriage, or perhaps she had tuned in on the girl through him.

"And what do you see?" he asked.

She laughed at the other end of the phone. "Don't worry about it," she said. "You're not going to marry her." And he didn't—the girl called it off.

But he was relaxed when the blow fell. He had been expecting it.

In death, too, psychics have been able to establish a helpful sense of harmony with the order of things. After their daughter disappeared mysteriously from an Eastern campus years ago, the girl's wealthy parents consulted Madam Bathsheba in the hope that she might be able to tell them where the girl was. There had been no clues. Bathsheba closed her eyes and saw woods and Indians. She was not quite sure what that meant. There were other readings. "Will I ever see my daughter again?" the mother implored. Finally, one day, Bathsheba gently told the mother: "I have something to tell you. You will see your daughter, but she will not know you."

The mother was elated at first, but as she thought it over, the words seemed to have an ominous ring.

"Will my daughter be found all right?" the mother asked again.

All Bathsheba could do was repeat: "You will see your daughter, but she will not know you."

Weeks later, the girl's body was fished out of a lake. She was dead. But she had still been alive when Bathsheba had made her enigmatic prediction—wandering about in Maine.

When the sad obsequies were out of the way, the mother visited the seeress' Carnegie Hall studio and thanked her. "After a while," she said, "I understood what you were trying to say. And it prepared me."

Bathsheba had been more than consoling. She had been instructive. "Without proper counseling," she said, "it is only fortune-telling." In their conversations, the mother had gradually gained an awareness of her oneness with the universe and of her own and her daughter's place in it. "The more we feel ourselves part of this continuous order of the universe," Bathsheba said, "the more we feel in tune with it, the greater security and content we will find, whatever happens."

Despite many theories, we still have no explanation of how precognition works, though the endocrine glands of the psychic may well be involved. And when we do find out, we may have a solution to other and greater mysteries. "The facts of prediction of the future lead us to the threshold of an unknown world," Nobel prize winner Alexis Carrel observed in his *Man the Unknown.* "They seem to point to the existence of a psychic principle capable of evolving outside the limits of our body."

But even granting a predictable future, there is still an obvious problem. At best, as only human instruments, the most accurate and disinterested of psychics are subject to error. It would surely be unfortunate to sell one's stock, and then discover that a psychic's conscious dislike of Wall Street or fear of the market had somehow caused her to incorrectly diagnose a falling market, or that, like a sensitive race horse, she was just having a bad day.

As the Catholic Church has warned, it can be dangerous to run one's life by astrology or clairvoyance, which may be even more fallible than the person's own indecision. Yet many successful businessmen—more than would care to admit it—have regularly consulted psychics before venturing into important transactions.

And it must certainly be exhilarating, at times, to be a Dave Kahn, with implicit confidence in a Cayce, almost reveling in the hazards of war because of that confidence, impressing others and yourself with your courage and high spirits.

But regardless of the evidence or proof, many people will never take seriously reported instances of psychic phenomena, or any other phenomenon that defies explanation by their five senses. As a matter of fact, even when the phenomenon has been established to the satisfaction of some of these senses—eyes and ears, for example—they still will sneer. The research scientists, too, almost incredibly, seem to place more stock in their own trifling laboratory experiments than in the spontaneous wonders happening on all sides of them. With all their experiments, public skepticism has changed little in the seventy-five years since Professor Henry Sidgwick, a leader of the British Society for Psychical Research, declared rather warmly: "It is a scandal that the dispute as to the reality of these phenomena should still be going on, that so many competent witnesses should have declared their belief in them, that so many others should be profoundly interested in having the question determined, and that the educated, as a body, should still be simply in the attitude of incredulity."

But when one considers the nonsense often offered as evidence of the psychic, it is no wonder that doubters prevail. Deliberately, I did not interest myself in levitation, trumpet-blowing, and the other spectacular accouterments of spiritualistic precognition. I did not see what a levitating force would prove except that a body could somehow, through a trick or otherwise, remain stationary in air. Yet, I was informed rather impatiently by one young collegian interested in the spectacular aspects of psychic research that levitation would establish that there was something to other forms of psychic phenomena. It reminded me of the story Arthur Ford passed on about the Indian whose brother had gone away to study the occult for fourteen years. When he returned, after enduring all manner of hardships in pursuance of his powers, he took his brother down to the banks of the river. And then, glowing with pride, he started to tread on the waves, saying: "Look, brother, I can walk across the river." The brother, in turn, took the miracle worker down the river a bit and boarded a ferry, giving the pilot a coin as they stepped aboard. And then, quietly, as the boat neared the opposite shore, he said, "You see, brother, you have gone through so much to achieve what I can do for a penny."

On the positive side, the possibilities of psychic communication are endless. Not only may they revolutionize crime detection, war, and diplomacy, as suggested, but they could also conceivably enrich our lives by divining hidden treasures of water, oil, and minerals, and intuitively solving intricate problems of science and chemistry, just as Edgar Cayce could help thousands without any knowledge of medicine. And in foreseeable time, as the distinguished British physician MacDonald Critchley has indicated, as we become more aware of these powers, we may eventually communicate with each other by thought from great distances, just as Dr. Spencer Thornton could sometimes communicate with his wife.

Though I had no way of measuring precisely, it did seem to me that this troubled generation, if not more psychic than its predecessors, was certainly more aware of this power. Confronted by the daily prospect of being blown to extinction, many appeared to be grasping intuitively for a faith they could not find through the orderly channels of the mind.

Thus sharpened and honed by uneasily sensed peril, the psychic or intuitive quality normally dormant appeared to manifest itself in many little ways.

How often have you known what somebody was going to say before he said it?

How many times have you thought of somebody, only to learn later he was thinking of you at precisely the same time?

Not much in itself perhaps, but a portent of something larger to be developed and explored—not just coincidence.

Perhaps there was something to womanly intuition. Women, generally, appeared to have more experiences that could be explained away only psychically. They were not as accustomed as men to rely on the logical processes of the mind, and were not so much prisoner to these processes. Was it thereby easier for them to take that giant step into the beckoning world beyond the mind?

We may be just beginning to glimpse a great natural law in its fullness. "What is so remarkable about man's future being predictable," the astrologers point out, "when science concedes an orderly course for the planets themselves, predictable thousands of years ahead?" Man, one astrologer pointed out, is as much a part of the natural law as the planets that contain him and other life. "Even in his disorder," he observed, "there is a certain order in his relationship to the planets, and this we call destiny."

It was stated another way, perhaps more intuitively, by the far-ranging intellect of Thomas Aquinas many centuries ago. There is a divine providence, and through this divine providence there is an orderly disposition of all creatures, and what is foreseen through prophecy, in tune with this providence, is neither fortuitous nor by chance. It was this implicit belief in the word of the prophet that instilled hope in generations of Jews parted from their homeland: "Fear not; for I am with thee; I will bring thy seed from the east, and gather thee from the west. And I will say to the north, keep not back; bring my sons from far, and my daughters from the end of the earth."

It was a prophecy fulfilled twenty-five hundred years later, in the latter times, as the Bible states, and today the world awaits as eagerly the fulfillment of other prophecies it only vaguely understands.

There is no reason, as spiritualist Arthur Ford points out, that the age of prophecies and visions should end with the Bible. The natural order continues. Among the modern-day clairvoyants, there may be some sufficiently endowed to carry a prophetic message, an Edgar Cayce perhaps, a Jeane Dixon, or only a child, ignorant and unlettered, like the children of Fatima. But, as the mystic Cayce once observed, of what purpose are these messages, unless man learns by them to work toward truth, seeking it first in himself?

As never before, multitudes of all faiths—and of no faith—are turning in fear and uneasiness to the approach of a new millennium, casting an eye to the Bible—and to modern "prophets"— for hidden meanings of doom and destruction and the dawn of a new and better day. But actually, in the sublime order of things what is there to fear? The future stretches on virtually endlessly, despite a few possibly unpleasant interludes, and the order is already established. Nothing we can do, perhaps, shall change it. All we can do is know what is coming and prepare. "I have declared the former things from the beginning, and they went forth out of my mouth, and I showed them; I did them suddenly, and they came to pass."

God receives no news from the world, Thomas Aquinas said, and nothing surprises Him. "If two servants, who do not know they need meet, are sent by their master to the same place, the meeting of the two servants, if referred to themselves, is by chance, but as compared to the master who had ordered it, it is directly intended."